# PAUL MARTIN

## CEO for Canada?

160201

## MURRAY DOBBIN

James Lorimer & Company Ltd., Publishers
Toronto, 2003

James Lorimer & Company Ltd. acknowledges the support of the Ontario Arts Council. We acknowledge the support of the Government of Canada through the Book Publishing Industry Development Program (BPIDP) for our publishing activities. We acknowledge the support of the Canada Council for the Arts for our publishing program. We acknowledge the support of the Government of Ontario through the Ontario Media Development Corporation's Ontario Book Initiative.

Cover design: Nick Shinn
Cover illustration: Aislin

**National Library of Canada Cataloguing in Publication**

Dobbin, Murray, 1945–
    Paul Martin : CEO for Canada? / Murray Dobbin.

Includes bibliographic references and index.
ISBN 1-55028-799-0

        1. Martin, Paul, 1938–. 2. Canada—Politics and government—1993–.
3. Canada—Economic conditions—1991–. I. Title.

FC636.5.M37D62 2003          971.064'8'092     C2003-903625-1

James Lorimer & Company Ltd.,
Publishers
35 Britain Street
Toronto, Ontario
M5A 1R7
www.lorimer.ca

Printed and bound in Canada.

# CONTENTS

# ACKNOWLEDGEMENTS

**B**ooks about politics and economics almost always rest on a foundation of the work of others and this book is certainly no exception.
Indeed, an enormous amount of excellent work has already been done
on Paul Martin and his time as Canada's most powerful finance minister. In fact there has been so much written about his policies and the
damage they have caused it is a wonder another book is needed. But it
is. Canada seems afflicted by a kind of collective amnesia about what
Paul Martin did as finance minister. Perhaps people just want to forget
what happened in the nineties, and if Paul Martin were retiring, we
could perhaps afford to forget. But he isn't, and we can't.

Numerous colleagues and friends have written about the Liberal government of the nineties and I am indebted to them all: Linda McQuaig,
Jim Stanford, Maude Barlow, Bruce Campbell, Seth Klein, Mel Hurtig,
and Armine Yalnizyan and others have all contributed to the debunking
of Paul Martin's economic rationalism, the deficit hysteria that preceded
his budgets and about the enormous impact all of this had on Canada.
Their work—and their advice—is much appreciated. People would be
well-advised to revisit their writings as a refresher course. The
researchers with the Alternative Federal Budget project, from both the
Canadian Centre for Policy Alternatives (CCPA) and the Manitoba

coalition Choices, have provided an amazing wealth of analysis of how we could have done things differently and better.

While we disagree about the legacy of Paul Martin, Edward Greenspon and Anthony Wilson-Smith's book, *Double Vision*, provided an invaluable insiders' look into the political process behind Paul Martin's powerful influence in the Chretien government.

Three students volunteered to help with aspects of the research for the book. Ben Millard, Letha Victor and Stephen Carley were all exceptionally generous with their time and dogged in their searching for often obscure and buried facts.

Others helped in various ways. Seth Klein, Steve Staples and Marc Lee read parts of the manuscript (with Seth doing so at the Vancouver Folk Festival, earning him undeserved teasing). Colleen Fuller, Elaine Briere, and Mike McCarthy all made my work easier and more interesting.

Deadlines and work schedules were a constant and terrifying companion from day one, no less so for the editors who made many sacrifices of their time and some, no doubt, of their sanity to get the book done. I thank Kristen Pederson-Chew and Jodi Lewchuk for work beyond the call of duty.

My partner, Ellen Gould, has the misfortune of also being a researcher and writer and thus gets dragooned into all of my projects at one stage or another. Four books later I now have an "unsustainable debt." I thank her for her forbearance, born of her commitment to social justice, and for her excellent advice and work on the book itself.

I dedicate the book to the 300,000 Canadians who were unnecessarily forced into unemployment through much of the 1990s because of Paul Martin's policies.

# INTRODUCTION

We live in dangerous times. As we approach a federal election, probably in the spring of 2004, Canada faces a rapidly changing, increasingly unpredictable and insecure world. While our closest neighbour and trading partner is embarking on an ambitious plan to consolidate its political, economic, and military power worldwide, our own country is experiencing a serious decline on all fronts, exemplified by our drop to eighth place in the UN's Human Development Index (from third last year and an eight-year number one ranking before that). Social inequality is now greater in Canada than in almost any other developed country except the United States. Working conditions are so onerous and stressful that millions of Canadians have delayed starting their families. The pressures facing single mothers in Canada are so profound that the UN is using unusually strong language in its reports to condemn our attitude towards the poor.

Closely tied to the state of our social well-being is the health of our economy. Despite recent boasts of Canada's economic stability, the truth is that times are about to get tough. After spending fifteen years hitching its wagon to the US through the FTA, NAFTA, and ever-greater integration, Canada now finds America in precarious shape. The declaration of a "New American Century" has occurred in tandem with skyrocketing deficits. The US is experiencing an unsustainable balance of trade deficits and historic levels of corporate and consumer debt. Regardless of the outcome of this volatile situation, Canada is in a very weak position to weather a crisis. If the US embraces protectionism and moves away from free trade, all our economic restructuring will have been for nothing; if the US strategy fails and its economy collapses, we are scarcely less vulnerable. Fifteen years of regressive labour policies mean we now have significantly more low-paying jobs and fewer industrial ones. Canadians currently have the highest rates of personal debt in the country's history and near-record-low savings rates. Furthermore, our physical infrastructure is deteriorating after twenty years of neglect. Restructuring our economy in the interests of trade has damaged the domestic economy badly enough that if trade falters—as it is already showing signs of doing—we will have little to fall back on. To deal with these issues, we will need a political leader with the vision and skill required to navigate the treacherous waters that clearly lie ahead.

This book poses the question: Is Paul Martin the man to provide the kind of leadership we need to face this dangerous and uncertain future?

Barring extraordinary political developments or an act of God, the former Liberal finance minister will become prime minister of Canada in February 2004, and will likely be elected in his own right a few months later. On the face of it, this succession should not present any surprises to Canadians. Save for actual prime ministers, few politicians have garnered as much attention as Paul Martin during his nine years as finance minister. Indeed, in an era preoccupied with deficits and debt and the "threat" of inflation, a finance minister's importance nearly eclipses the party leader's. In the 1990s, this circumstance was more true in Canada than in almost any other developed country. Paul Martin put his personal stamp on the Liberal government in such a decisive manner that it is only a slight exaggeration to say that he has already been prime minister.

Given this high-profile political career, it would seem that Canadians should know all they need to about the man who will lead their country. Yet, Paul Martin remains something of an enigma. A close look at his politics, his business ethics, and his dual personas reveal startling contradictions. There are significant inconsistencies between his political reputation and his actual political record; between his career as a corporate mogul and his aspirations for political leadership; and between his engaging personality and the ruthless tactics of his leadership campaign. By examining these contradictions and inconsistencies, this book will try to determine who Paul Martin really is and what kind of prime minister he would likely be.

Take, for instance, the astonishing disconnect between people's perception of Paul Martin's performance as minister of finance and what he actually did in that position. The discrepancy is between Martin's widespread popularity across the political spectrum (in a Fall 2002 poll conducted by EKOS Research Associates, 63 per cent of respondents said Martin would make a good prime minister) and his actual record, which includes deep cuts to social spending, cultural programs, farm subsidies, foreign aid, health and environmental protection, and a long list of other programs and public institutions that had defined Canada in the post-war period.

Despite his legendary status as the man who slew the deficit dragon, Paul Martin was actually much more proud of a goal that few Canadians are even aware he had. Yet he said it for all to hear in his 1995 budget speech to Parliament, and repeated it many times after: "Indeed, as far as we are concerned, it is [the] reform in the structure of government spending, in the very redefinition of government itself that is the main achievement of this budget.... This budget overhauls not only how government works but what government does."[1]

This was Paul Martin's "greatest" achievement: not defeating the deficit, but permanently redefining the role government would play in the lives of Canadians and their communities. He could not conceal his pride in taking Canada back fifty years in terms of social spending. "By 1996–7," boasted our next prime minister, "we will have reduced program spending from $120 billion in 1993–4 to under $108 billion. Relative to the size of our economy, program spending will be lower in 1996–7 than at any time since 1951."[2] When he spoke these words in 1995, he did not mention that Canada was more than twice as wealthy per capita than it had been in 1951.

Paul Martin was determined to preserve what he had accomplished. At the end of the decade, when low interest rates and a low dollar stimulated growth, Martin was suddenly faced with a "surplus crisis." Huge budget surpluses meant he could have easily restored every program he had cut and even launched new ones. Instead, he implemented the largest tax cuts in Canadian history, with the bulk of the benefits going to large corporations. Seventy-seven per cent of the personal income tax cuts went to those earning over $65,000 per year—the richest 8 per cent of the population. When he still had billions left over, he spent most of it paying down the debt, a policy even mainstream economists found questionable.

Prime Minister Jean Chrétien gave Paul Martin free rein to implement these policies. Any minister who complained was quickly brought to heel—even threatened—by a prime minister who made it clear from day one that Paul Martin was not only in charge of the finance department but, by virtue of his particular mandate, virtually in charge of determining the direction and capacity of almost every other government department. In the months leading up to his 1995 budget, Martin presented each and every minister with a one-page instruction sheet that outlined not only by how much, but sometimes by what means, they would have to cut their expenditures.

One of the enduring myths about Paul Martin is that he turned the economy around and brought prosperity to Canada. Certainly nine years is more than almost any other finance minister in Canadian history has had to make policies work. Yet economic performance in Canada in the 1990s was worse than in any other decade of the last century except the 1930s. GDP growth per capita, private investment, productivity growth, unemployment levels, and Canadians' standard of living all declined, even though Paul Martin's policies were intended—by his own declarations—to strengthen the economy.

But what is an economy for, if not to serve its citizens? The average annual national unemployment rate increased from 5 per cent in the 1960s to 6.7 per cent in the 1970s, 9.3 per cent in the 1980s, and 9.6 per cent in the 1990s. Real personal disposable (after-tax) income per person actually fell by 3.3 per cent per year in the 1990s, down from an annual average *increase* of 1.1 per cent in the 1980s, 3.0 per cent in the 1970s, and 3.9 per cent in the 1960s. The gap between the rich and poor grew faster in the 1990s than in any period since the Great Depression. Particular groups were hit especially hard. For example, there has been no increase in the real annual earnings of Canadian men working full time for more than twenty years.

One of the most disturbing aspects of Paul Martin's record is his complete repudiation of the Liberal Party platform, the famous "Red Book" he co-wrote for the 1993 election. Unprecedented in Canadian election history, it was a very detailed book of promises that summarized the Liberal Party's contract with Canadians to reverse the economic course set by the reviled Brian Mulroney. It promised to attack the scourge of unemployment, lower interest rates to spur economic growth, and reinvest in social programs, including a plan for national child care. In short, Paul Martin's Red Book pledged to deliver what Canadians said they wanted. Instead, the transition from Brian Mulroney to Paul Martin was virtually seamless—as Mr. Mulroney delights in pointing out whenever he can. Reminded by a staffer of a Red Book pledge months before his 1995 budget, Paul Martin declared, "Screw the Red Book!"[3] It was, he said, never intended to be a policy book. It was intended to get the party elected.

Paul Martin's pride in reducing government spending to levels not seen since 1949 has a lot to do with his political apprenticeship. That apprenticeship was singular and intensive: twenty years as a CEO and twelve years as owner of one of Canada's largest shipping companies, Canada Steamship Lines. His first job with the enormously influential Power Corporation of Montreal involved "firefighting," or taking over ailing companies and "restructuring" them to make them profitable. Many business people become politicians, but few deliberately choose a long career as a CEO to prepare for running the country. As finance minister, Martin more resembled a CEO restructuring a large conglomerate—getting rid of many business sidelines and "refocusing" on core functions—than he did a political leader with a positive vision for building the nation. In the tradition of the modern CEO, Paul Martin created a "mean and lean" country.

It is also on a personal level that Paul Martin is fraught with inconsistencies. He is known—even among those most critical of his policies and record—as a charming, intellectually curious, and decent man. He loves to debate. He seems to listen to his public and will engage people in discussions about economics at any opportunity—in airport lounges, on the street ... almost anywhere. He exhibits genuine enthusiasm for ideas. He is personally gracious and friendly.

How to explain, then, the ruthlessness and ferocity of his leadership campaign, in which his hand-picked team has engineered rules that give him enormous advantages over opponents? And how to interpret his determination not just to win, but to crush all opposition by raising millions of dollars, Americanizing Canadian politics in the process? How do we understand such a sophisticated and experienced political animal who must know—who does know—that judgment is everything in politics, yet seems unable to personally calculate when enough is enough?

Many of Paul Martin's long-time friends are just as puzzled as casual observers by this schizophrenic behaviour. A former senior Liberal official says, "I have known Paul Martin for thirty years and he really is a very nice person. But he allows these people to act in his name. I have heard people ask him, 'Why do you let these people leak information about the prime minister, and hold secret meetings, and speak for you?' But he always seems ambivalent about it.... Paul Martin is a man who doesn't seem to know who he is or just what he believes."

Yet we already know what he has done and what he stands for. Martin rarely, if ever, reveals a comprehensive vision of what he thinks Canada should be, yet he has refashioned the country in ways that are unmistakably in conflict with the values the majority of Canadians hold. Martin's popularity may stem from a Canadian political culture in which values have had little currency in the past ten years. What makes the prospect of Martin becoming prime minister both interesting and problematic is that this culture is changing. As the economy comes out of a decade characterized by government-imposed recession and deficit-induced downsizing—not to mention the moral free fall of corporate America under oil executive President George W. Bush—Canadian values are coming to the fore once again.

Frank Graves of EKOS has stated that Canadians currently demonstrate "a stronger sense of identity and greater national confidence than at any time in the past decade." And at no time since the late 1980s have they been so keen to see the government return to its role as creator of the commons—or, in Graves' words, "Canadians still want government to deal with the really big problems that are too onerous for them to manage on their own." EKOS's extensive surveys, along with several others, also show that Canadians are increasingly rejecting the neo-liberal, free-market ideology that has dominated the media and Paul

Martin's policies. They simply don't buy trickle-down.

In fact, even some of the wealthiest Canadians seem open to a return to a more activist government—especially at the national level. In an EKOS poll, only 11 per cent of Canadians questioned agreed with the following statement: "Now that the economy is getting stronger, we no longer need to worry as much about child poverty issues." Prime Minister Chrétien's concern for his legacy is based on more than nostalgia—he reads the polls, too. After suffering the 1990s, a decade plagued by deficit propaganda wars, a steady decrease in quality of life, and false promises about the market bringing them endless prosperity, Canadians have had enough. They want their government back. Not the old government, which is seen as wasteful and unaccountable, but an active government that still cares for community.

In the last chapter of this book I address the question "Could Paul Martin have acted differently?" This answer is important not just for judging his record as finance minister, but also for predicting where he will likely take the country if he is elected prime minister. In asking whether the deficit could have been eliminated without forcing Canadians to suffer persistent nine to ten per cent unemployment and cuts to medicare, education, unemployment insurance (UI), and social assistance, the answer is an unequivocal 'Yes.' Many mainstream economists presented such alternatives to Martin and criticized his cuts and his fixation with inflation. But in asking if Paul Martin could have acted differently or taken a different approach, given his background and political context, the clear answer is 'No.'

Paul Martin had a role to play. In 1994 the Business Council on National Issues (BCNI) presented the finance minister with "A Ten-Point Growth and Employment Strategy for Canada." The list included slashing UI, cutting social spending, keeping inflation low and unemployment high, cutting taxes for the corporate sector, minimizing government, and expanding privatization and deregulation. Paul Martin delivered on every one of the BCNI's demands; as finance minister, he concluded that Bay Street would accept nothing less. For the man who was determined to be prime minister the message was clear: slash government spending and permanently restructure the government or we will not support you. There is little doubt that the $6 to 9 million Paul Martin's leadership campaign will raise from big business is in warm recognition of his delivering on the BCNI's plan, and incentive to keep delivering.

Where will CEO Martin take us if we give him an electoral mandate in 2004? The BCNI—now called the Canadian Council of Chief Executives—has another project waiting for Paul Martin to manage. It is called "deep integration," and it is a plan that will see Canada further assimilated into the United States. Corporate Canada sees trouble ahead under the rule of the new American Empire. It has failed to compete successfully with its US counterparts despite fifteen years of free trade, the driving down of Canadian wages, and huge tax cuts. Now it fears being shut out. It sees no other recourse but to join the US in whatever ways it can. Cooperating with the US on foreign policy, defence policy, immigration and perimeter security, continental energy, and Star Wars II—this and much more is Bay Street's agenda for the next ten years.

Everything we know about Paul Martin tells us he will deliver. Paul Martin, CEO, may engage you on Main Street, but he belongs to Bay Street. As if to signal that he understands what he has to do, Paul Martin has early in his leadership run pledged to support plans for the US National Missile Defense system, the first step in America's plan to ultimately militarize and control space. Where Paul Martin will take Canada is no mystery: he will lead us further down the road we have already travelled. If we let him.

# 1

# WHO IS PAUL MARTIN?

Paul Martin is a political phenomenon: he is a politician people actually like. While that sounds like a minimal requirement for someone shooting for the job of prime minister, it does wonders for a man whose actual policy record includes both the largest cuts to social programs and the biggest tax cuts for the wealthy in Canadian history. Paul Martin is one of the most popular politicians the country has seen in the past twenty years, racking up approval numbers that are stunning for a public official who has already exercised power. It is easy to imagine Paul Martin as prime minister: after all, we want our prime minister to be presentable, likeable, articulate, and intelligent. Martin's recent predecessors didn't leave good memories. Brian Mulroney was hated so viscerally that Canadians still revile him. Kim Campbell was a bad flash in the pan; people wanted to like her, but were prevented from doing so by her condescending manner. Jean Chrétien has hardly been an inspiration. One of the most enduring images of his time as prime minister is of him grabbing a hapless demonstrator by the throat just for standing in his path.

In fifteen years of electoral politics, Paul Martin has managed to persuade a large number of people, often personally, that he truly understands their interests and concerns and is willing to reflect those viewpoints in his decisions. There is no shortage of testimonials to this effect. Typical is the opinion of James Laxer, one of the founders of the 1970s' left-wing Waffle movement in the New Democratic Party (NDP): "One-on-one, Paul Martin is completely genuine. I have spoken to many politicians over the years who said they wanted to pick my brains about something or other, yet when we got together they would spend three hours pontificating. Paul Martin is not at all like that. He does not come across as a know-it-all. He is genuinely interested in you and what you have to say—it's an amazing political gift."[1] A friend of mine calls Paul Martin a "serial seducer," a man who so needs to be liked and admired that he engages everyone he meets.

How to explain, then, why so many progressive people who express this view of Martin never saw any of their ideas implemented in his budgets? Martin believed in medicare, cared about the environment, and was appalled at poverty in Canada, even declaring on one occasion, "You have to wonder about a society where people are sleeping on sidewalk steam vents while the limousines roll by." Yet in spite of everything he said he believed, Paul Martin set Canada back nearly fifty years by reducing program spending to the same percentage of GDP as in 1949.

The explanation for this contradiction is simple enough. The man who chatted people up in airport lounges and conference hallways was Paul Martin the civilian. Paul Martin the Opposition critic was also one of us, with his values front and centre. However, the man who walked into the government's finance department every morning was Paul Martin the CEO. Finance Minister Martin had a country to fix, like many of the companies he had managed: restructuring the country, refocusing "the business" on its core operations, getting rid of unprofitable divisions, and making the operation efficient. Like most contemporary CEOs, Finance Minister Martin left his feelings, and his intellectual curiosity, at the door.

Paul Martin will just be official retirement age when he starts his job as prime minister in the winter of 2004. He came to politics relatively late, at age fifty, after having been a businessman for most of his life. Martin was born into one of Canada's most pre-eminent political families. His father was Paul Martin Sr., whose career began in the 1930s when he was an MP for Windsor, Ontario. By 1945 he was health minister in Mackenzie King's post-war government. He would go on to serve two other Liberal prime ministers, Louis St. Laurent and Lester Pearson, and is most often associated with the rich social policy era of the 1960s. Paul Jr. has often said that his father was the most influential person in his life. He once told a story about driving with his father past fields full of people picking tomatoes. "Thank God I don't have to pick tomatoes for a living," he commented. The next day, his father had him doing just that. "He taught me at an early age what life was about," said Paul Jr.[2]

But that lesson would have to compete with something much more powerful: his decision to gain experience—and economic security—in the business world as a precursor to entering politics. By 1988, when Paul Martin Jr. first ran for Parliament, he was reportedly worth at least $20 million. Picking tomatoes was a symbolic lesson, but twenty years as a CEO was an indelible experience.

While Paul Martin came to know formal political power later in life, he was immersed in one of Canada's most influential informal political institutions very early on. Just after he graduated from University of Toronto Law School in 1966 at age twenty-eight, he joined Power Corporation of Quebec. Martin was hired by Maurice Strong, former assistant to Paul Martin Sr., CEO and member of the Canadian and global elite. Paul Desmarais began running the company the next year, and within three years he had appointed Martin vice-president. At age thirty-one, Martin was given the kind of position and power only a handful of people twice his age ever experience.

## GROOMED FOR POWER

In Liberal Party politics, being mentored by Paul Desmarais means that you are being prepared for public office whether or not you choose to go that route. Desmarais runs a virtual training ground for prime ministers and premiers in Canada; Paul Martin will be the fourth politician this Quebec billionaire has groomed for or financially assisted into being prime minister.

Firmly committed to Canadian unity, Desmarais provided a sizeable chunk of money for Jean Chrétien's leadership campaign and was also instrumental in smoothing the way for Pierre Trudeau's leadership run. Still, Desmarais's political objectives were defined not so much by partisan principles as by corporate interests and a unified Canada. As a result, he also helped Brian Mulroney become leader of the Tories. Mulroney is now a lawyer and lobbyist for Desmarais's Hong Kong–based Asia Power Corporation. Former Quebec Liberal Premier Daniel Johnson also worked his way through the ranks of Power Corp. under Demarais's tutelage.

Paul Desmarais chooses his protegés for bigger things than Canadian business or Canadian politics. Desmarais's billionaire status and his abiding interest in politics make him an international player. Through the financial arm of his firm, Desmarais controls a significant portion of Canadian corporations such as Great-West Life Assurance Company, London Life Assurance Company, and Investors Group Inc. He also owns an international holding company headquartered in Geneva, and companies in England, France, and the US. He has a partnership with Albert Frère, one of the richest businessmen in Europe. The Desmarais-Frère holdings overtly control or strongly influence corporate assets worth over $140 billion.[3]

Paul Martin entered this rarified atmosphere just as the corporate imperative for a new elite consensus was beginning to take shape. The post-war consensus, the "social contract" between the elite and society as a whole, was in the early stages of breakdown. By the early 1970s, the global political and economic elite, led by its US members, decided that a new consensus was necessary, one that would put power back into their hands and "rebalance" the distribution of wealth between private capital and labour. Corporate profits had hit post-war lows, governments were introducing more—and more expensive—social programs, and governments and employers alike were facing ever-increasing expectations from ordinary working people. For corporate leaders, these trends were unsustainable. The result was what became known as the "Washington Consensus," a new blueprint for how the global economy and national democracies would work. The four pillars of this new order were free trade, privatization, deregulation, and a significant reduction of government's social and economic role.

In this era of the Washington Consensus, the kind of economic clout and political interest represented by the Desmarais family often becomes an admission ticket to global forums where the shape of policy is worked out before it finds its way into formal political institutions and government legislation. These forums include the Rockefeller family's

Trilateral Commission, the Bilderberg Group, and the World Economic Forum, which are the top three elite venues for CEOs to meet with the most influential members of the world's political elite. Most of the Desmarais graduates—Mulroney, Chrétien, and Martin (Trudeau wasn't that interested)—have been to one or more of these globalization talk shops. If you are whom you hang around with, being at one of these forums means you are among the fifteen hundred most influential people on the planet.

When Paul Desmarais took over Power Corporation from Maurice Strong, he recognized in Martin a man who had a talent for dealing with troubled operations. According Robert Chodos, co-author of a 1998 political biography of Martin, "Despite his relative lack of business experience, Martin became a sort of corporate firefighter, sent to various subsidiaries and divisions that needed an injection of management skill." Martin ended up doing stints at various Power Corp. companies, including Dominion Glass and Consolidated Bathurst. At the latter "he took on the role of slasher, closing several mills and taking an axe to the payroll...."[4] By the time Martin left in 1973, the papermaker was profitable again.

In 1973, Desmarais made Martin president of Canada Steamship Lines (CSL), a century-old company with a rich and sometimes shady history. (CSL was criticized in the final report of a special inquiry established by John Diefenbaker to investigate lawlessness on the Great Lakes.)[5] Martin became head of CSL at a time when it was already shrinking, in the process of eliminating much of its shipbuilding business and removing itself entirely from the passenger ship and hotel industry. Later, in 1981, Desmarais needed money for a planned takeover bid of the much larger Canadian Pacific empire. He decided to sell CSL and told Martin to find a buyer. Martin said he wanted it and quickly found a partner in Quebec millionaire and shipping magnate Laurence Pathy. Even with Pathy's backing, much of the $195 million asking price had to be borrowed from the Royal Bank—with Desmarais as the loan guarantor. While the term "leveraged buyout" was not in common use at the time, the purchase of CSL was effectively that. The purchase of the company was a high-risk venture: interest rates were over 22 per cent and Martin later admitted that if they had gone much higher, he would have been ruined.

Paul Martin is a wealthy man—the low-end estimate of his current wealth is $70 million—and by definition that makes him a successful businessman. Nonetheless, it is important to examine not only his business success, but also his business methods and ethics to gain insight into the kind of finance minister he later became. As owner of the company, Martin could run it as he chose—what would he do? Take a risk and grow CSL or remain cautious and shrink it further?

After buying CSL, Martin faced the same problem that all businesses purchased through leveraged buyouts face: he had an enormous debt that required a steady and substantial cash flow to service. CSL was a conglomerate, with sales of $500 million and six thousand employees. Two of the businesses under the CSL umbrella were Voyageur Bus Lines, the second-largest bus service network in North America, and Kingsway Transport, a large trucking subsidiary. The bus and trucking companies together accounted for half of CSL's revenue in 1984. In a feature article in *Canadian Business* that year, David Olive wrote that while both Voyageur and Kingsway had had some tough recession years, both were advancing.[6]

Yet both these large and apparently growing companies would disappear within a few years as Martin's debt and his need for cash to expand the shipping portion of CSL forced him to sell them. Martin also got rid of CSL's last vestige of shipbuilding. As president he had already closed the company's subsidiary shipbuilder, Davie Shipbuilding, but had left one yard at Collingwood, on Lake Ontario's Georgian Bay, in operation. Over one hundred years old, it had built over seven hundred ships, and was one of the companies that Martin turned around in his earlier role as a "firefighter" at Power Corp. Now, four years after buying CSL, he decided to close down the Collingwood operation. Orders for new ships were not coming in fast enough, so after a series of negotiations—and according to Chodos, a generous severance package for the remaining workers—CSL's last shipbuilding operation folded in 1986.[7]

There were underlying economic reasons for most of these decisions, which effectively downsized CSL from a conglomerate to a single-focus shipping company, even though the bus and trucking operations were doing well and could have been maintained had it not been for the huge debt. Wherever a problem might have been solved by an infusion of capital, the debt load made that extremely difficult if not impossible; the only other solution was to sell the assets. This pattern—solving debt crises through reduction rather than growth strategies—would repeat itself in Martin's career both in and out of the corporate world. In 1988, just as he was running for office for the first time, Martin's holding company took possession of all of CSL's common shares, adding millions more to the company's debt. His experience as a firefighter and head of his own company seemed destined to make Paul Martin a cautious manager.

In the mid-1980s, Martin assembled a company team to determine where new business could be generated for CSL, as he was considering moving the company back into its previous role as a deep-sea carrier. He earlier had pushed the idea of a deep-sea fleet with Desmarais, but his old boss declined the proposal. Now that he owned CSL himself, Martin could pursue his ambition of having a truly international company. A shrinking Canadian shipping market, CSL's expertise in loading technology, and Martin's own declared conviction that international trade was the key to Canada's future prosperity led him into international shipping. As Chodos and his co-authors also point out, "The further goods have to travel, the greater the revenues that accrue to the owners of ships."[8] This new plan involved developing a niche market in international shipping commerce by capitalizing on CSL's "bulk self-loading" technology for shipping raw products.

There was yet another financial advantage that Paul Martin very likely had his eye on when he decided to move into international shipping. Shipping on the high seas was characterized by the use of flags of convenience (FOC), an arrangement that allowed ship owners to ignore the taxation, labour laws, and other regulations of national jurisdictions. The additional profits to be made from FOC ships were much more attractive—in the neighbourhood of US$700,000 a year for each ship, according to some analysts.[9] However, the ethical price of those extra profits was just as great.

## FLAGS OF CONVENIENCE, SHIPS OF SHAME

Flag of convenience ships are registered in one of more than twenty-five countries around the world that provide legal and cheap registration and then promise virtually no taxes, regulations, or standards will be imposed on the companies that use them. The conditions on the worst of these ships have led to their being called sweat ships or, even worse, slave ships.

The Centre for Seafarers' Rights, an organization that tracks the abuses in the FOC shipping industry, investigated one case after receiving a letter from a Kenyan man. His contract showed that he was obliged to work a 48-hour week for which he received $80, and 124 hours of overtime a month for which he was paid an additional $30. He had no vacation. If he worked 365 straight days without a day off, he would receive six days vacation pay of $17.75. This was in 1986.

FOC ships are also a hazard to any nation with an extensive coastline because they are often in ill repair and vulnerable to rogue waves that can break them apart. One of the most infamous recent examples of an FOC ship was the 2002 sinking of the *Prestige* oil tanker off the coast of Spain. According to the *Observer* newspaper, "The *Prestige* [sinking] has exposed the international framework of maritime regulation and attitudes of many shipping companies ... This was a vessel chartered by the Swiss-based subsidiary of a Russian conglomerate registered in the Bahamas, owned by a Greek through Liberia and given a certificate of seaworthiness by the Americans. When it refuelled, it stood off the port of Gibraltar to avoid the chance of inspection. Every aspect of its operations was calculated to avoid tax, ownership obligations, and regulatory scrutiny."[10]

When Paul Martin decided to focus his company's expansion on the high-seas trade in 1986, he certainly knew the advantages—and ethical choices—he would face. The employees on his Canadian-flagged ships were all unionized, and by most accounts CSL lived up to the labour standards of the Canadian industry. That would not be the case, however, for the FOCs. The timing, too, cannot have escaped Martin's attention; just as he was contemplating entering politics in a serious way, he launched into a very controversial area of shipping that demonstrated the worst kind of corporate behaviour. FOCs are responsible for a disproportionate percentage of fatalities, casualties, crew exploitation, oil spills, pollution, and security breaches on the high seas. FOC shipping has also been cited for a wide variety of criminal activities, including money laundering.[11]

Conditions on Paul Martin's FOC ships do not compare to the dire situations on many of the others, and no one is accusing Martin of money laundering or any other criminal activity. Most of Martin's eighteen high-seas ships have agreements with the International Transportation Federation (ITF), which does protect the rights of FOC seafarers. Although these vessels are covered by labour agreements, typically all FOC mariners' contracts can require up to one hundred hours of overtime a month, and the wage rates are at less than a quarter of the Canadian wage. Regardless of the conditions on CSL's ships, what makes the CSL story amazing is that Paul Martin managed for so many years to avoid any serious media scrutiny of his company, which deliberately avoided Canadian labour, tax, and environmental regulations.

## PLAYING DIRTY DOWN UNDER

In the spring of 2002, CSL was front-page news for weeks in Australia, embroiled in the most controversial dispute in the company's modern history. After several years of working in relative harmony with the country's cabotage laws (laws that require ships in Australian waters to obey Australian laws), CSL suddenly reversed course. It used a loophole in Australian law, and the tacit support of union-busting Prime Minister John Howard, to change its two Australian-flagged cement-hauling ships to FOCs. By doing so, it thought it could quietly rid itself of its unionized Australian workers and replace them with cheaper Ukrainian sailors. The plan didn't work out quite the way CSL had hoped. CSL's tactics earned it the wrath of Australian unions, the mainstream media, the Queensland state government, the Australian Shipowners' Association, and even CSL's own cement company customers. CSL had stirred up a hornet's nest.

The loophole that CSL managed to find was a system that allowed foreign-flagged ships or FOCs to ply Australian coastal waters if no Australian ship was available to do the job. These permits were virtually always one-off trips, from one coastal port to another. However, there were very few ships that could compete with CSL's self-unloaders; if they reflagged, there were no Australian ships to do the job competitively. As a result, these same ships, now FOCs, could apply for a permit that became a virtual permanent licence for Australian coastal shipping. CSL reflagged its first ship, the *Pacific* (formerly the *River Torrens*), by taking it out of Australian waters for a year and then bringing it back with a Bahamian flag. This tactic was so successful that CSL decided to accelerate the process with its second ship, the *Stadacona* (formerly the *Yarra*), and tried to execute a crew change in Port Pirie, a small, isolated port on the Queensland coast.

However, Port Pirie is a very strong union town and the *Yarra's* sailors were not in the mood to lose their jobs. Diane Kelly, one of the crew, remembers the moment they were ordered off the ship: "We were just told, 'Get off and the new crew, [a] Ukrainian crew, will be joining.'"[12] The crew refused to leave the ship, sparking a sit-in that lasted fourteen days. When management cut off food, power, and sewage services, the townspeople pitched in with provisions and generators. Ken Madigan, the town's mayor, set up a picket line.

CSL had no intention of changing its tactics, despite being portrayed in the media as a ruthless multinational depriving Australian seafarers of work on their own coast. The company started suing the crew for refusing to leave the ship, and according to senior union officials, even began proceedings to seize workers' homes as compensation. It threatened other unions into backing away from active support of the Maritime Union of Australia (MUA) members occupying the ship. "They sought an injunction which restrained the union from taking any action which would damage CSL," said Paddy Crumlin, the MUA's national secretary. "And they have tried repeatedly to [claim] our statements are damaging to their company. It's an attempt to violate free speech."[13]

The incident surrounding the reflagging of the *Yarra* was the subject of numerous Australian Industrial Relations Commission (IRC) hearings and court proceedings. In April 2002, the courts rejected an attempt by the MUA to get an injunction on the sale of the *Yarra* from CSL's Australian arm to another subsidiary, the Singapore-based CSL Asia (where Paul Martin's son is a senior executive). However, the IRC did rule in favour of a union submission that the Ukrainian crew should receive Australian wages and conditions while working on that country's coast. CSL is now appealing that decision to the Supreme Court of Australia. If CSL wins, says Crumlin, "the other companies will say, 'Well, how can we compete in a market where there is no floor?' It has huge ramifications for what happens in Australian coastal shipping."[14]

What seems to genuinely shock Crumlin, though, is that CSL already had a monopoly in the cement-hauling trade. The two ships it purchased, the *River Torrens* and the *Yarra*, were self-unloaders built twenty years earlier precisely for that trade. "CSL is spending a fortune on the court case and for what?" asks Crumlin. "They didn't have any serious competitors, so that argument is just bogus. They were making a good profit.... Why do they have to go down this anti-labour, highly confrontational, highly politicized, conspiratorial road?"[15]

It didn't take long for the two CSL ships to demonstrate the difference between unionized crews and the cheap labour FOCs pay for. On February 18, 2002, a seaman sustained life-threatening injuries on the CSL *Pacific*. According to the union website, a government report on the incident accused management of "a significant failure of the safety management system." The report also noted that before the *Pacific* was reflagged, the vessel had a record free of any serious accidents.[16] The issues regarding CSL's FOC ships don't apply to their unionized Canadian-flagged vessels, which observe Canadian labour standards.


## WHAT, AND WHEN, DID MARTIN KNOW?

Did Paul Martin know about the actions of his company in Australia and if so, could he have done anything about it? Martin was subject to a blind trust, examined in more detail below. According to the rules of the trust, administered by Ethics Counsellor Howard Wilson, Martin could, on occasion, get briefings about his holdings whenever major decisions were going to be made, but he was bound by the rules not to intervene. Whether or not the situation in Australia was ever discussed in such a briefing will never be known—Howard Wilson says it is a private matter.

However Martin's son, Paul Martin III, is director of business development for the Asian division of Canada Steamship Lines, to which ownership of the two CSL Australia ships was eventually transferred. No one knows if he talked to his father about a conflict that was all over the Australian media and generating costly legal fees. If Paul Martin III did not mention the controversy, it is possible that Martin's political staff, always alert to the potential for bad publicity, would have said something to their boss.

Martin had at least one source of information because he intervened in mid-2002 when the situation threatened to get out of hand in Canada. The MUA's struggle had become international, and the ITF

issued a statement in April 2002 that attacked the Australian government for backing CSL's union-busting tactics. The statement also
pledged support from worldwide affiliates.[17] Later that spring, the ITF
was having a major congress in Vancouver, and Paul Martin happened to
be in town. A resolution condemning Martin had been written for the
convention and the placards had already been made for a demonstration
by all the delegates.

Ultimately the delegates, including MUA National Secretary Paddy
Crumlin, agreed instead that an effort would be made to resolve the
matter behind the scenes by appealing directly to Martin through
respected Canadian Auto Workers President Buzz Hargrove. Hargrove
offered to intervene at the highest levels and have Martin arrange a
meeting between the MUA and senior CSL management to resolve the
dispute. According to Crumlin, "They basically agreed to actually
resolve it. Not that Martin would act directly, but I was assured that
Martin would understand the situation. It was made clear to me that
Martin was in full knowledge of it and that he was concerned and
would use whatever influence he had within the company to ensure that
a high-level meeting was organized to deal with the question."[18]

According to Buzz Hargrove, his contact with Martin was indirect: "I
arranged [the meeting] through a Liberal Member of Parliament, a
friend of mine who is close to Martin, and I got a call back from the
chief executive officer of CSL, a French guy, whose name I have for-
gotten."[19] In the end, however, no meeting with top-level management
was ever arranged. Says Crumlin, "We eventually had a meeting with a
guy named Gerry Carter who was just the Australian shipping operator.
He was half the problem in Australia—he was very pugnacious, a know-
it-all, and I reckon a lot of this stuff was his call in the first place."[20]

Despite its front-page status in Australia, there was barely a mention
in Canada of an issue that reflected directly on one of the country's
most prominent and powerful politicians. At the time, only the *National
Post* gave the story independent coverage; the CBC aired a brief radio
report, and the mostly small city newspapers that printed anything at all
had to use an Associated Press wire story.

Over a year later this media silence ended in dramatic fashion with a
full documentary on *Disclosure*, a CBC television documentary program.
Larry Zolf, a veteran journalist, wrote about the media's self-censorship

after the exposé aired: "The media sat on the Martin story for years. In media circles, nervous jokes about Martin's 'navy' were common. But the media sat on [it] … because they knew that, above anything else, Paul Martin was an honest and dedicated businessman … Integrity, complete solid integrity, both in business and in politics, was the Paul Martin trademark."[21] For the Canadian media, evidence to the contrary was counterintuitive, so it declined to bring the story to Canadians.

Yet this was a case of more than just voluntary censorship. The hard-ball tactics of Paul Martin's personal strategists and media advisors are legendary in Ottawa. Reporters who wrote unflattering stories about Martin often found their access to the finance minister denied. The *Disclosure* documentary was a classic example of this strategy. Just two hours before the program was to air, CBC News editor-in-chief Tony Burman ordered the show pulled. Elly Alboim, consultant to Martin and former CBC Ottawa bureau chief, called Burman to complain about *Disclosure*'s efforts to question Martin at a public event. The broadcast was postponed for two weeks.

Again, there was barely a ripple in the rest of the media despite the apparent intervention by CBC brass on behalf of a powerful politician whose business practices were being revealed. Burman claimed pulling the program had nothing to do with the call from Alboim. In an internal memo to all CBC journalists, Burman stated, "There was nothing unusual or inappropriate in receiving this communication from Mr. Alboim…. So to repeat: the piece was delayed because we felt it needed more work. There were no outside pressures involved in this decision … Delays in complicated pieces often happen."[22] Delays do happen, but this piece was pulled two hours before broadcast after having been intensely promoted all day.

The only people who knew about this story were those who read the *National Post* piece or saw the *Disclosure* documentary: Paul Martin was never seriously tagged with his company's union-busting activities in Australia. Martin would eventually take a public hit for tax avoidance, however, which arose from the use of offshore companies to own ships. More than once the political opposition pointed to the hypocrisy of Canada's finance minister owning a company—even if it was at arm's length—that was structured specifically to avoid Canadian tax laws.

## TAX HAVENS, POLLUTION, AND SCANDAL

*Disclosure*'s investigation found that CSL was a thorough practitioner of tax avoidance. It also found what seemed to be an obvious conflict of interest involving Martin's role in bringing about changes to tax laws that directly benefited CSL.

According to *Disclosure*, in 1992, when Martin was still in Opposition, CSL set up five companies in the small African country of Liberia. "The companies had names like 'Atlasco Shipping' and 'CSL International Inc.' They had no employees and no offices, but they did help CSL avoid paying Canadian tax."[23] Liberia's laws, in concert with Canada's, allowed companies to declare profits in that country and then bring them back into Canada tax-free. It would have been difficult for Martin not to have known that just as CSL was establishing its Liberian shell companies, Canadian Auditor General Denis Desautels was pressing the Tory government to shut down these tax havens, which were costing Canada hundreds of millions of dollars in lost revenue. In 1993, a Commons committee put added pressure on the government to remedy the situation.

In 1994, it seemed the new Liberal finance minister had truly heard the complaints. In his first budget speech, Paul Martin announced his plan of action: "Certain Canadian corporations are not paying an appropriate level of tax. Accordingly, we are taking measures to prevent companies from using foreign affiliates to avoid paying Canadian taxes which are otherwise due."[24] But according to *Disclosure*, "Martin didn't shut down all the tax havens. Across the Atlantic, he kept Barbados open, and that's exactly where CSL went next."[25]

The tax avoidance and union-busting issues were not the only controversies to dog CSL and Paul Martin in 2002. On March 6, one of Martin's ships, the CSL *Atlas*, was caught trailing an oil slick 15 metres wide and 40 kilometres long through an area off the coast of Nova Scotia containing sensitive marine wildlife. The ship's officer denied responsibility, but the government had photographic evidence to the contrary. CSL was fined $125,000, one of the largest penalties ever levied by the transport department. The same ship had been fined in 1991 for a similar infraction.[26] A year later, another CSL ship was caught polluting an extremely sensitive ecological zone in a bay near prime salmon stocks on the BC coast.[27]

It was also revealed in 2003 that Martin had been informed about a deal in which CSL was preparing to purchase three new ships that would have an exclusive contract hauling coal for an independent electricity producer in Indonesia called PT Jawa Power.[28] Bambang Trihatmodjo, son of Indonesian president and dictator Suharto, convinced the company to give him a 15 per cent interest for virtually no investment. Forced to purchase electricity at above-market rates from Jawa, Indonesia's state-owned power company eventually collapsed into bankruptcy. Those politically enforced above-market rates provided CSL with very lucrative contracts. Martin and CSL claimed they knew nothing about the Suharto family's involvement in the scandal even though US Ambassador to Indonesia Robert Barry said it was "common knowledge in Jakarta that Bambang had been cut in on Jawa Power."[29]

These stories highlight the astonishing disconnect between what Paul Martin says about his corporate ownership and the company's actual practices. When he gave up ownership of CSL to his sons in March 2003, Martin said in a statement, "I have always believed in the underlying principles of corporate social responsibility. Indeed, those [companies] that embrace their obligations to environmental stewardship, progressive labour relations and the highest of safety standards are companies that ultimately enjoy greater success."[30] Earlier, he had also stated, "I have always followed the rules. I have always gone far beyond the rules."

In choosing these words, Paul Martin claims that his company is not just ethical by average standards, but exemplary. Yet reports of union-busting, tax avoidance, environmental infractions, safety violations, and dubious dealings in Indonesia show how CSL is just the opposite. Ironically, Martin was, in fact, in an excellent position to run a model corporation: he owned the whole company and had no outside shareholders to whom he had a fiduciary responsibility to maximize profits. He had the opportunity to create any corporate culture he chose. He has made his choice clear.

## THROWING IN THE TOWEL
On March 13, 2003, after weeks of pressure, Paul Martin was finally forced to divest himself of CSL as a result of Canadian conflict-of-inter-

est laws affecting cabinet ministers. When he finally relinquished the company to his sons, Martin showed no sign that he actually understood why he had to give it up—he did it because politically he had no other choice. Many commentators argued that the new ownership of CSL represented little or no improvement, that the conflict still existed because Martin's sons owned the company. Almost every time he was accused of being in a conflict of interest, he gave the impression he simply didn't comprehend the problem: namely that public officials can't perform their duties properly when those duties intersect with their business interests.

Wilson claims that Martin never gave any instructions to the CSL management team while he was finance minister. Yet the whole concept of conflict of interest is tied to perception. It isn't enough that conflict doesn't take place, the public has to see that conflict doesn't take place and couldn't take place. The conflict here exists not because Martin could make a phone call to CSL management, but because he was allowed to be in a position of knowledge to make that call. Even so, this is what Howard Wilson told *Disclosure* about Martin: "He didn't come into public life to enrich himself. I mean, the fact of the matter is he was already a wealthy man when he came in. And his concern was to in fact achieve some important goals for Canada."[31]

Wilson's very subjective judgment about Paul Martin's character raises serious questions about his role as ethics counsellor. If he believed Martin to be beyond reproach, how could he judge him otherwise? Wilson's assessment of Martin is similar to the mainstream media's—Paul Martin is a man of integrity, incapable of unethical behaviour. The Ethics Counsellor's unusual take on conflict of interest has worked extremely well for Paul Martin. On every occasion, he has been absolved of any conflict, perceived or otherwise.

## OTHER CONFLICTS?

As Robert Chodos and his co-authors have pointed out in their political biography of Paul Martin, when a politician with business interests as extensive as Paul Martin's occupies a portfolio like finance, which has an almost limitless range of impacts on every sector of the economy, "it is virtually inevitable that the possibility, suggestion or appearance of conflict of interest will arise at some point."[32] In this case, it wasn't just Martin's businesses that gave rise to the possibility of conflicts, it was also his membership on the boards of several large firms. One of those firms was Manufacturers' Life Insurance Company. While Martin was finance minister, the insurance industry successfully lobbied the finance department to defer changes to the Bank Act that would have allowed Canada's chartered banks to sell insurance. Had the plan gone ahead, it would have provided serious competition for the insurance industry. Martin was no longer on the board, but did former board colleagues have privileged access to Paul Martin, and was he especially sympathetic to the industry's needs?

Martin had also been a member of the board of Imasco, a holding company that owns Imperial Tobacco, the dominant player in the Canadian cigarette market. Soon after Martin took over as finance minister, the federal government was facing the problem of large-scale tobacco smuggling from the US. Tobacco companies were shipping huge quantities of cigarettes to the smugglers' US suppliers in what was a transparent effort to pressure the federal government to lower its tobacco taxes. The scheme worked, and the government dramatically lowered the tobacco tax, resulting in the loss of tens of millions of dollars in revenue and a rapid spike in the number of teenaged smokers. While the Liberal cabinet approved the move to lower the tax, there is every likelihood Paul Martin, the most powerful minister in the cabinet, could have refused to buckle in the face of what the government now claims was a criminal conspiracy by big tobacco.

Martin's ownership of three (now two) movie theatres in Vancouver raised explicit questions of conflict of interest in the spring of 1994 when the Canada Development Investment Corporation (CDIC) sold Toronto textbook firm Ginn Publishing to its former owner, Paramount Communications. The finance department was responsible for the CDIC and a Martin company had direct business dealings with Paramount subsidiary Famous Players, which leased his theatres. More importantly, the sale of Ginn effectively completed the sell-off of Prentice-Hall (a process begun by the Mulroney Tories), increasing Paramount's already large market share in the Canadian textbook industry.[33] The Commons went into an uproar over the issue and Martin's connections with Paramount, but the finance minister was absolved again by Ethics Counsellor Wilson.

Said Wilson, "He's in a landlord relationship with Famous Players, not an investment relationship."[34]

In 1999, Martin would face yet another charge of conflict of interest. Though the charge would again arise out of Martin's career as a businessman and a corporate board member, it related more to politics than business. The company in question was the Canada Development Corporation and the alleged conflict was Martin's possible role in one of the worst health scandals in Canadian history, the tainted blood tragedy of the 1980s.

## BAD BLOOD, BAD BUSINESS

In 1981, the Liberal government chose Paul Martin to be one of its four nominees to the board of the Canada Development Corporation (CDC). During the six years Martin sat on the CDC board, a company in which the CDC held a controlling interest would play a central role in Canada's tainted-blood scandal.

The Canadian Hemophilia Society estimates that through the 1980s, 1,100 Canadians were infected with HIV through the blood supply: hundreds died after subsequently developing AIDS, and thousands more contracted hepatitis C.[35] Andre Picard's book, *Gift of Death*, chronicled much of the story, but also repeatedly brought readers back to what is central to this tragedy: the horrific and mostly avoidable suffering many Canadians endured because they were treated with blood containing the HIV virus and other infectious agents.[36]

Paul Martin's connection to this tragedy was through Connaught Laboratories, one of fifteen in the CDC's stable of companies. The federal government established the CDC in 1971 as a holding company to foster leading-edge Canadian businesses and create profit-making opportunities for Canadians. The investment in Connaught was an effort to nurture a domestic health-care industry.

The contaminated blood products that were linked to so much suffering and death were supplied by Connaught Laboratories to the Canadian Red Cross during the years that Paul Martin sat on the CDC board. In his 1997 report on the causes of the tainted-blood tragedy, Justice Horace Krever revealed that those responsible for Canada's blood supply could have reduced the scale of the disaster.[37] Working from the findings of the Krever Inquiry, the RCMP created a special unit, the Blood Task Force, and launched its own five-year investigation. This investigation has so far resulted in thirty-two criminal charges, with the possibility of more in the future. To date, Connaught has escaped criminal charges, but it is named in a billion-dollar lawsuit by hemophiliacs who contracted hepatitis C from tainted blood products.

Two years after Krever published his report, it was revealed that Paul Martin had a connection to the issue. Opposition claims of a conflict of interest were investigated by Ethics Counsellor Howard Wilson. Martin's response to the claims was essentially a denial of any responsibility. He maintained his role on the CDC board did not involve the details of Connaught's operations and he had "no recollection" of tainted-blood problems ever being mentioned. Martin himself asked Wilson to investigate, promising complete cooperation and the provision of all documents related to the issue. While Wilson concluded there was no conflict, the details surrounding the scandal and actions by Martin's political staff raise serious questions about Paul Martin's role on the CDC board.

## FOLLOW THE MONEY

One contributing factor to Canada's tainted-blood tragedy was the political pressure to have a Canadian manufacturer of blood products, but little comparable commitment to ensure that high safety standards were met. Another possible factor was the coincidental drive to create a commercially successful health business out of what had been a non-profit Canadian research institution.

Between 1914 and 1972, Connaught Medical Research Laboratories (as it was known after 1946) was a self-supporting, non-commercial part of the University of Toronto. In 1972, the university sold Connaught, famous for its development of insulin, for $24 million to the CDC. The Red Cross had reservations about the sale: "The transfer of [Connaught] to the private sector placed the Red Cross in the position of answering one million volunteer blood donors as to why profits should be made on their gift."[38]

One reason the University of Toronto sold Connaught was that its laboratories had become antiquated and required expensive upgrades.

There were problems in particular with Connaught's blood facilities, which separated blood into its components for different therapeutic uses. These problems would plague Connaught right up until the CDC sold the company in 1987.

When Martin joined the CDC board in 1981, Connaught had already generated nearly a decade of headaches for the CDC that should have been part of any file Martin received as a new director. Right from its very first years under CDC ownership, Connaught repeatedly got negative evaluations from government health inspectors.[39] A CDC insider commented to the *Globe and Mail*, "Crowding, exposed piping and peeling paint ... It is no wonder that contamination has been a recurring problem with our plasma product."[40] In 1976, investigative journalists at CBC-TV's *The Fifth Estate* did a major exposé on Connaught, documenting how the company made $500,000 exporting a blood derivative at a time when the Red Cross said it was in short supply in Canada.

In the two years just before Martin joined the CDC board, Connaught was engaged in a very public fight with the Red Cross over a contract for factor VIII concentrate, a blood product used to treat hemophiliacs. The Red Cross wanted to build its own factor VIII plant in Canada, but in the interim had hired a US company to do the job. The Ontario government intervened and forced the Red Cross to contract part of the work to Toronto-based Connaught. Red Cross officials objected to a commercial lab like Connaught being given a central role in what was supposed to be a non-profit blood system. Connaught argued private industry would view the creation of non-profit factor VIII facilities as a government "nationalization," making Canada less attractive to pharmaceutical companies.[41] Paul Martin could have scarcely missed the widespread media coverage of this battle.

By the time Martin began serving on the CDC board, Connaught was a high-profile, controversial company with a public record of serious problems. This hardly fits with Martin's later description of Connaught as a "subsidiary of a subsidiary" as though it barely hit the radar screen of CDC board members. While Connaught's deficiencies were certainly not the only factor in the tainted-blood tragedy, the Krever Inquiry would document specific defects in the way Connaught operated during Martin's tenure on the CDC board that played a role in the disaster.

## CONNAUGHT'S FAILINGS

The Krever Inquiry revealed that, in the early 1980s, "Connaught was unable to achieve a reasonable yield of factor VIII concentrate, and, as a consequence, large volumes of domestic plasma were wasted."[42] The company's inability to make efficient use of plasma provided by the Red Cross meant it had to buy additional plasma on the international market. In making purchases from international blood brokers, Connaught would be both undermining the non-profit character of the Canadian system and relying on riskier sources of blood.

Unlike Canada, where the Red Cross had stopped collecting blood from prisoners in 1971 due to their high rate of hepatitis B infection, the US still was meeting part of its blood supply needs from prison sources up until 1982. But, in March 1983, the US Food and Drug Administration (FDA) informed Connaught of the new guidelines it had established for American blood suppliers. These guidelines recommended against collecting prisoners' blood because of concerns about HIV contamination.[43] In August, Connaught discovered one of its main suppliers, Montreal-based Continental Pharma-Cryosan, had been buying plasma that came from Arkansas prisoners. Connaught alerted the Red Cross to this discovery, and the charity immediately cancelled Connaught's contract. Although the Red Cross would subsequently reinstate the contract, its cancellation in September 1983, two years into Martin's appointment, created a major crisis for Connaught.

Connaught's apparently unintentional use of prison blood was not the only problem, however. Connaught had stopped doing its own inspections of blood collection centres in the US, and instead was supposed to be relying on FDA reports. Except, as the Krever Inquiry discovered, nobody at Connaught actually looked at the reports: "The Food and Drug Administration inspection reports were obtained, but they were not reviewed."[44] The result was that US blood rejected as too risky for use by Americans was being supplied to Canadians through Connaught.

Connaught had assured the Red Cross in March 1983 that none of its US suppliers were collecting blood in areas with a high incidence of AIDS. Connaught officials claimed in a letter to the Red Cross that they were "keenly aware of the potential risk of AIDS for the hemophiliac."[45] However, around the time it was offering this assurance, Connaught was getting supplies from a blood bank in San Francisco, a city that was on the FDA's warning list because it was located in one of the world's highest-risk areas for HIV infection. Connaught supplied the Red Cross with blood products from this source until 1985.[46]

The conclusion of the Krever Inquiry was unequivocal: "Many of the lots of commercial factor VIII concentrate made by Connaught during 1983 and 1984 contained plasma that came from prisons and the Irwin Memorial Blood Bank [in San Francisco]. Those lots had a higher risk associated with them than would have been the case if plasma from those sources had not been used."[47]

In his April 2000 report on Martin's alleged conflict of interest, Ethics Counsellor Howard Wilson shifted the blame for the prison blood fiasco from Connaught—and by extension, the members of its CDC parent board—to Continental Pharma-Cryosan. Wilson said that while Continental Pharma was informed by the FDA in June 1983 of potential problems with plasma it had supplied to Connaught, it did not initiate a recall and did not inform Connaught until two months later. Wilson concludes in his report that if Continental Pharma had acted more promptly, "subsequent difficulties for Connaught and the Canadian Red Cross might have been avoided or at least minimized."

However, Wilson's focus on the 1983 prison blood incident ignores the underlying problem, identified by Krever: Connaught did not read FDA inspection reports about any of its US sources. This included high-risk blood banks, which were supplying it independently of Continental Pharma. Furthermore, if directors at Connaught and the CDC were shocked by Continental Pharma's purchases of prison blood and failure to recall potentially contaminated supplies, their subsequent behaviour did not show it. Instead of severing relations with Continental Pharma, mere months after the prison-blood revelation Connaught entered into negotiations to launch a multi-million-dollar joint venture with the company's president, Thomas Hecht. Connaught President Alun Davies wrote a letter on February 2, 1984, addressed to "Tom," informing him that Connaught was "prepared to enter into a long term arrangement" with Continental Pharma, and would consider a "joint venture company." The CDC board would almost certainly have been involved in planning this new venture, as it involved a significant new investment.

Perhaps CDC board members, including Paul Martin, were never provided with the federal health department report on Canada's blood brokers. This 1977 report had warned, "It is evident we are dealing with more than technical violations, but rather a calculated and deliberate business designed to take advantage of legal loopholes providing possibly hazardous products on the world market, which could include the Canadian market."[48] Perhaps health officials had never passed on the information they had received about an FBI investigation that found Continental Pharma had "violated the law."[49] And perhaps they had never heard about the RCMP investigation that resulted in Continental Pharma pleading guilty in 1980 for falsely labelling blood as coming from Swedish donors when it had actually been extracted from Russian cadavers.[50]

Yet, as shown earlier, Continental Pharma was not an unknown quantity for CDC board members. In 1982, Continental Pharma President Thomas Hecht joined long-time CDC Director Murray Koffler on the board of an Israeli bank's Canadian subsidiary. When Connaught was developing its joint venture plan with Continental Pharma, Hecht and Martin sat on the board of Concordia University together. It is possible, of course, that Martin had no knowledge of the long-simmering blood story. But it seems unlikely.

As well, CDC board members could hardly have been unaware of the prison blood incident, since this discovery had resulted in the cancellation of Connaught's all-important Red Cross contract, on which its blood business depended. As well, articles about AIDS and the possibility of infection through the blood system started appearing in Canada in the spring of 1983; Martin was a CDC director until the end of 1987. A concerned and alert CDC director might have raised the issue at a board meeting, asking whether its subsidiary, Connaught, was doing all it could to avoid transmitting HIV through its blood products—such as avoiding any blood supplied from sources that did not meet the FDA's guidelines. When asked about his role on the CDC board during the time of the tainted-blood tragedy, Paul Martin's response is that the issue never came up while he was a director. Given Connaught's central role in the Canadian blood system, the question is, "Why not?"

## THE POLITICIAN AND THE BLOOD SCANDAL

Connaught abandoned the blood business joint venture it had discussed with Continental Pharma, and the CDC sold the company in 1987. Martin quit the CDC board that same year and ran for office in 1988. A decade later, Martin had to deal with the blood scandal when the federal cabinet learned that Justice Krever intended to assign blame in his final report. Krever had sent notices to Connaught, the Red Cross, and health department officials informing them that they would potentially be cited for wrongdoing; if they were, criminal or civil prosecution was a possibility. Martin participated in the cabinet decision to pursue Krever all the way to the Supreme Court of Canada to block him from assigning such blame, but was cleared of conflict-of-interest charges by Ethics Counsellor Wilson. Krever ultimately won the court case, but was cautioned on the extent to which his report could identify instances of criminal negligence.

Martin was also cleared of conflict-of-interest charges when he participated in the 1998 cabinet decision that denied compensation to those who contracted any blood-born disease before 1986 or after 1990—a total of between 20,000 and 39,000 victims. Justice Krever had recommended that all those infected by the blood supply be compensated on a no-fault basis. The government justified its decision to limit compensation by saying that there was no effective blood test for hepatitis C before 1986. But this decision ignored evidence in the Krever Report that Connaught failed to take available measures to ensure its blood products were not contaminated. Government compensation of victims who were infected before 1986 might have been perceived as official acknowledgment that organizations linked to the government—including Connaught—had done something wrong. In short, compensation could have been used in lawsuits against Connaught and/or the CDC.


## TO BE CONTINUED ...

It was not until May 25, 1999 that Martin's connection with the blood scandal was revealed in the media.[51] Opposition MPs immediately charged that Martin had been in a conflict of interest because of his past connections with Connaught. They pointed to the two tainted blood-related decisions that Martin had to participate in as a cabinet minister.

Martin responded to the accusations in the House of Commons with this statement: "I was a director of the Canada Development Corporation. Connaught Laboratories was a subsidiary of a subsidiary of the Canada Development Corporation. Each of the companies had their own independent boards of directors. As I have already stated, I have no recollection of any discussions at the CDC board level on this matter."[52] However, as annual reports for the companies show, the governing bodies of the CDC and Connaught overlapped. To ensure CDC supervision, CDC directors and officers sat on the board of each of its major companies, with Connaught's board having several CDC representatives. These overlapping appointments would have given CDC directors ample opportunity during board meetings to get answers about what was going on at Connaught. Martin had opportunity to question any of the CDC members on the Connaught board, and despite his effort to downplay the company's importance, it was far from an obscure sideline. The CDC owned 100 per cent of Connaught, and Connaught accounted for 85 per cent of the CDC's revenues from its health sector division. Connaught's blood business was the key component of its growth strategy and was described by company executives themselves as a "major operation."[53]

Ethics Counsellor Wilson backed Martin's description of his role when the Opposition asked for a conflict of interest ruling. In his April 2000 statement, Wilson said he did not see a conflict, citing the 1983 CDC annual report that described the CDC as not being involved in the "day-to-day management" of its companies.

Yet Wilson could have selected other descriptions of the CDC's mandate that would have given a different perspective on the role of directors like Paul Martin in overseeing CDC companies. For example, the annual report for 1981, the year Martin became a CDC director, stated clearly, "To be successful itself, CDC has never hesitated to take full responsibility for the policies and major operating decisions of the companies it controls." In 1991, the Kingston *Whig Standard* did an in-depth profile of Connaught based on extensive interviews with CDC and Connaught directors. The CDC is described as "actively involved in strategy. CDC was never a passive holding company; it worked on business plans and financial plans and marketing plans and research plans and budgets."[54]

## BLOOD SECRETS

Unfortunately, Canadians may never know the whole story of the tainted-blood tragedy, despite all the effort that went into the Krever Inquiry and the subsequent RCMP investigation. Unidentified persons have gone to extreme lengths in an apparent attempt to destroy documents related to the story. On May 18, 1999, the Montreal offices of the Canadian Hemophilia Society were burglarized.[55] A computer and all the materials relating to the blood tragedy were taken. On that same evening in Pine Bluff, Arkansas, the medical clinic owned by US tainted-blood whistleblower Michael Galster was fire-bombed, destroying all his tainted-blood files. Galster had written an exposé based on his work at the Cummins Prison in Arkansas, a major source of the contaminated blood purchased by Continental Pharma and sold to Connaught.

Less dramatic, but perhaps more effective, has been the stonewalling of Access to Information requests. When Paul Martin's connection to the scandal was revealed in the media, the Hemophilia Society's vice-president Mike McCarthy and others requested the CDC board minutes from the government. The finance department claimed "a thorough search" turned up no such records. Unsatisfied with this response, McCarthy filed a letter of complaint to Federal Information Commissioner John Reid.

What follows is the chronology of events as described in the Information Commissioner's annual report for 2001–02. In July and August, all requests for the CDC board minutes received the same reply: "I must inform you that after a thorough search, no records were found to respond to your requests." There the matter would have rested had Reid not come across a memo referring to a conversation between finance officials and the Ethics Counsellor's office. Finance had obtained a set of CDC minutes as a result of shadowing the Ethics Counsellor's staff, who found them while investigating the conflict of interest complaint against Martin.

The memo indicated senior finance officials—including the deputy minister and two assistant deputies—reviewed the minutes and then tried to give them back to the Ethics Counsellor's staff, who refused to take them. According to Reid, "It is the Commissioner's view that senior officials of Finance Canada were concerned about the 'optics' of being in possession of records obtained by the Office of the Ethics Counsellor...."

The Information Commissioner's annual report is devastating in its assessment of the behaviour of finance department officials: "The commissioner ... concluded that the answers given to the requests for CDC board minutes were so bereft of helpful information that he found them to be intentionally misleading.... The most senior officials of the department were aware of the 'disconnect' between the facts and the responses.... Finance Canada was neither embarrassed nor apologetic when these facts came to light." Reid later discovered that, in fact, the finance department had two sets of CDC board minutes: one from the Ethics Counsellor and one they had all along in their own files.

In his full report on the matter, leaked to the Canadian Press, in March 2002, Reid went even further, directly blaming Martin's political staff for drafting the misleading responses: "The Minister's senior exempt staff, Ms. Thorkelson and Mr. [Scott] Reid, knew of and were involved in the preparation of the 'no records' responses."[56] Scott Reid subsequently denied the "no records" response was his decision. He later became one of Paul Martin's senior campaign organizers.

The minutes McCarthy was finally able to obtain from the finance department were incomplete, missing out the crucial years when the tainted blood tragedy unfolded. McCarthy has spent years trying to track down these documents, but his efforts have so far been unsuccessful. Unless copies of the missing CDC minutes finally get unearthed, Paul Martin will always be able to say that he has "no recollection" of the board discussing the tainted-blood tragedy.

It is worth noting that not all politicians connected to the blood scandal were eager to deny responsibility. Monique Begin, Minister of Health and Welfare under Pierre Trudeau, was granted immunity by Justice Krever. Begin waived her immunity, however, noting in a letter to Krever: "I consider it my duty to take my share of the responsibility."[57]

The story is not over. The search for CDC minutes and other documentary evidence of Paul Martin's knowledge of the tainted-blood tragedy continues. The billion-dollar lawsuit against Connaught and Continental Pharma is ongoing. Eventually, people will be called to testify under oath about who knew what, and when.

## EDGING INTO POLITICS

During his fight to keep CSL, Paul Martin suggested that his critics were attacking all business people. He asked, "Do we want to say, 'Everyone who has built a business cannot go into public life'? I don't believe so."[58] No one was saying that business people should not be in politics, but many would say that each businessperson who goes into public life has to answer for his or her record in business and their ethical standards, just like anyone else seeking public office. It's the kind of businessperson you are that matters.

We can and should take Paul Martin's record as a businessman and corporate tycoon into account when assessing his ethical make-up and his judgement. Most business people who end up in politics seem to have little trouble recognizing the difference between the two vocations. While no one suggests that business people are not appropriate in public life, they are ultimately expected to understand the difference. Part of that difference is in ethical cultures: the bottom line versus the public interest. Yet as this book shows, instead of providing Paul Martin with an advantage in serving the public good, his long experience as a CEO may have made it more difficult for him to see just what that entailed. Having immersed himself in the highest echelons of the corporate world at a time when its attitude towards democracy and activist government was undergoing profound change, his business experience would have instilled in him the imperative of the day—radically reducing the role of government in the economy and society.

The defining moment for Martin's entry into politics was somewhat serendipitous. While Martin was not a publicly identifiable Liberal in 1981, he was nevertheless attracting attention from those in the party searching for potential leaders in a post-Trudeau era. At the time, many Young Liberals were becoming critical of what they viewed as an increasing disregard for internal party democracy by the party hierarchy. Looking for a conference speaker, three members decided to approach Martin, a relative outsider, but a man with power and prestige. The three—Alf Apps, Terrie O'Leary, and Peter Donolo—called on Martin with the message, "The party needs you, the country needs you."[59] Their visit and his acceptance of their invitation to speak at the conference are said to have been a decisive moment in Martin's political evolution.

Martin had thought about running for the leadership in 1984, but decided he had no chance of winning. Yet even then he would have had enthusiastic support, for he had impressed the Young Liberals. According to Apps, "Though we were centre-left Liberals, we thought the party needed to address fiscal responsibility issues."[60] By sheer chance, Martin had made a strong and durable connection with a group of young, smart, and ambitious political activists, the new generation of Liberals who would help him define the party in the new political era. It was just a matter of time.

# 2

# HIDDEN AGENDA

One prevailing myth about Paul Martin has it that he is his father's son. To be sure, Paul Martin was devoted to his father and has often referred to Paul Martin Sr.'s "legacy," but that is where any substance to the story seems to end. The alleged conflict between Paul Jr.'s respect for his father's legacy and his determination to fight the deficit would, in the real world of Finance Minister Martin, turn out to be virtually non-existent. Paul Martin's immersion in the business world, and his protracted career as a CEO, created an unbridgeable gap between his father's social liberalism and his own dedication to business principles and agendas.

Time and again, Paul Martin demonstrated that he was willing to sacrifice the philosophy of social liberalism, the value of social programs, and even the broad objective of nation-building for the fundamentals of the corporate-driven Washington Consensus. However, there is good reason for the persistence of this notion of a Paul Martin mired in conflict: he was largely responsible for both the left-wing policy platform that got the Liberals elected in 1993 (the famous Red Book) and the right-wing blueprint that guided their governance.

## THE "SOCIAL" LIBERAL

Paul Martin's reputation as a social liberal (at least within the party) may have its roots in the days of the 1990 Liberal leadership race, which coincided with the final battle over the Meech Lake Accord.

Meech Lake was a Mulroney government initiative in constitutional change that would have both given Quebec "distinct society" status and radically decentralized the Canadian federation. Martin was among Meech Lake's strongest supporters and was able to make that support very high profile because the deadline for its ratification—June 30, 1990—was the same day as the Liberal leadership vote, in which he and Jean Chrétien were the main contenders. Though the accord eventually fell apart (prompting some Martin supporters to wear black armbands at the convention to symbolize its death), and Chrétien won the leadership (leaving a bitterness between the two men and their staffs and advisors that would last thirteen years until the next convention), Martin's campaign was a magnet for progressive elements in the party.

While Chrétien had tried to reconcile the regional tensions and anti-Quebec bias developing around Meech Lake by proposing amendments (one of which rendered the distinct society clause benign), Martin had taken a different position: "The main challenge for a post-Trudeau vision is to reconcile the desires of Canadians for a strong national government ... with their genuine aspirations as members of ethnic, cultural and regional groups."[1] Many saw this "soft" approach to Quebec sovereignists as progressive, particularly those who supported Quebec's right to self-determination. However, Martin's stance went beyond a simple question of political rights for Quebec. Mulroney had also appealed to soft nationalists—a strategy that won him and the Tories the province of Quebec in two elections. Though some accused Martin of being "soft" on Quebec, he was actually hard on political strategy: the Liberals had traditionally stayed in power by dominating Quebec.

Another element of Martin's leadership campaign was his promotion of what he saw as the crucial relationship between government and business in creating economic growth for the country. Martin was especially impressed with what Quebec had accomplished with government institutions like the Quebec Stock Saving Plan and the Caisse de Depot, which had helped to develop an indigenous business class. Martin was acquainted with the key individuals in this grand experiment and commented, "What Quebec has created in the past twenty-five years is nothing less than an economic revolution ... Canada is desperately in need of the same kind of revolution."[2]

The most legitimate part of Paul Martin's reputation as a social liberal comes from his time in Opposition and shadow cabinet positions, especially as environment critic. It was here that Martin's legendary charm and his real engagement of the issues were most in evidence. Many environmentalists remember Paul Martin in his role as environment critic as one of the most enthusiastic supporters of the cause. Karen Mahon, a long-time environmental activist in the early 1990s, met with Martin many times. "He was by far the most responsive environment critic I ever dealt with," she recalls. "He listened to everything we said very carefully. He would even spend hours at meetings and conferences sitting on those hard chairs listening to endless speeches. He was very charming and unassuming for a politician. Everyone was really impressed with him and his grasp of the issues. I think most people would have credited him as a genuine environmentalist."[3]

Martin took over as environment critic just as Canadians' concerns about the environment was peaking. Concerns about climate change and the thinning of the ozone layer were high-profile public issues, and the historic 1992 Earth Summit in Rio de Janeiro provided Martin with his first significant opportunity to impress the Canadian public. He became a passionate advocate of sustainable development and defined the issue in Brazil with the rhetorical question, "Will the focus of international trade shift from raw market forces to the needs of sustainable development?" Martin attacked the Mulroney free trade deal for the extremely weak protection it afforded the environment, declaring that environmental protection should trump free trade as an inherent value. He challenged the Tory MPs to ask why "Germany is both the environmental leader of Europe as well as the economic leader.... One follows the other."[4] To everyone involved in environmental issues, Martin seemed a genuine, and effective, champion of their cause.

Like the environmentalists, anti-poverty activists also experienced Martin's convincing advocacy. This time the issue was social housing, and Martin co-chaired a Liberal Task Force on Housing in 1989–90. The task force visited nine cities over a six-week period in the fall of 1989 and produced a major report, "Finding Room: Housing Solutions for the Future," which made twenty-five detailed recommendations for solving the housing crisis. Martin lambasted the Tories: "The housing crisis is growing at an alarming rate and the government sits there and does nothing.... The lack of affordable housing contributes to and accelerates the cycle of poverty, which is reprehensible in a society as rich as ours." Quoting the Universal Declaration of Human Rights, Martin stated, "The Task Force believes that housing is a fundamental human right: all Canadians have the right to decent housing."[5] It was a passionate and persuasive expression of the Trudeau Liberals' "just society."

## POLITICS FOR REAL

Being in Opposition is one thing; being part of the governing party is decidedly another. Ultimately, it was both exercising power and maintaining it that tested Paul Martin's philosophical mettle and his legendary internal struggle.

When the Liberals swept to power in the 1993 election, they did so on a platform that ridiculed the free-market policies of the Tories under Brian Mulroney and denounced Kim Campbell's claim that the government couldn't solve the problem of unemployment. Ironically, while there were some mild hints of social liberalism early on in Paul Martin's tenure as finance minister—he presented a mildly stimulative 1994 budget—Canadian politics eventually took a hard right turn with Martin holding the financial reins.

On the face of it, there was no contradiction; the Liberals had a long history of getting elected on a run-from-the-left, govern-from-the-right strategy. Yet there is enough of a puzzle in Paul Martin—posed by some politically astute activists who are not easily duped—that it begs to be explored. The contradiction in Paul Martin wasn't between values; it was between roles. When he was in Opposition and running on the Liberal platform, Martin was free from his responsibility—and his persona—as a CEO. In this context, his best personal values found their fullest expression. There was no fiduciary duty to get in the way, no concern with costs. Martin's time in Opposition and on the campaign trail was like a sabbatical. When he got elected and entered cabinet—and took on the finance portfolio—he picked up his CEO identity just as quickly as he had dropped it. It was then that values became problematic, for he had a business to run.

More than anyone else, Paul Martin contributed to the formula that got the Liberals elected and to the contrary policy development that laid the plans for how they would actually govern. The progressive Paul Martin may have co-written the Liberal Party's Red Book platform, but it was Paul Martin the CEO who was key to a policy conference that dictated how the Liberals would run the country.

## THE RED BOOK: SELF-DECEPTION?

Co-authored by Paul Martin and left-leaning Liberal Chaviva Hosek, the Liberals' Red Book, an extensive policy document, appealed to what they knew to be Canadian values: strong communities, equality, medicare, education, and the elimination of child poverty. The Red Book was crystal clear in its criticism of the Tories' economic and fiscal policies. Above all, it attacked them for being "obsessed" with the deficit and inflation to the exclusion of any consideration of the resulting costs in terms of poverty and unemployment. Second, the Red Book claimed the Tories were too ideologically rigid and relied too much on the market for solutions to economic problems. The Liberals proposed to take a more balanced approach and reclaim an activist role for government. The third criticism flowed from the first two. The Red Book stated that the solution to Canada's economic problems, including the deficit, was not wholesale cuts to social programs and "diminished expectations," but "immediate measures to make our economy grow and create jobs."

The Red Book left no doubt about the pain and suffering that would follow if the government continued down the Tory path of radical inflation-fighting and deficit-cutting: "Unless Canadians get back to work, the cost of lost production, unemployment, and welfare will inevitably increase the deficit as it has in the course of the Conservative mandate.... Faster economic growth and reduction of unemployment is a prerequisite for sustained deficit reduction." Economic growth would solve all of Canada's fiscal problems and put people back to work—this was the unmistakable message found throughout the Red Book. That message was consistent with what Martin had said in Opposition, attacking the Mulroney government for its obsession with ideology:

"This administration claims that its hands are tied by the deficit. That is garbage. Its objectives are not economic, they are ideological, an ideology that went out with the potato famine of the 1840s. The deficit is a problem and it is a very real one, but its solution does not lie in taking a broad axe to our social safety net."[6]

The Red Book's economic policy promised an industrial strategy—the same kind of policy that had built Canada's modern economy from the post-war period through to the early 1980s. It was the policy option most reflective of Canadians' values: at its core was a commitment to create jobs for Canadian workers. This commitment was a value in itself and fit with the broad notion of the rights of citizenship—or at least with the expectation that the government would act in the interest of its citizens, even if it failed in that effort. It was a restatement of government objectives in the 1960s and 1970s to work towards full employment.

And there was more in the famous Liberal book of promises. One of the eight sections was devoted to the environment and sustainable development, likely reflecting Martin's active role as environment critic. In another, the Liberals promised to renegotiate NAFTA; if that was impossible, they said they would consider abrogating the deal. Another major promise in the 112-page book was clearly intended to capitalize on the issue that made Mulroney the most hated prime minister in Canadian history: the Liberals would get rid of the GST. Actually, the Red Book said the Liberals would "... replace the GST with a system that generates equivalent revenues, [and] is fairer to consumers and small business," but Sheila Copps claimed the government would abolish the hated tax and that is what stuck in the public's mind.

The Red Book dominated the 1993 election like no election platform document had before. No doubt Brian Mulroney's legacy was the biggest asset of the Liberal election campaign, but it was in the Red Book that the Liberals played on that legacy and the epithet that tormented Mulroney wherever he went: "Lyin' Brian." The importance of the Red Book was twofold: it provided a genuine vision of the country and it put in writing what the government was going to do. The Liberals' pollster, Michael Marzolini, concluded from his focus groups and polling that the desire for accountability would be the measure people used to judge the parties in the election: "Verbal promises were not enough to satisfy the electorate. They wanted accountability—a written contract, signed and costed..."[7] And Chrétien used it in exactly that manner, employing it as a prop for every speech, waving it at his audiences and repeatedly promising that if the Liberals won the election people could bring it to him in four years and hold him to account.

Within eighteen months of the election won on the Red Book, almost all of its promises were not only broken but were smashed. It was hardly the first time that election promises had not been kept; indeed, most prime ministers have notoriously retracted their word—Trudeau promised never to implement wage and price controls, and Brian Mulroney pledged never to sign a free trade deal. Yet given the foundation upon which the Red Book was laid, it seems that the document may have been nothing more than a tool designed to take advantage of Mulroney's legacy of deception and scoop votes from the NDP.

As a policy-platform process, the writing of the Red Book by Martin and Hosek was preceded by another process, one designed not for the electorate but for the Liberal Party and its future direction. The 1991 thinkers' conference in Aylmer, Quebec, was held exactly thirty years after a similar gathering, the famous 1961 Kingston Conference. Each reflected the times in which it was held and each laid out a policy framework that very accurately predicted the actual direction of future Liberal governments. The Kingston Conference set out the philosophy and objectives that would find their way into the governments of Lester Pearson and Pierre Trudeau for nearly twenty years.

However, the two conferences were profoundly different in terms of their ideological and political thrusts, and in the way they were organized. Tom Kent, a key figure in the Kingston Conference, recalls that the gathering was just a starting point and was followed by extensive involvement of the party membership: "Aylmer did not play the same role—[it was] a very different affair. It was much more top-down. Kingston was a gathering of liberally minded thinkers and was a free-for-all academic conference. Most importantly, it went on to a great national party rally for which over two thousand people came to Ottawa. In those days all the parties were actually democratic organizations. There was a very strong grassroots spirit in the 1960s. But it faded quickly in the late '70s."[8]

With the Kingston Conference, the party took a sharp turn to the left, largely because of the threat posed by the Co-operative Commonwealth Federation (CCF), which was about to join with organized labour to form the NDP. The conference was the inspiration and the wellhead of ideas for the Canadian version of the welfare state, which included expanding government social programs, meeting and encouraging high expectations, and seeding the notion of entitlement that, thirty years later, was the precise target those gathered at Aylmer had in their sites.

The Aylmer Conference unfolded under a very different notion of democracy and process. Says Kent, "The Aylmer Conference was structured more or less as a series of lectures by outside experts, with much less time for discussion.... But even as a think-tank event, the most important thing was that it was not followed up by a party policy conference. All it was followed by was the writing of the Red Book, which was also a top-down operation."[9]

Aylmer was overwhelmingly dominated by business Liberals and free-market advocates. Despite the Liberals' opposition to free trade, the only people at Aylmer knowledgeable about the issue were Brian Mulroney's two key FTA negotiators, Simon Reisman and Gordon Ritchie. Finance executives were well represented with Ken Courtis of Deutsche Bank capital markets and Dr. Martin Barkin, a partner in Peat Marwick Stevenson International. The right-wing economist John Crispo was there, as was Michael Phelps, the highly political CEO of BC's Westcoast Energy and member of the C.D. Howe board.[10] Two of the most influential speakers at the conference were Paul Martin's favourite thinkers.

The keynote speaker was, symbolically, an American—Lester Thurow, dean of the Alfred E. Sloan School of Management at Boston University. While he admitted, "I haven't studied Canada," he nonetheless assured those gathered that the country's way forward was increased economic integration with the US, "a carefully thought-out consensual strategy for economic growth for America"[11]—by which he apparently meant both Canada and the US. Thurow's ignorance of Canada was not a problem for those gathered at Aylmer. Such was the nature of a one-size-fits-all neo-liberal ideology that considered a country's history, traditions, and values as secondary to economic progress.

The same message was delivered by the most forceful and dynamic speaker at the conference, Bank of Nova Scotia Vice-President and former Nova Scotia Finance Minister Peter Nicholson—whom Martin invited personally to address the conference. His speech was not so much an analysis of the global economy and a formula for how Canada could best navigate its difficulties as it was a declaration of surrender. Entitled "Nowhere to Hide: The Economic Implications of Globalization for Canada," it was a hardball public relations assault on any hope that Canada might preserve what it had built in the post-war period. Nicholson developed a theme that would become a key objective in Martin's reign as finance minister: the need to change the role of the nation-state. Calling for a "reappraisal of the role of the nation-state," Nicholson left little room for any social role: "Societies that fail to respond effectively to the market test can, at best, look forward to a life of genteel economic decline, and, at worst, a descent into social chaos." He went on to offer six "guideposts" for Canada. They were a simple listing of the elements of the Washington Consensus—from fiscal restraint and labour "flexibility" to the expansion of free trade and a "social policy overhaul." In a back-to-the-future recommendation, the corporate state became the practical solution for dealing with the global economy: "Our foreign and commercial policy should be reunited with the private sector."[12]

The Aylmer Conference was not intended to be a debate about where the government would go; it was an opportunity to lay to rest any residual social liberalism lingering in pre-Mulroney elements of the party. Nicholson employed the TINA argument the Tories had saturated the country with in the free trade debate: "*There is no alternative....* The world is in the thrall of global forces that cannot be defied by a relatively small, trade-dependent and massively indebted country like Canada [italics added]."[13] Nicholson's hyperbole seemed like a plea to social liberals to simply give up, to surrender for the good of the country. He was staking out the territory of the new elite consensus. His speech and Thurow's were intended to ensure that no one who wanted to be taken seriously by the party would dare challenge such a self-evident declaration.

And few did. Jean Chrétien, who made a point of attending the whole weekend conference, wrapped up the gathering with words and a tone similar to Nicholson's. Chrétien's political instincts obviously approved of such a clear, uncluttered, ruthlessly simple message. In his interpretation of the weekend's neo-liberal theme, he revealed why he liked it: it was practical, not ideological. "Protectionism is neither left-wing or right-wing. It is simply passé," said the future prime minister. "Globalization is neither right-wing or left-wing. It is just a fact of life."[14]

For the business Liberals, the weekend had been a complete success. Especially happy were Roy MacLaren, John Manley, and Paul Martin (dubbed "The Three Ms" by MacLaren) because all three believed the party clearly had to rethink its position on free trade—not just accept it, but embrace it is a guiding principle. Thirty years after the hard left turn to the democratic welfare state, the party was about to take a hard right turn. "Aylmer was the watershed," remembers MacLaren. "Once Aylmer happened and the leader of the opposition endorsed its discussion, as he so clearly did in the summing-up speech, to a real degree the debate was over."[15]

Lloyd Axworthy, the party's pre-eminent social liberal, didn't stick around for the celebration of globalization, dismissing it as a "cover for right-wing ideology." Axworthy and others on the left of the party had not given up. Despite the ideological tone of the conference, they believed there was in fact flexibility with regard to public policy-making—including deficit reduction—which could preserve much of what the Liberals had built in the post-war period. But the conjuncture of forces was not propitious for such flexibility. The hostility to the old world order was considerable, not only within the party and among its corporate backers, but also in the overwhelmingly pro-market mass media. Furthermore, the business Liberals had in their arsenal the political equivalent of a nuclear bomb: the deficit.

The federal civil service, especially the key departments of industry, finance, and trade, had been implementing the market agenda for a full nine years. In the 1970s and even the early 1980s, senior and middle levels of bureaucracy were still able to provide a mix of policy options to ministers and their political staffs. However, by the time the Liberals took office in 1993, the bureaucracy had been transformed: that mix of policies and the arguments for them had largely disappeared. Any economist promoting traditional notions of economic growth, full employment, or any objective other than "economic efficiency" had either recanted under relentless pressure from the free marketeers or simply retired. The Chrétien government would leave this Mulroney-inspired bureaucracy absolutely unchanged—right up to keeping the deputy ministers largely responsible for implementing Mulroney's policies in their posts.

While many of the backbenchers in the caucus owed their 1993 election to fighting free trade, the next batch of MPs—especially the ones from Ontario—would be overwhelmingly business Liberals. This shift to the right was due in part to the other key political factor driving the party. In the days of the Kingston Conference, the Liberals were forced to move their traditional "centre" to the left because of the threat from the NDP. In the early 1990s, the NDP had been marginalized and the new threat came from the right-wing Reform Party, which, for all its populist trappings, was run by a man as dedicated to pure neo-liberal ideology as any Bay Street CEO or Fraser Institute warrior.

The Red Book turned out to be a broken campaign promise. There were still Liberals, like the book's co-author Chaviva Hosek, who were determined to defend the social programs and the activist role of government they had always supported. However, the real policy agenda had been set at Aylmer, and at Aylmer there were very few social Liberals. The key players in the existing bureaucracy and in the Liberal party were of one mind—they knew where the government was going. They also knew they could not get elected by running on that plan. The Red Book would get them elected. The next day they would have to start figuring out how to break those promises and get away with it. It was an aide to Jean Chrétien who revealed this hidden agenda. In a conversation with *Globe and Mail* reporter Edward Greenspon just days after the election, the aide said, "You have to remember we were not elected on the deficit in any way, shape or form. So [Chrétien] has to bring everyone onside—caucus, cabinet, everyone."[16] It was a frank admission that the party's election win had been based on deception.

## THE RELUCTANT MINISTER

No one knew following the Aylmer Conference, or even following the 1993 election victory, what a pivotal role Paul Martin would play in ridding the party of its election promises. When Martin was running for election in 1993, he had imagined becoming the industry minister. He was still influenced by growth economics and economists like Robert

Reich (US President Bill Clinton's labour secretary) who had written that deficit-cutting should not be done just for the sake of it, that its purpose had to be kept foremost in mind lest it produce the very opposite of the desired results.

According to Edward Greenspon and Anthony Wilson-Smith, the authors of *Double Vision: The Inside Story of the Liberals in Power*, it took a whole series of personal interventions and forceful arguments to get Martin to finally accept the finance portfolio. Several experienced political figures tried to convince Martin that the industry department was no longer the driving force it had been when C.D. Howe ran it and used it to build the country in the days of the Mackenzie King Liberal government. The key argument may have come from Arthur Kroeger, once the most powerful bureaucrat in Ottawa and the head of a policy think-tank in 1993. He told Martin that "finance differed qualitatively from any other job in government. As a finance minister, through the budget, you could define the content of the whole government."[17]

The authors of *Double Vision* reveal that even though Martin expressed extreme distaste for a finance job involving little more than "slashing and burning," there were people in the government and the bureaucracy who were determined to have him in finance precisely because they knew slashing and burning were the order of the day. Principal among them was Jean Chrétien, who had tagged Martin for the post right from the beginning. Chrétien needed someone both credible with big business and strong in their own right. Another who insisted on Martin was none other than David Dodge, the deputy minister of finance. He staged an intervention with Ed Lumley, a boyhood friend of Martin's and a former industry minister. Dodge told Lumley it was essential that Martin take the job because the critical deficit situation required someone who could stand up to the prime minister if necessary. Just hours before Chrétien was to publicly announce his cabinet, Martin finally acquiesced. But, by all accounts, he was not happy.

## SHOOTING DOWN JOHN CROW

Martin immediately started preparing for his job by going through hundreds of pages of briefing books, followed by talking to his officials about his first budget with his junior minister, Doug Peters, at his side.

This Paul Martin was still concerned with economic growth and even before the budget was finished, this side of Martin would reveal itself in a major decision: not to renew the seven-year term of John Crow, the Governor of the Bank of Canada. Martin effectively fired Crow, but according to Doug Peters, it was mostly because of a personality clash. The difference between Crow and Martin on the inflation target range was only about half of one per cent. The new governor, Gordon Thiessen, was hardly a dissenter; as Crow's deputy he was in almost total agreement with his boss. However, he was considered less arrogant and less preoccupied with what the international financial community thought of him, which made him easier to work with.

Martin's move to dump John Crow seemed like a relatively risky move for a finance minister barely three months into the job, but Bay Street barely twitched. It was another sign that might have put the financial crowd on yellow alert. In a speech to the Commons on February 1, 1994, just three weeks before his first budget, and only three months after the November election, this is what Martin said about the deficit:

> We have clear priorities: to create jobs, to increase economic growth, and to help those who are truly in need. The debt and deficit problems of our country present severe difficulties and severe obstacles in the way of meeting these priorities.... The question is: How do we get the deficit down? Let me frame the challenge. There are those who blame the public service. They are wrong.
>
> We could let every public servant go. We could discharge every soldier. We could board up every government building. We could shut the whole show down and we would still have a deficit. There are those who blame the poor. They are wrong. We could abandon all the major programs we have in place to help the elderly, to help those who are unemployed, to help those who are in need, and the deficit would still be with us.
>
> I would hope no one in the House today would argue that the deficit should be brought down on the backs of those who are most in need. If they did I would simply point out, as my colleague the Minister of Human Resources Development pointed out yes-

terday, that not only is slash and burn morally wrong economically, it will not work.[18]

A few weeks later, Martin's first budget did reflect his statement to the House of Commons—but only partially. It was a mildly expansionary budget. Martin took nearly $2 billion out of the defence budget and applied it to program spending in the domestic economy, even giving Human Resources Minister Lloyd Axworthy an additional $800 million for innovations in social policy. On the other hand, he revealed his willingness to slash social programs by hitting the Unemployment Insurance (UI) program for $2.5 billion, continuing a pattern begun by the Tories and premised on the ideological premise that UI was too generous and discouraged people from seeking work.

## REALITY CHECK

Martin's '94 budget was pretty much the last anyone saw of Paul Martin Sr.'s son—at least the son who promised never to betray his father's legacy. In his place would appear the CEO of Canada Steamship Lines, the man who wanted to be admired by his peers, and most of all, the politician who wanted to be prime minister. The '94 budget can be seen as the opening battle between those two forces within Paul Martin as finance minister. Over the next months that internal war would intensify—and then be over almost before it started.

While most of the media and the ubiquitous financial markets were actually quite easy on Martin for at least not making the deficit worse, two deficit-warrior camps were very unhappy: Martin's own crew of free market, inflation-fighters in finance, and the equally ideological editorial board of The Globe and Mail, the critical media voice in the country from which other media often took their lead. The finance bureaucrats, led by David Dodge, had to be somewhat muted in their criticism of their boss and were mostly reduced to muttering among themselves. Not so The Globe and Mail. Still, a good cop/bad cop routine was just what the deficit doctor ordered. Within four months Martin would be planning and implementing the biggest budget cuts in Canadian history.

A week after the budget Martin went to a meeting of the Globe editorial board where he was promptly blindsided. How it was that the *Globe*'s board had become so obsessed with cutting social spending as the only way to get rid of the deficit isn't clear, but William Thorsell, the editor-in-chief, led off with an attack on Martin for daring to use a growth strategy instead of budget cuts to bring down the deficit.[19] The brutal two-hour session featured Martin on the defensive the whole time, with *Globe* members taking turns denouncing his budget. Andrew Coyne, the paper's acerbic neo-liberal wünderkind, commanded the assault. Numerous observers have suggested that this single meeting with the country's leading newspaper was a seminal event in the finance minister's evolution. If Martin was going through an internal struggle over policy options, an attack by this leading media outlet would have made him feel vulnerable. Doug Peters confirms that assessment: "Paul was very shaken by the interview with the *Globe and Mail* editorial board after the '94 budget. That was quite an event in his early stages as finance minister."[20] From that point on he was defensive about his first budget—the first and last that would balance the principles of social and business liberalism.

In the next weeks, *Globe* editorials reignited the deficit hysteria that had preceded the election. Business pundits who had given Martin an easy ride on his first budget were suddenly changing their minds. Other major media outlets took their lead from the *Globe*, repeating its message that Martin would have to do a lot better. The *Globe*'s assault on Martin signalled that the deficit war was on again. The business world, its expectations of what was possible on the rise, let it be known that if Martin didn't come up with something better the next time, his reputation on Bay Street might suffer.

## POLICY-MAKING IN A TIME OF DEFICIT WARFARE

The renewed attack led by the *Globe* was no surprise given the campaign the deficit warriors had waged in the four years leading up to Paul Martin's '94 budget. The assault had used a whole series of phrases designed to become part of the citizenry's political lexicon: "Canada will hit the debt wall"; "The debt is reaching crisis proportions"; "Foreign debt threatens the nation's sovereignty"; etc. The campaign had flogged a sense of urgency: nothing was more important than the deficit, and it had to be dealt with immediately.

All the major corporate players and their organizations played a role, as did every corporate print and broadcast media chain. The Business Council on National Issues (BCNI), the Canadian Manufacturers' Association, and chambers of commerce and boards of trade were all engaged in the deficit hysteria campaign. The corporately funded C.D. Howe and Fraser Institutes, along with the Canadian Taxpayers Federation and the National Citizens Coalition, all took on active roles. In the three years preceding the '94 budget, literally thousands of articles, reports, columns, and statements by prominent academic economists had railed against the deficit.

For a long time, the public resisted this unprecedented assault on its political consciousness. The deficit just wasn't a compelling issue for most people, as it did not appear to affect them directly or immediately. Up until 1988, less than 2 per cent of Canadians ranked the deficit as their top concern. With the Tories and Reformers campaigning relentlessly on the issue, concern about the deficit peaked at 20 per cent in 1993. However, by October 1994, just as Paul Martin was putting together the biggest program-slashing budget in Canadian history, deficit concern was ranked as the number one issue by just 10 per cent of Canadians. Unemployment was the top priority for 38 per cent, and 15 per cent cited the economy.[21] While the deficit was a huge problem for the government, its continuing unpopularity as an issue may have been due to its twin: cuts to social spending. The media-driven deficit crisis was always attached to the need to curtail social spending as the only solution to the problem.

While the corporate elite was having trouble reaching ordinary Canadians with its message, it was having greater success behind the scenes with party and government leaders and officials. With institutions like C.D. Howe and Fraser offering academic legitimacy to a goal of zero inflation—an extreme aspiration even for neo-liberals[22]—those in power who stood to gain financially from the results of deficit reduction had a solid rationale for carrying out that plan. These corporate outlets appealed to a sense of citizenship and morality: deficit-cutting was about democracy, courage, decisiveness, resoluteness, prudence, and "helping" people free themselves from a dependence on welfare. Who could disagree with such values?

As a result, "The Courage to Act: Fixing Canada's Budget and Social Policy Deficits," a C.D. Howe study released in mid-1994 as Paul Martin was deciding on his 1995 budget, gave a positive spin to the notion of gutting social programs (and it was only one of many influential corporate reports released at this time). "The Courage to Act" also demonstrated just how expressly political the corporate think-tanks had become. Unlike economic studies of the past, which simply provided economic prescriptions and left it at that, these corporate-sponsored documents specifically advised governments to act decisively and quickly in order to undercut opponents' abilities to organize against proposed cuts.

## THE IMF WEIGHS IN

Another organization that had a significant impact on the course of Paul Martin's career in finance was the International Monetary Fund (IMF). Canadians are generally familiar with the IMF's role in determining policy for the Third World. These underdeveloped countries, almost all of them burdened with enormous foreign debt, are at the IMF's mercy for refinancing. In return for more loans to pay off the interest on previous loans, countries are obliged to carry out "Structural Adjustment Plans," or SAPs. These plans are extremely onerous and generally involve cuts to social programs, layoffs for pubic employees, privatization, and trade liberalization, which removes any protection of local industries. In effect, the IMF is the enforcer of the Washington Consensus' prescription for the global economy.

Canadians might be surprised to know, however, that the IMF isn't just concerned with the Third World; it puts together SAPs for industrialized countries as well, including Canada. In the fall of 1994, the IMF delivered its latest prescription for "economic efficiency" to Paul Martin and his finance department. Article IV in the IMF's statement advised Martin "to consolidate the federal fiscal position by ... cutting government spending.... It is critical that fiscal policy take the lead."[23] While the report arrived too late to have impacted Martin's first budget, it would end up looking like the blueprint for the budget Martin would present in 1995.

In fact, the IMF prescription was so finely detailed—deep cuts to UI;

elimination of the Established Program Financing for provincial health care and post-secondary education; elimination of the Canada Assistance Plan in favour of (unaccountable) bulk funding; reduction in federal transfers to the provinces for health care, post-secondary education, and social assistance; and more—it seemed to have been written by an insider. And it almost certainly was. What is not generally well understood about the IMF's SAPs for Canada is that they are produced in close consultation with the government. According to economist Pierre Fortin, "This is always the case. These mission statements are only written after interaction with the Bank of Canada and the finance department. When you hear something coming from the OECD [Organization for Economic Cooperation and Development] or the IMF, very often it's actually coming from the conservative branch of the finance department. Most journalists don't even know this, so it looks like independent advice."[24]

The deficit warriors in the finance department and at the Bank of Canada didn't need convincing to make huge cuts to social programs, to privatize, and to maintain tight control over inflation: these were their preoccupations. What they needed were more allies to convince their political masters to implement these policies and convince the public to accept them. Working behind the scenes to get the IMF to issue supposedly independent advice to Canada was one of the ways to get the country on board with neo-liberal policies.

## YES, MINISTER

To deal with the renewed attack by the deficit warriors and prepare for the 1995 budget, Paul Martin had to rely heavily on his senior officials. While he had his political staff, it was his officials—the people available to carry out policy—who determined to a considerable extent which policies were pursued. People fundamentally hostile to the notion of growing a country out of deficits could not be expected to effectively carry out such a strategy with any enthusiasm, if at all, and Martin's officials were convinced that a growth policy was anathema to their goal of "economic efficiency." This was the political world satirized on the British TV series *Yes, Minister*, in which politicians come and go, but the deputy ministers and their associates run the government.

Doug Peters, Martin's junior minister, represented the last best chance for any moderating influence on the finance department's neo-liberal orthodoxy, and he was well placed to exert it. Peters was at least as qualified in the area of government finance as any of the bureaucrats in the department, including Deputy Minister David Dodge. He had a Ph.D. in public finance and had worked as the senior economist for the Toronto Dominion Bank for many years before deciding to run in the 1993 election. Peters had made a reputation for himself in the normally staid subculture of Canadian banking by being an extremely outspoken critic of John Crow and the Bank of Canada's monetarist policies, especially the use of high interest rates to control inflation, which he called "almost incoherent." Despite his strong dissenting voice (Peters claimed other bank economists agreed with him but declined to do so publicly), he was supported by his bosses at TD and highly respected by his peers. The federal finance department thought otherwise.

Linda McQuaig tells Doug Peters' story in her book *The Cult of Impotence: Selling the Myth of Powerlessness in the Global Economy*. Peters quickly discovered a department utterly convinced that if Canada did not reduce spending to control the deficit, international investors would either pull their money out of the country or impose such a huge "risk premium" on loans that the country would be brought to its knees. Finance officials, led by Dodge, were telling a government just elected on a platform of job creation that such a program was out of the question. Peters, confident that he knew as much as any official about finance, deficits, and the state of the country, argued that while the deficit was a problem, the greatest obstacle facing the Canadian economy was unemployment, but the officials would hear none of it. In McQuaig's words, "Peters now found himself confronted by a group that seemed even more inflexible in its views than the crowd on Bay Street. Indeed, Bay Street was starting to look like a virtual commune of free-thinkers compared with this deficit-fixated isolation cell in the nation's capital."[25]

Peters was simply ignored and effectively isolated by Deputy Finance Minister David Dodge and his senior officials.


## THE NAIRU DOGMA

Doug Peters took the position that if the government dealt with the most important problem, unemployment, it would solve the other problem, the deficit, simply through the creation of more wealth, more tax revenue, and the reduction of spending on the social safety net. By his calculations, the Canadian economy was operating between 10 to 12 per cent below capacity, equal to a yearly $70 billion loss of output. In other words, with a different policy mix that capacity could be stimulated back into use. The reason for high unemployment was straightforward: a lack of sufficient consumer demand. The way to deal with such a huge gap in potential output was to increase spending and stimulate the economy, decrease interest rates, or a combination of both. Given the deficit, the obvious approach was to encourage the Bank of Canada to dramatically lower interest rates.

The finance department officials took the opposite, supply-side view, and the theory underpinning their analysis is starkly revealing of the counter-revolution in government thinking that had been taking place for ten to fifteen years. David Dodge and his senior economists adhered to the controversial and largely untested theory represented by the acronym NAIRU: the non-accelerating inflation rate of unemployment. By this economic theory, Canada had to keep unemployment high so that inflation would remain low. In other words, four decades of government efforts to create full employment, something most Canadians who work for their income would probably support, were overturned and replaced by a government objective of keeping unemployment high enough to hold inflation down.

The government deliberately used policy tools, and primarily Bank of Canada interest rates, to actually create more unemployment if too many people were working. For good reason, this change in the government's purpose was never debated in any election, nor promised in any party platform. By keeping NAIRU an obscure theory, meant only for experts and ensconced in the inaccessible bunker of the Bank of Canada, probably 95 per cent of Canadians were unaware of the economic policy that dominated their national governments for almost ten years.

According to NAIRU, the cause of unemployment was not a lack of consumer demand, but unmotivated workers. The welfare state—overburdened with "entitlements" for ordinary working people—was simply too generous. Over a period of many decades, workers and their unions had managed to convince governments to provide UI, workers' compensation, and labour standards legislation, which established binding rules largely intended to protect unorganized workers from exploitation at the hands of unscrupulous employers. To free marketeers, however, these same protections were seen as "labour market disincentives." By reducing these protections, the desperation level of unemployed workers increased, and they returned to the marketplace to sell their labour. The euphemism for this increase in the desperation of unemployed workers is "labour flexibility." The issue of where the jobs come from is never seriously addressed by this theory. The implication is that workers' labour would be so cheap and "flexible," employers couldn't afford not to hire them.

The NAIRU theory was mostly just that, a theory, especially in other countries. But in the finance department, it was so radically applied that Dodge and his officials considered 8 per cent unemployment the 'natural rate' of joblessness. In other words, anything even approaching 8 per cent was unacceptable, as it would immediately lead to increasing inflation. Even though Martin had rid the country of John Crow, the Bank of Canada's inflation target was still about 2 per cent, extremely low given the nation was barely out of a recession. Still, finance officials were so fearful of inflation that even if the unemployment rate began to drop from its 1994 rate of 11 per cent to 10 per cent, they started to worry.

While the Bank of Canada is supposed to be independent from the finance department in establishing inflation targets, and thus NAIRU levels, in reality the two work together closely. In a speech to the IMF Interim Committee in 1995, Martin acknowledged this collaboration: "The Government and the Bank of Canada have jointly established targets of 1 to 3 per cent for inflation over the 1995 to 1998 period, and have geared monetary policy to ensuring that inflation does not leave this range."[26]

The cost to the economy was staggering. The federal Human Resources Development Department calculated that excessive unemployment cost the country's GDP $77 billion in 1993—even more than Doug Peters' estimate of $70 billion, and these were not the only sources confirming the huge loss of national income. Pierre Fortin, a distinguished economist at the Université du Québec à Montréal was also publicly critical of the government's obsession with inflation and its extreme application of NAIRU theory. (He would later calculate that NAIRU cost the economy $400 billion between 1990 and 1996—a third of the losses of the Great Depression.) The Canadian Centre for Policy Alternatives (CCPA) analysis put the 1993 loss to GDP at $109 billion. The CCPA study calculated the total loss to all levels of government in foregone revenue and increased social security costs at $47 billion.[27]

As Linda McQuaig points out, David Dodge, in defending the government's policies in an internal memo, claimed the cost to the economy was much lower (*"only* $45 billion"[28] [original italics]). Here was a frank admission of the cost of his policies—$45 billion in lost wealth—just to keep inflation from rising a single point. Nowhere in Dodge's defence of his guidelines was there any mention that actual Canadians were part of this dance of numbers. Yet the difference between a NAIRU rate of 8 per cent and Doug Peters' calculation of 6 per cent was an additional 300,000 Canadians without work—and in reality, a 6 per cent level of unemployment would not have budged inflation at all.

The US government also used NAIRU estimates as one of many guiding principles for its monetary policy. It had set its NAIRU at 6 per cent, but discovered that as unemployment actually dropped from 5.5 per cent, to 5.1 per cent, and ultimately to 4.7 per cent, there was no increase in inflation.[29] Unlike Canada, the US Federal Reserve did not panic and drive interest rates through the roof at the first sign that more people were working. In resisting such a knee-jerk response, it effectively proved that NAIRU was, at best, a very unreliable guide to making interest rate policy. At worst, it was a simplistic ideology that could not possibly encompass the complexities of a modern economy as a predictor of economic activity.

Yet Canada's finance department continued using NAIRU for years, right through the late 1990s, maintaining the magic figure was 7.5 to 8 per cent unemployment despite evidence to the contrary in the US. The continued adherence to this high NAIRU rate fuels suspicions that what was driving the finance department was not inflation at all, but the much more political and largely unspoken objective of labour flexibility—that is, ensuring labour did not regain the economic power and political leverage it had when Canada was near full employment.

But, as Doug Peters experienced first-hand, the actual value of NAIRU in determining policy was ultimately not as important as who captured the minister's thinking on the issue. Here, the fight for Martin's ideological loyalty was lost almost before it began. As others have pointed out, including Peters, there was a genuine conflict in Paul Martin—"I've always felt that Paul was much more of a liberal than any of his budgets indicated,"[30] Peters admits, but when it came to making policy decisions, Martin would show again and again that his attraction to contrarian ideas was sporadic and superficial.

With the single exception of pressing for debt relief for developing countries at the international level, Martin was ideologically consistent on literally every important policy question throughout his term as finance minister. As minister, he had complete control over who was on his staff. Had he studied in-depth the alternatives to the NAIRU dogma, had he resisted giving up his earlier instincts about economic growth, and had he listened to the arguments of Doug Peters and Pierre Fortin he might have—and could have—hired staff to balance the singular advice from his officials. But that didn't happen.

Martin the politician had no interest in such a struggle. Paul Martin's enormous ambition does not come across in his public persona. Yet virtually from the day he lost the leadership to Jean Chrétien in 1990, Martin has been preparing and organizing for the next contest. The people around him—his political staff at the finance department, his supporters in the party, key Bay Street players—were never far from his thinking when he weighed how any particular action or inaction would impact his desire to become prime minister.

Finance department policy was invariably strategic policy for Paul Martin's leadership ambitions, and from day one Martin used the Earnscliffe Group, a lobbying and consulting firm, to refine and vet every policy that came out of his department. The company, which also had many clients who were affected by finance department decisions, had a virtual veto over finance decisions if they weren't saleable. The Earnscliffe staff was, in effect, the core of Martin's leadership team, and it worked as much, or more, for Martin the candidate as it did for Martin the finance minister.

In this context, the deficit issue was actually what neo-conservatives like to call a "useful crisis." The deficit "crisis" was the weapon of choice for downsizing democracy and eliminating the culture of entitlement. The way the deficit was cut was more important than actually cutting it—decreased spending was the ultimate agenda of Bay Street. The Paul Martin who was proud of what his father had accomplished concluded very quickly—within a couple of months of his first budget —that he could never be prime minister.

In a sense, Martin knew all of this when he finally, reluctantly, took the finance position. He accepted the post because friends persuaded him that deficit-cutting would make him the most powerful man in cabinet. With David Dodge encouraging him to make cuts and restructure the government, and Peter Nicholson warning him against the "social chaos" that results from failing to pass the "market test," (Martin had asked his mentor from the Aylmer Conference to join him at the finance department as a sort of policy guru) it is easy to see how Doug Peters' single voice for economic growth was drowned out early in the battle for Paul Martin's ideological allegiance. While Dodge was responsible for making Martin comfortable with the NAIRU approach to the deficit, Nicholson was probably the decisive voice that persuaded Martin he could sell it. According to Linda McQuaig, it was Nicholson who "convinced Martin that tackling the deficit—not creating jobs— was the truly heroic, visionary course for the 1990s."[31]

## A FEW SHORT STEPS INTO THE PRIESTHOOD

If there really was a struggle going on within Paul Martin, one rooted in the conflict between his father's legacy and his experience as a CEO, it was an extremely short one. Within weeks of delivering his 1994 budget, Paul Martin was already showing that he was coming around rapidly to the finance department's way of thinking. The battle was so short it was like driving through a prairie town: if you blinked, you missed it.

Martin's political experience had been limited to being in Opposition for five years; he had no experience actually running a government department. He did, however, have twenty years' experience as a CEO and corporate owner. Once he clearly understood the lay of the political land—the agenda of the party's Bay Street backers and the corporate media that marched in lockstep with them—it was pretty simple. Freed of the shackles of his romantic attachment to his father and his father's political philosophy, Martin very quickly fell back into his CEO persona. The deficit and the debt could only be dealt with by restructuring the company (read: country) and permanently protecting it from the kinds of mistakes that got it into trouble in the first place.

As the heavily indebted owner of the Canada Steamship Lines conglomerate, Martin had had only one choice. He could not "grow the company"—that would have put him ever further in debt. He had to restructure—that he had done many times before for his boss Paul Desmarais. He had reinvented CSL by lopping off whole divisions and refocusing on the single core business: shipping. It was the perfect experience for his new job. Cutting the deficit was boring and even unpleasant, but it was something that prepared the mind for a more interesting job: restructuring the government/company. Paul Martin, with the help of David Dodge, Peter Nicholson, and his eager promoters at Earnscliffe, suddenly saw his job and his mission unfold in front of him. He would take it on with an energy and a determination—and an amazing effectiveness—that surprised even his teachers.

# 3

# HARD RIGHT TURN

**P**aul Martin's legacy as finance minister would be the most radical restructuring of the Canadian nation-state in its history. After promising to reverse the course of the hated Tory government, Paul Martin actually went on to embrace the policies of that administration with breathtaking enthusiasm, refashioning the role of government to an extent never dared by Brian Mulroney. Just as only right-wing US President Richard Nixon could get away with recognizing Communist China, only a Liberal government could pull off such a reversal of forty years of nation-building. And Paul Martin, the serial seducer, would carry out this stunning task with uncommon brilliance.

Hugh Mackenzie, an economist with the Steelworkers' Union and a keen student of Paul Martin's long career, has drawn parallels between the Mulroney-inspired Meech Lake Accord and Martin's finance policies: "What struck me about Martin as finance minister is how closely his budgetary policies dovetailed with the radical decentralization of the federation implied by Meech Lake. I've often thought that one of the real ironies of the Chrétien-Martin regime is that Chrétien fought to the death against Martin over Meech Lake and won, only to have Martin effectively implement the financial side of Meech Lake as his finance minister.... Right wingers love being pushed into doing what they want to do. In this case, the fight against the deficit pushed Martin to do two things that he really wanted to do: reduce the size of government and decentralize the federation."[1]

It's not clear exactly when Martin developed his passion for reducing the size of government, but it certainly predated the writing of the Red Book. In a 1992 interview, Martin told author Peter C. Newman that "central governments such as Canada's have become too small to deal with the big, global issues, yet they remain too large and distant to deal with the problems of local concern. So the challenge is to redefine the role of the central government as an institution that can do a limited number of things well."[2]

Though the neo-liberals and free marketeers railed against it, the deficit was the perfect tool for their goal of downsizing the government and diminishing the power of the nation-state. Indeed, there is evidence from other jurisdictions that suggests deficits were deliberately created for just this purpose. David Stockwell, an official in the Reagan government, later admitted that at the behest of their corporate friends the administration "deliberately increased the deficit so that [we] could justify later cuts in social program funding."[3]

Deliberate or not, the huge federal debt and the ever-increasing annual deficits added to it were touted as a "crisis," allowing a government intent on cutting social programs to appeal to citizens' better instincts, asking them to accept changes to their communitarian culture and the social programs that reflected it for the good of the country. As long as citizens didn't know where the deficit came from or how it might otherwise be dealt with, it was a surefire strategy. With the able assistance of a media consumed by debt hysteria, it was a strategy that Paul Martin finessed better than any other finance minister.

## THE DIRTY LITTLE DEFICIT SECRET

The actions of the Canadian government caused the so-called deficit. The problem is that there was never a public debate about exactly *which* actions of the government caused it. The overwhelming message of the deficit warriors was that we were paying a price for our attachment to social programs. However, as many studies revealed at the time and since, this wasn't the case. The crisis, if there was one, was initially a crisis of falling revenue, which was then exacerbated by compound interest.

By 1975, Canada's accumulated deficit—the debt—was just 22 per cent of GDP, an important measure because it indicated our ability to pay it off. After the war it had been at 138 per cent, the highest level ever. It gradually came down as the defence budget was slashed to peacetime levels, the economy grew, and near full employment unburdened social security. Real interest rates were also low, keeping debt servicing charges at a minimum. In the mid to late 1970s, however, the Liberal government, responding to a fall in the profitability of corporations, introduced a flurry of corporate tax breaks. Finance Minister John Turner also indexed programs like pensions to inflation, which increased their costs over time. By 1978, government revenue had dropped by 20 per cent to a 1968 level.[4] It was the start of Canada's deficit situation, and by 1980, the debt had gone back up to 27 per cent of GDP. Even when spending actually decreased, it was not enough to match the dramatic fall in government revenue.

What really caused the debt to rise was neither spending nor the revenue decline of the late 1970s, but a change in policy at the Bank of Canada. Its governor, Gerald Bouey, decided to launch an all-out war on inflation, which was running at a post-war high of 11 per cent at the time. Bouey's solution was to adopt the monetarist approach to the deficit: using high interest rates to lower inflation, following the example of the US Federal Reserve. By 1981, Bouey had radically increased interest rates to 22 per cent. In doing so he certainly beat inflation, but he also created the worst recession in the Canadian economy since the 1930s.

The recession meant that revenues fell even more and social welfare costs skyrocketed. The high interest rates also had the effect of exploding the government's interest charges on its debt, forcing it to borrow more just to pay the interest on the old debt. While the federal government used to do significant borrowing at near-zero interest rates from the Bank of Canada, that policy had changed too, and it was forced to borrow almost exclusively from private banks, including foreign ones.

When John Crow replaced Bouey as governor in 1988, he pursued the goal of zero inflation with even more zeal. While Bouey had faced a real inflation problem, Crow was facing a very different scenario. The economy was experiencing a burst of growth, inflation was at 4 per cent, and the deficit was actually decreasing, from 8.7 per cent of GDP in 1984–5, to 4.5 per cent in 1989–90. Bay Street financial analyst George Vasic suggested in a column for *Canadian Business* magazine that the deficit would continue to decrease and the debt would be quite manageable by the mid-1990s.[5] Despite this and similar predictions, Crow raised interest rates from 8.8 per cent to 14 per cent in just two years—more than twice the rate in the US and enough to impede any economic growth. In a critique of Crow's approach, economist Pierre Fortin commented, "We were almost there. But the recession blew us out of the water."[6]

By the time the Liberals took office in 1993, the economy was on its knees. Estimates of the loss to the economy from taking inflation to below 1 per cent ranged from $70 billion to $109 billion for 1993 alone—over 10 per cent of GDP. While still in power, the Mulroney government had coped with this loss of revenue by raising taxes and cutting spending, so that in strict deficit terms, there was a $32 billion program-operating surplus (revenue minus program expenditures) over that government's nine-year reign. Even the finance department's own calculations showed that the growth in the debt from 1985 onward was entirely due to interest on the original debt. StatsCan produced a study showing that 44 per cent of the debt accumulated between 1975 and 1991 could be attributed to revenue decline, and 50 per cent to interest charges. As for social spending, the study pointed out that "expenditures on social programs did not contribute significantly to the growth of government spending relative to GDP."[7] The Dominion Bond Rating Service confirmed these studies with its own, concluding that the entire accumulated program deficit was created between 1975 and 1985.[8]

## RULE BY DEFICIT

Once the deficit came to dominate political discourse, its source became irrelevant. Canada's deficit had become a huge problem; reaching over 70 per cent of GDP, it was one of the highest in the developed world and unsustainable for any nation serious about its future. At the time of the Liberal victory in 1993, the economic and political elite had made cutting the deficit the issue of the day, creating a political context for a new government in which the finance minister would have enormous power.

The contrast to the last time the Liberals had been in power was striking. In the 1960s and 1970s, there was a genuine political equality between ministries. Health ministers, environment ministers, and ministers of industrial development, agriculture, and regional development had real mandates and resources to carry them out. The result was genuine debate in cabinets and among senior policy bureaucrats over what government would do—which was the key point: government was expected to initiate policies that enhanced communities and the lives of Canadians. Both the public and politicians had high expectations. To be sure, finance ministers were encouraged to be cautionary even in those days, but the 1960s and early 1970s were nonetheless days of public policy-making.

Once the government's prime objective was defined as deficit reduction by budget-cutting, that political culture of activist government was put on life support. Ministers and their ministries—those that still had public policy-makers in them—effectively went into defensive mode. Policy-making was reduced to a desperate effort to defend what existed and to justify program spending. Instead of imagining policy, departments were engaged in triage, determining what could be cut while retaining the essential mandate of the department.

## PAUL MARTIN HEADS THE WAR CABINET

The peculiar combination of the political times and the particular way in which Jean Chrétien ran his government meant that Paul Martin effectively controlled the direction of the Liberal administration right from the beginning. The political ascendancy of finance ministers was a feature of most Western governments preoccupied with inflation and deficits, especially English-speaking ones, but nowhere was it more evident than in Canada. Even when Chrétien disagreed with Martin, he refused to contradict him or step in and dictate policy. Only once in nine years, on the issue of pension reform, did Chrétien refuse to back his finance minister's agenda. While Chrétien had broad and vague notions of where he wanted the government to go, these ideas were rarely expressed in terms of actual policy options. He wasn't an ideologue, but working for a large business law firm during his political hiatus in the 1980s would have immersed him in the corporate agenda of downsizing government. He wasn't a politician who would try to change the political context to adopt a vision; the vision was as flexible as necessary to take advantage of the existing political culture and remain in power.

In Chrétien's government, Martin didn't just decide how much had to be cut from total spending in the critically important 1995 budget; he and his senior officials actually decided how much each department would have to give up. It was not a collective political exercise in which Chrétien and his ministers sat around a table and discussed what was and wasn't essential for the country before Chrétien gave final approval to particular policies. By allowing Martin and finance officials to make all decisions, Chrétien, in effect, handed the reins of government to his finance minister. He was still formally responsible for the decisions, but in a very real sense he abdicated the traditional role of prime minister. He was largely absent from the decision-making process of his own government.

The politics of power, rather than the mechanics of government, were always foremost in Chrétien's mind. According to Edward Greenspon and Anthony Wilson-Smith, Chrétien's relationship with his finance minister was governed by his own experience in the finance job while in the Trudeau cabinet. Chrétien himself had demonstrated a commitment to fiscal conservatism in 1979. Faced with the option of introducing a budget that would have loosened the purse strings in the run-up to an election, he decided instead to hold spending to the existing levels.

Perhaps more importantly, he had experienced being sucker punched by Trudeau the year before, an experience he never forgot. After attending an economic summit in Germany, Chrétien returned to Canada while Trudeau stayed behind. Arriving in Ottawa a few days later, Trudeau announced what was then a huge budget cut of $2 billion in a high-profile address to the nation without informing Chrétien. In his autobiography Chrétien wrote, "I was made to look like a fool. Normally a finance minister would resign in such an embarrassing situation. I decided not to because I was worried about the effect of a French-Canadian senior minister resigning when a separatist government was in power in Quebec."[9]

Chrétien was determined to never expose a minister to that sort of humiliation. He intended to give Martin enormous leeway as a minister, and Martin knew it. One example of Chrétien's resolve to let Martin set policy occurred during the preparation of the 1994 budget. Chrétien was notified by Clerk of the Privy Council Glen Shortliffe about an item being discussed in finance. Shortliffe had correctly anticipated that Chrétien would disagree with the direction finance was taking. Nonetheless, Chrétien declined to intervene, telling Shortliffe, "I am not going to tell my finance minister what to do."[10]

Martin wasn't the only one who knew Chrétien was behind him all the way—every other cabinet minister knew it, even those with years of experience and significant political status and clout. When Martin decided to implement a budget freeze in the spring of 1994, Chrétien told him he disagreed with the decision but would support it anyway. When Martin announced the freeze at a cabinet meeting the next day, one of the ministers brought up a project that clearly required additional money. Chrétien cut him off. "'Didn't you just hear the minister of finance?' he asked. 'Just ten minutes ago, he said there wouldn't be any more money.'" Another ten or fifteen minutes went by and another minister made mention of a new spending initiative. This time Chrétien, as he did on many occasions, simply bullied his cabinet into submission. "'Didn't you hear *me* ten minutes ago? ... I said there was no money. Can't you guys understand that? I said there is no money. The next one who asks for new spending, I'm going to cut their budget by twenty per cent.'"[11]

This intervention by the prime minister had the effect of signalling to Paul Martin that his agenda would be the government's agenda. When Martin spoke, it was as if the words were coming out of Chrétien's mouth. The ferocity of this support would not have been lost on the key bureaucrats in finance such as David Dodge, who were in the process of designing, with Martin, their radical program on the deficit, interest rates, cuts to spending, and the restructuring of the federal government. The Liberal Government, Inc. had Jean Chrétien as chair of the board and Paul Martin as chief executive officer.

Once Martin was absolutely certain he had Chrétien's backing, he simply withdrew from cabinet discussions of budgets and spending priorities. Assured of his authority to act, he fell back into CEO mode, and the CEO didn't need to be at the meetings of corporate department heads. According to Doug Peters, Martin's junior finance minister, "Paul never went to cabinet committees—I went to them. That's where all the arguments happened and he didn't like hearing them. At one point the cabinet committee wanted to authorize an expenditure. I said, 'That's not in the budget, you can't authorize it.' The chair of the committee, who was one of the senior ministers, said, 'Well what the hell are we doing here in this cabinet committee if we can't authorize spending?'" The issue was serious enough that it ended up in the Prime Minister's Office for resolution. "The answer came directly from the PMO: 'You can reallocate your budget any way you like, and you can go around to other cabinet colleagues and get them to contribute something from their budget, but you cannot initiate any new spending.'"[12]

Whether by design or by happenstance, Chrétien made other major changes that strengthened Martin's position even more. First, the PMO abolished all but two cabinet policy committees: social development and economic development. Previously, the many cabinet committees were power centres in their own right because they created formal and authoritative policy forums where ministers could come together not only to discuss policies, but, more importantly, to create alliances that could fight for them. Without this formal arrangement, individual ministers were isolated from each other and had to rely on whatever informal conversations and temporary alliances they might be able to build.

Without these committees, Martin's finance department could, in effect, pick off each department one by one with its budget-cutting targets. As Maude Barlow and Bruce Campbell observe in *Straight through the Heart*, "Every government department had been enlisted to serve Martin's budget-cutting agenda: Marcel Massé must undertake massive layoffs in the public service; Ralph Goodale has to wind down farm subsidies; Doug Young is selling off transportation services; Art Eggleton must put infrastructure plans on hold."[13] Martin's role gave him great power not only over his own department, but also over the direction of every other federal department.

When the Liberals took office, there was no effort to examine the senior levels of the civil service for compatibility with what was supposed to be a new political regime—a regime defined by the Red Book promises and philosophy. According to Doug Peters, "The Liberals, during that seventies period, had virtual control of the public service for such a long time, and they brought in people appropriate for their policies. Prime Minister Chrétien failed to take control of the public service when he came to office in 1993. He should have made some major changes; he should have brought people in from the outside and didn't do so."[14]

Paul Martin's Red Book of political promises, with its emphasis on growth and jobs and its critique of Tory free trade and fiscal policies, would clearly have run up against a stone wall: an entrenched free-market, neo-liberal bureaucracy. The Mulroney government, dedicated to privatization, free trade, deregulation, and downsizing public service and social programs, had been in power for nine years. That was more than enough time to completely transform the civil service into an administrative body ideologically committed to dismantling the post-war modern state. That Chrétien and his advisors did nothing to change this bureaucracy indicates they had no problem with its makeup or its dominant economic philosophy. In the economic ministries of foreign affairs and trade, finance, and industry, this tacit endorsement of the market-oriented public administration philosophy would prove especially significant. The mere fact that there were no significant changes in the senior ranks of the civil service would have emboldened those in key positions and the perspective they held.

This is not to say that there were no other powerful ministers in the new Liberal regime. Lloyd Axworthy, Sheila Copps, and Herb Gray were all very experienced politicians, but none of them had been in a ruling government for almost ten years. Their lack of recent administrative experience (Copps had none), was aggravated through yet another Chrétien move that would weaken political opposition to Martin's budget-cutting. Not only did Chrétien leave the Mulroney era bureaucracy untouched, but he also reinforced that bureaucracy's influence over its ministers by dramatically decreasing political staffs. Doug Peters recalls the shape of the new government: "The prime minister, when we were elected, reduced ministerial staff by a huge amount. I had a staff of three and my predecessor had a staff of sixteen. The prime minister felt very strongly about the public service bringing forth policy ... and then the politicians look after the political side of it, selling it to the public."[15] This shift, said Peters, severely weakened ministers' ability to influence policy. It is hard to imagine that Chrétien would not have recognized that he was leaving his cabinet ministers extremely vulnerable to the bureaucracy Brian Mulroney had created to carry out his free-market agenda. While he may have been motivated by a desire to avoid conflicts between or gaffes by inexperienced ministers, an undeniable effect was to increase bureaucratic power.

Chrétien also eliminated the position of ministerial chief of staff, the political equivalent of a deputy minister, viewed by the prime minister as a "disruptive layer between ministers and their deputies."[16] In effect, the ministers were instructed to meet daily with their deputy ministers and were left alone to deal with the highly trained senior officials of each department. There was no equivalent instruction to meet with any-one who could speak to the issue of public expectations. Historically, the role of political staff has varied, but in general the staff has been chosen to reflect the minister's political interests, which meant it had to be sensitive to public opinion. While that sensitivity was often charac-terized by opportunism rather than idealism, it at least implied that the public's will should be factored into the policy equation.

Ironically, the highly politicized policy-making of the Mulroney era may have had a moderating effect on the implementation of the Tory government's agenda. The Tories traditionally didn't trust the bureau-cracy because it was associated with long periods of Liberal rule. Political staffs would, by their nature, put any policy through a filter of political consequences for the government. With no ministerial chiefs of staff under Chrétien and Martin, policy-making was completely depoliticized, which made it even more rigidly ideological. The whole nature of the civil service began to change in the late 1970s under Trudeau. The Public Service Commission used to hire for the whole government, recruiting people who had self-selected for the public service. But, according to political economist Duncan Cameron, "Under Simon Reisman's reign as deputy finance minister [in the 1970s], the government began hiring directly out of the economics departments of universities. These [departments] were dominated by monetarists and economic rationalists." Instead of recruiting people who had explicitly chosen to serve the public interest, government departments "were recruiting people who had gone through the brainwashing process of academic economics. With the growth of government and its complex-ity, the culture of the policy advisor changed from mandarin as policy-thinker to mandarin as manager. Once you're into that management mode you are into the business ethic."[17]

As the economics profession began to dominate public debate about the role of government, what had begun as a practical set of business administration tools gradually became a philosophy of government. Economic efficiency became the predominant criteria for assessing governance. Social equality was anathema to efficiency; as such, it virtually disappeared as a guiding principle for public policy.

## THE 3 PER CENT SOLUTION

Even after being softened by the deficit hysteria campaign, the Liberal cabinet and the public were judged not ready for the kind of cuts the finance department had planned. Selling the cuts would require the equivalent of declaring war. Of course, this war would not be as compelling as a war on poverty or unemployment—wars that Canadians said they would actually support. So, Paul Martin and his staff figured they would attach core Canadian values like determination, resoluteness, and courage to the campaign. With any luck, people would focus on these values and wouldn't notice the war was actually being waged against health care, education, the poor, the environment, and foreign aid to developing countries.

Victory in this war had to be clearly defined so people would know what they had to sacrifice and when they had won. The victory was specified as lowering the deficit to 3 per cent of the GDP within three years. That rate had been mentioned in the Red Book (with a timeline of five years), though it had never been elevated to the status of an all-consuming goal, and was never mentioned on the campaign trail. However, finance officials believed the deficit was going to worsen in the fall of 1994 as a result of interest rate projections. Consequently, the finance department saw the 3 per cent figure not as a guideline but as an "anchor," a goal that had to be achieved if the department, and Martin, were to retain any credibility with the deficit warriors. Martin himself later said, "Without a target to which we were all irrevocably committed, the natural reluctance of ministers to accept cuts in their own domain would likely have caused things to unravel."[18]

Once the 3 per cent solution was identified as the concrete target and war was declared, the finance department was transformed into the war department, a department with absolute control. In *Double Vision*, Edward Greenspon and Anthony Wilson-Smith tell the dramatic story of how the cuts went down in the eight-month run-up to budget day in February 1995. Finance was not taking any chances; they began the process in June. Each minister was asked to come by the department with their deputies to discuss "program review." Martin and his partners in the process, Cabinet Minister Marcel Massé and Deputy Finance Minister David Dodge, presented each minister with a single sheet of paper on which was printed "little more than a small table of numbers, two lines over three years. The table laid out the current budgetary allocation … and the amount by which it was to be reduced in the 1995, 1996, and 1997 budgets under review. The size of the required cuts left the ministers gasping: in many cases, the they were well above 50 per cent."[19]

Alberta Minister Anne McLellan, a bona fide business Liberal, realized in the short meeting that "they were going to destroy the Department of Natural Resources and remove any meaningful federal role in the resource sectors of this country."[20] All the ministers were given their numbers—the percentage by which they were required to reduce their departmental budgets. They were to come up with plans for cuts over the summer, which would be examined by a new Program Review Committee to be chaired by Marcel Massé.

Massé proved to be almost as important a figure as Martin in the redefinition of government. A long-time bureaucrat, Massé was a former Canadian director of the International Monetary Fund (IMF), and a hardliner on structural adjustment. He once stated: "It isn't just the third world that needs structural adjustment … we *all* do, in one form or another. We should avoid the temptation to let our desires for justice in the world obscure the view of reality."[21] Where Martin had a mandate to reduce the size of government and only vague notions of how to do it, Massé knew exactly what had to be done. Massé had been appointed by Jean Chrétien to "renew" the public service; specifically, "he was charged with both restructuring the operations of government and reordering relations with the provinces."[22] Massé argued forcefully against across-the-board cuts, favouring instead the reduction of the size of particular departments. He was also instrumental in eliminating the ministerial chiefs of staff. He was, as the authors of *Double Vision* point out, a perfect partner for Martin: a skilled architect for reinventing government, but one with no political ambition. Once he attained Martin's trust, the two became the most powerful team in the government: Massé had the plan, and Martin had the authority to implement it.

The Program Review Committee's makeup revealed Chrétien's political savvy: it was almost equal parts social liberals and business liberals, and its members included Sheila Copps and Herb Gray. Balanced or not, it came to be known throughout the government as the Star Chamber. Once the cuts were established, what better way to legitimize them than by having some of the most progressive ministers in cabinet eventually sign off on the plans? And those ministers would reinforce the process by reducing their own departmental budgets.

If the exercise had really been about simply cutting the deficit, as Martin and the government publicly maintained, the cuts would have been more or less across-the-board, but an examination of the disproportionate cuts reveals that Martin and Massé were carrying forward their plan to radically alter the role of the Government of Canada. When the package of cuts was implemented, Canada would be left with a political economy much like the one in the US: a system reconfigured to enhance and support the role of private capital and less influenced by the state agencies of social development and economic regulation and planning.

## "SCREW THE RED BOOK"

If his stated goals coming into government in 1993 are taken at face value, it is obvious that Paul Martin, working in the finance department, had come around 180 degrees. Far from promoting growth economics, he was implementing cuts with the zeal of a convert. In the early months, some of his staff were still referring to the Red Book as a rough guide when policy questions arose. However, Martin had already moved on, and, according to the authors of *Double Vision*, often screamed at those who dared mention it: "Don't tell me what's in the Red Book. I wrote the goddamned thing. And I know that it's a lot of crap."[23]

The numbers assigned to the Department of Industry demonstrated the full extent of Martin's conversion. Martin had originally wanted the industry portfolio, and up to a few weeks before the cutting process began he had been urging his fellow business Liberal John Manley to "find ways to support growth-oriented companies in adopting new technologies or identifying new export markets."[24] Now he was virtually demanding that the department commit suicide with a budget cut of 60 per cent.

Even his closest friends in the government and cabinet were furious with his program. Ralph Goodale blasted the Program Review Committee for its arrogance: "What gives you the right to act as judges on what generations of people have created? The futures of thousands of people are going to be decided by you nine here. From what divine right do you derive the power to decide that fifty of my scientists will be without work tomorrow? How come you think you know ... what is in the national interest or not?"[25] Goodale was livid that Transport Minister Doug Young, in meeting the committee's "number" for his department, was eliminating the Crow freight-rate subsidy for grain farmers, a program as important as medicare in the Prairies' history. Regional agencies, a core set of programs aimed at ensuring the economic integration of regions into a national economy, received the deepest cuts, losing 65 per cent of their budgets. The Departments of Natural Resources and Transport, both considered critical departments for defining the nation and making it work, were cut by about 50 per cent.

The mid-range cuts—from 20 to 30 per cent—were targeted at heritage and culture, agriculture, fisheries and oceans, the environment, and international assistance. Environment Canada, Martin's old critic posting, had its budget slashed by 30 per cent after it had already been cut to the bone by the Tories. The departments that received the smallest cuts corresponded with what neo-liberals and economic rationalists traditionally saw as the core activities of the market state: justice, immigration, solicitor general, and foreign affairs and international trade took hits of between 10 and 15 per cent.[26] These were still large cuts by historical standards, but small in comparison to those social and economic departments arguably responsible for nation-building and holding the federation together. The cuts went a long way toward transforming Canada from a nation governed by the democratic will of its citizens through their government into a market economy managed by the government.

While government still had a role in regulating the economy, that role was dramatically reduced, and the budget cuts heralded a major step in the continuing shift of economic decision-making authority from elected government to Bay Street. Private capital would decide where to invest, largely unencumbered by national or regional social objectives. Keeping a key corporation and its technology in Canada or moving it to the US would be a business, not a government, decision. Workers, their families, and their communities would be left to fend for themselves. If an individual wanted a job, they'd better be prepared to relocate for it; if a community wanted to survive, it'd better be prepared to do whatever it took to attract the next factory or corporate franchise. If Martin still remembered the Quebec revolution that had so excited him, the one involving a close working relationship between government and business, it was fading quickly. The new revolution could be summed up easily: get government out of the way.

At the end of the budget-cutting process, the minister hardest hit was Lloyd Axworthy; radical changes to his mandate were the most decisive sign that the business Liberals were in complete control. The evolution of the Chrétien era has been portrayed by many commentators as a battle between Martin and Axworthy for the soul of the government. Chrétien and Martin had agreed early in 1994 to charge Lloyd Axworthy, the most prominent and respected social Liberal in the cabinet, with an extensive social policy review, in which Martin wanted to integrate social welfare policy with education and job training. To Axworthy, this was a mandate to conduct a progressive review.

The authors of *Straight through the Heart* reveal just how out of the picture Axworthy was as he worked away on his reform plans throughout 1994: "On the morning of October 5, 1994, the day he was to present to the House of Commons a major policy review that was already seriously watered down ... Axworthy was floored by a newspaper headline revealing rumours of what turned out to be a treasury board estimate pointing to heavy social spending cuts in the coming years.... Axworthy would be proposing something that had already been squelched by financial constraints that went beyond what he had anticipated."[27]

The changes were to be announced in 1995, and came into effect in 1996. They would see cash transfers to the provinces drop from the 1995 level of $17.3 billion to $12.9 billion in 1996 and then $10.3 billion in

1997—a 40 per cent cut in two years. Mulroney had cut Ottawa's contribution to health, education and welfare programs from 20 per cent to 15 per cent of provincial spending in nine years; Martin would cut it to 9 per cent in four.[28]

The authors of *Straight Through the Heart* provided some evocative examples of what cuts might mean to individual provinces—just for 1996. Newfoundland lost $73 million, the equivalent of more than half of all payment to physicians; Nova Scotia lost $118 million, or twice the provincial spending on mental health services; Quebec saw a $1.1 billion cut, the equivalent of half of all payments for doctors' services. Ontario took the biggest hit at $1.4 billion—twenty times the amount spent on community health centres—and Manitoba lost $139 million, the amount it takes to operate the provinces sixty-five smaller hospitals.[29]

Yet that wasn't the half of it. Instead of introducing a bold new plan for social programs, Axworthy would find himself dismantling a generation of federal government initiatives, including the Canada Assistance Plan (CAP), which had provided national guidelines for social assistance since the era of Lester Pearson. The long-standing (1977) Established Programs Financing (EPF), the method by which Ottawa provided accountable funding for health and post-secondary education to the provinces, was to be eliminated as well. These two programs were to be delivered in a single lump sum to the provinces with no strings attached, in what was to be called the Canada Health and Social Transfer (CHST).

The CHST initiative had enormous implications and was more far-reaching than all the other changes combined in the 1995 budget. The CAP and EPF enshrined the very philosophy of 1960s and 1970s nation building. That philosophy was universality, the principle that everyone, regardless of income, would receive key public services and that they would be paid for through progressive taxation. In this single move, Paul Martin and Marcel Masse signalled that the federal government was, with the stroke of a pen, reversing possibly the most important core principle of Canadian social democracy. Federal initiatives had originally provided powerful incentives for provinces to join these programs. The practical implications of the CHST were difficult to overstate, for the elimination of these two programs had the effect of freeing provincial governments from any commitment to the national project. It was a policy of balkanization—Paul Martin's dream of massive decentralization fulfilled.

## THE FINAL ASSAULT

Paul Martin and his advisors from Earnscliffe, a private consulting firm, had worked assiduously not only on how to sell the budget, but on how to sell it effectively. To do this, they developed a whole new strategy: budget by strategic leak. Bit by bit, the media and the public learned what would be in the budget so by the time it happened there would be no surprises. By leaking the government's intentions, Martin effectively gave the details permanence so that ministers could not fight behind the scenes to make last-minute changes. By the fall of 1994, the drive to cut the budget was unstoppable. Martin was fully committed and it was unlikely that anything could have knocked him off track.

This firmness of purpose was in spite of embarrassing evidence produced by powerful and contrary outside voices coming to bear at just the wrong time. As Linda McQuaig points out in *The Cult of Impotence*, in September 1994, a report arrived in the finance department. Not only did it give Canada an unexpectedly good grade with regard to its debt, but it also said the deficit situation would be one of the best in the developed world if Canada successfully pursued full employment. This was not a report from some left-wing special interest group that could be easily dismissed; it was from Goldman Sachs, one of the world's leading brokerage firms, and a company that ordinarily would have the finance priesthood genuflecting.

Written by Senior Analyst William Dudley, the report didn't expressly reject the NAIRU faith, but it did bluntly state a long-accepted principle of public finance: so long as a nation's debt is shrinking relative to the size of its economy, it is becoming more manageable. Goldman Sachs approached the question by looking at the gap between a country's budget and what is required for fiscal "sustainability," and concluded that Canada's gap was a "relatively modest" 2 per cent. Dudley concluded that "the budgetary problems of ... Canada may not be quite as severe as many assume."[30]

However, it was something in the study's examination of how Canada might address its "relatively modest" problem that should have embarrassed Paul Martin, David Dodge, and the finance department. A country's budget gap was not an absolute; if its economy was not producing at full capacity, the gap could be overstated, and that is exactly what the Goldman Sachs study found. Using a model called the Full

Employment Budget Gap, the report determined that with full employment, "the budget gap of Canada vanishes." It went on to show that if Canada achieved full employment, its deficit situation would be one of the most envied in the world.

The study confirmed in spades exactly what Doug Peters had been telling Martin for months: Canada's economy was operating well below capacity, and growing the economy would reduce the deficit faster than cuts ever could. As if to puncture the last two balloons holding up the finance department's rationale for its policies, the Goldman Sachs report virtually ridiculed the Bank of Canada's interest rates as "far higher than what was justified by the pace of economic activity and inflation."

A stock finance department defence for high interest rates was that they were needed to attract foreign investors to Canadian bonds—a so-called "risk premium." Wrong again, said Goldman Sachs. Canada's bonds were rated Triple A by most bond rating agencies, including Moody's in New York. This was the top rating, given only to the twenty-four countries in the world with the least risky bonds. By comparison, the debt of the corporate sector was far riskier; in the fall of 1994, only six large corporations worldwide managed a Triple A rating for their bonds.

But nothing so unglamorous as a thirteen-page report from Goldman Sachs was going to budge the finance minister. The budget cuts had already been imposed on the various departments; the die was cast. In any case, almost no one knew about the report, as Goldman Sachs was not inclined to promote it and the Canadian media were not motivated to give it any attention. The study was swept aside in the heady rush to war on government spending.

Symbolic of Martin's dedication to the impending cuts was the book he commissioned Peter Nicholson to write. Known as the "Purple Book," the document became the Liberal government's new economic and fiscal plan, and a kind of public *mea culpa* for Martin's co-authorship of the Red Book's policy prescriptions. The Purple Book's title, *Agenda—Jobs and Growth: A New Framework for Economic Policy*, made it sound as if Martin had changed his mind about economic growth and the deficit, and was on the verge of creating thousands of jobs for the unemployed, but no such reversion had actually taken place; the Purple Book was all semantics and public relations.

Written by Nicholson and reworked by Martin and Martin's trusted assistant, Terrie O'Leary, the book was intended to sell the government's new policies, which would be unveiled in Martin's upcoming budget. Linda McQuaig writes that the document was "full of pop references about 'the globally integrated economy,' 'round-the-clock capital markets,' the 'revolution in technology based on the microchip,' and 'knowledge and information on the cutting edge,'"[31] all of which were employed as arguments not for, but against, using growth to bring down the deficit. It was almost as if the Liberals were releasing their real election platform book a year too late for Canadians to consider it before they voted. The Liberal Party, true to form, had run from the left with the Red Book, and intended to govern from the right with the Purple Book.

The approach revealed just how enamoured Martin was with the NAIRU economic theory, which deliberately kept unemployment high in order to keep inflation low. While the Tories had promised that interest rates could come down once inflation was conquered, no such promise was issued from Paul Martin. He maintained that growth and jobs would have to wait until his historic struggle with the deficit was over. In a letter to the Canadian Labour Congress's Bob White, Martin argued against growth spending, saying, "Experience has shown that allowing inflation to rise does not create lasting jobs, just more inflation."[32]

## CANADA AS MEXICO NORTH

The political gods were with the deficit slayers as budget day approached. In December 1994, just before Christmas, the Mexican peso virtually collapsed, losing half its value in a matter of weeks. In preparation for joining NAFTA, the Mexican government had allowed it to float on the open currency markets, which set off panic selling. The rush to get rid of Mexican pesos destabilized financial markets around the world. Even the Canadian dollar fell, forcing the Bank of Canada to raise interest rates. The Mexican crisis provided the deficit warriors with the perfect opportunity to scare Canadians even more: "See, this is what 'hitting the debt wall' looks like." Of course, those scare tactics didn't take into account that Canada had a Triple A debt rating while Mexico's was close to junk-bond status.

A timely article in the *Wall Street Journal* gratuitously compared Canada to Mexico, saying it had become "an honorary member of the third world. Canada could hit the debt wall ... and have to call in the International Monetary Fund." Not many Canadians read the *Wall Street Journal*, but the *Globe and Mail* reprinted the article by John Fund the next day. As the authors of *Straight through the Heart* disclose, Fund was a friend of *Globe* editorial writer Andrew Coyne, and had provided him with the material from his original article.[33] (It is curious to note that Canada's deficit warriors aren't busily writing about the US government's 2003 deficit of $500 billion—the equivalent of a $75 billion deficit in Canada.)

Another attack soon followed. Toronto currency speculator Albert Friedberg warned that the dollar might collapse. Then analysts with the Deutsche Bank Capital Corporation, Solomon Brothers of New York, and the British-based Barings Bank joined in the international chorus of high-profile capitalists enlisted to convince Canadians that the only way to save their social programs was by slashing them. Almost daily the assaults continued, preparing the way for the budget cuts coming in February.

The timing of the wave of media stories gave the distinct impression of a coordinated attack. As Linda McQuaig reveals in *Shooting the Hippo,* New York bond-raters were constantly being harangued by Canadian business figures and financial analysts to downgrade Canada's debt. Vincent Truglia, a senior analyst at Moody's told McQuaig in the summer of 1994, "[Canada] is the only country I handle where usually nationals want the country downgraded on a regular basis."[34] While the world's financial markets were undoubtedly skittish, the notion that Canada's debt was in trouble was nonsense. University of Toronto economist Peter Dungan stated that the chances of Canada defaulting on its debt were about as great as "a [nuclear] meltdown ... at the very same hour that there is an earthquake ... and a tornado that carries the stuff to Ottawa."[35]

The negative clamour about Canada's deficit was having its desired effect: the dollar was falling as speculators drove down its value. The Bank of Canada dutifully raised interest rates to protect it, bringing them dangerously close to the recession-inducing levels of the early 1990s. This action made the deficit situation look even worse, as higher interest rates increased debt-servicing charges. Moody's was forced to put Canada's debt on a "credit watch." For the first time in history, a plurality of Canadians said the deficit was a top concern. The timing was perfect. Paul Martin saw his budget pass the pro forma cabinet vote unanimously; dissenters, like ordinary Canadians, were duly cowed by the deficit hysteria campaign.

## BUDGET DAY

Paul Martin began his budget speech on February 27, 1995, with the following words:

> Mr. Speaker, there are times in the progress of a people when fundamental challenges must be faced, fundamental choices made, a new course charted. For Canada, this is one of those times. Our resolve, our values, our very way of life as Canadians are being tested. The choice is clear.
>
> We can take the path too well-trodden of minimal change, of least resistance, of leadership lost. Or we can set out on a new road of fundamental reform, of renewal, of hope restored.
>
> Today, we have made our choice. Today, we take action.[36]

In reading this moving paragraph out of context, it would be easy to conclude that the minister was launching a bold new nation-building initiative, a leap into a future filled with hope, renewal, and political leadership. Yet Paul Martin was about to reduce Canada's spending to a level not seen since well before most living Canadians had been born. But Martin's reform was not limited to spending cuts; it included a change in the role of government:

> We need to redesign the role of the government in the economy to fit the size of our pocketbook and the priorities of our people. What is that role? It is to provide a framework for the private sector to create jobs through responsible policies on inflation, on taxation, regulation, trade, and the labour market. It is to see an aggressive trade strategy as central to Canada's industrial strategy.... It is to do only what government can do best, and leave the rest for those who can do better, whether business, labour, or the voluntary sector.

It is difficult to imagine a more sweeping statement about abandoning such large portions of the commons. This new role of government was primarily to facilitate business. Martin also highlighted the role of "an aggressive trade strategy," by which he meant that all previous efforts to develop industry would now be subsumed into a single economic development policy: promoting trade and the free trade agreements that accompany it. Martin was careful to cast these profound changes in terms of the fiscal situation:

> If we are to ensure durable fiscal progress, building towards budget balance, that can only happen if we *redesign the very role and structure of government itself. This budget secures that reform irrevocably. Indeed, as far as we are concerned, it is this reform in the structure of government spending in the very redefinition of government itself that is the main achievement of this budget.... This budget overhauls not only how government works but what government does* [italics added].

The budget speech was probably as bold a political statement of intent as had ever been made in the House of Commons. Certainly, it was the budget cuts that received the most attention, but Martin was obviously confident enough in public opinion—and in the impact of the deficit hysteria campaign that had assailed Canadians—that he felt no need to downplay what he and his government were actually doing. They were implementing such a radical top-down revolution that even the clinically cool Preston Manning was left grasping for something to say. Indeed, the program described in the budget speech was the Reform Party's platform almost to the letter.

Of course, Martin's basic assumption, that "durable fiscal progress" could only be achieved by a revolutionary and permanent downsizing of government, was not true. In fact, that assumption would be disproved so quickly in the next two years that Martin would scramble to figure out what to do with the huge government surpluses that resulted from a surge of economic growth. Those surpluses started accumulating once the Bank of Canada lowered interest rates (forced to do so to counter the near-recession caused by Martin's budget cuts) and the de facto growth strategy was put into effect.

While it did not get much press, if any, another part of Martin's speech virtually institutionalized the new predominance of the finance department in government. Other ministries were reduced to an almost vassal-like state, subject entirely to the finance minister and his officials:

> Departments will have to prepare business plans for three years forward. Those plans will be subject to Parliamentary, and therefore public, scrutiny. That transparency and that accountability will mark a major departure from the past.... Individual ministers are being asked to alter their funding approach accordingly. They will be held accountable for their decisions and those decisions will be reviewed annually.

While the spin promised that Parliament would scrutinize department spending, the process all the ministers had been put through during the budget's creation left little doubt as to whom the departments would be accountable. It was almost as if the whole government, except for finance, was being put under trusteeship. No longer trusted with the taxpayers' dollars, and no longer able to claim legitimacy in the new fiscally conservative world order, the mainline departments were suddenly subjected to a kind of internal political feudalism under Paul Martin. Ministers responsible for transfers to the provinces, economic development, regional equality, international aid, transportation, natural resources, agriculture, environment and fisheries effectively became supplicants before Finance.

And then came the numbers:

> In short, overall departmental spending will be cut by almost 19 per cent in just three years. And let me emphasize, these are not the phoney cuts we saw so often in the past—measures that pretended to define a slower rate of increase in spending as actual cuts. These are real cuts in real dollars.
>
> Over the next three fiscal years, this budget will deliver cumulative savings of $29 billion, of which $25.3 billion are expenditure cuts. This is by far the largest set of actions in any Canadian budget since demobilization after the Second World War.... By 1996–97, we will have reduced program spending from $120 billion in 1993–94 to under $108 billion. Relative to the size

of our economy, program spending will be lower in 1996–97 than at any time since 1951.

Nowhere in substance or tone was Martin apologetic; he did not express regret at having to take such measures. Instead, he boasted about them again and again. This was Martin in his best CEO mode: bragging to the shareholders about reduced costs. He seemed so blinded by the beauty of what he had accomplished that it didn't even occur to him to express regret over what he would later say "he had to do."

In attacking government, he borrowed an old trick from Preston Manning and others in the right-wing populist camp. He portrayed government almost as an enemy of citizens, one that took their money for itself. Martin characterized the government as being parasitic, an out-of-control entity that had to be disciplined, rather than a demo- cratic body, an expression of Canadian society:

> In the last recession, every household, every business, every volun-
> teer group in the country was forced to face up to hard choices
> and real change. But the Government of Canada did not. In this
> budget, we are bringing government's size and structure into line
> with what we can afford.

The budget also contained major commitments to other principles of the neo-liberal Washington Consensus model. Hidden within the cuts to many departments was the biggest deregulation at the federal level in fifty years. Many agencies responsible for studying and protecting aspects of Canada's heritage and regulating the corporate activity related to them simply disappeared; other agencies experienced cutbacks so extreme that they could not possibly do the job assigned to them. Then there was the commitment to privatization and commercialization, well beyond any- thing Brian Mulroney's Tories had committed to:

> The government is committed to privatizing and commercializing
> government operations wherever that is feasible and appropriate.
> This is a matter of common sense. Our view is straightforward. If
> government doesn't need to run something, it shouldn't. And in
> the future, it won't.

Martin then listed the first items on the chopping block: privatization of CN Rail, the country's 70 per cent interest in Petro Canada, and the commercialization of the Air Navigation System across the country. The privatization initiative, which Martin promised was far from over, was never mentioned in the Red Book and had nothing to do with the deficit. Martin did not even connect the two in his speech. It was, however, a fundamental principle of the Washington Consensus and a high priority for Bay Street, which stood to make tens of millions of dollars in fees for this sell-off of Canadian assets.

While privatization was to be expected from a federal government run by a major business party, the commitment to "commercialize" government operations was extremely significant. Though Martin did not elaborate on what he meant, it would become clear over the years that government departments would be run on commercial, business principles superimposed on their traditional mandates.

Thus, as Martin promised, the whole purpose of government would be changed. The commercialization imperative would, in effect, mutate the original mandate of the department or agency in question. To take a single example of what the government had in store for Canadians, the Canadian Food Inspection Agency would be given two mandates: (1) the commercial promotion of Canadian food products and (2) the protection of the health of Canadians from tainted food. Rather than directly weaken or eliminate the agency mandated to protect Canadians, the "redesigned" Canadian government simply made it subservient to corporate, commercial interests. It was as if the budget had changed the very DNA of government. No other government in Canada, not even the right-wing administrations of Ontario and Alberta, managed to devise such an assault on democratic governance.

## WRITING THE NEW CANADA IN STONE

Paul Martin's 1995 budget was really three budgets in one, as it set out the cuts to every government department for the period 1995 to 1998. It was a stroke of political and strategic genius against those who might have fought the program—no one can maintain such a fight for three full years. Other budgets introduced by Paul Martin would contain significant features both in terms of cuts and even some new expenditures, but the '95 budget was the watershed budget for the continued corporatization of Canada, the balkanizing of the Canadian state, and the radical retrenchment of social programs that the majority of Canadians had come to expect and still supported. The only other significant budget action was Martin's record-breaking tax cut program in 2000, designed to permanently lock in his spending revolution, by ensuring that there would be inadequate revenue to restore programs in the future.

Paul Martin and the committed free-market advocates in the Liberal cabinet and in the bureaucracy had truly seized the moment. They took brilliant advantage of a major, if temporary, shift in the Canadian political culture, one that relied on an unprecedented ideological assault on Canadian citizens by the corporate sector and its media voices, think-tanks, and right-wing political parties. People really did seem willing to sacrifice for the good of the country, to tighten their belts, and to do the right thing in the face of a crisis.

In doing so, however, they signed a contract whose fine print they did not read. The changes wrought by Paul Martin's budgets, and the ripple effect they had in virtually every provincial government and municipality across the country, were equal to any so-called left-wing "social engineering" experiments that governments of the 1960s and 1970s were accused of implementing. Though those rich social programs were attacked by the right as efforts by governments to change the social fabric of the country from above, they had real popular support—they never could have happened otherwise. Paul Martin's social experiment was driven purely by an economic rationalist ideology in the interests of the very wealthiest of Canadians. Its effects on ordinary working and middle-class Canadians would be enormous.

# 4

# PAUL MARTIN'S CANADA

There is no denying Paul Martin's legacy of ridding Canada of its deficit. It is his other legacy that he has never had to answer for, a legacy that changed the very shape of the country. As a former CEO, Martin was used to striding into troubled companies as the man who would turn around their ailing financial situations. To him, that was Canada: a troubled company with financial difficulties rooted in the dangerous practice of straying from its core business. What Martin seemed unable to grasp was how cutting back on those "fringe" businesses and restructuring the government affected more than just the bottom line—they affected real people.

After the Council of Canadians' Maude Barlow made a speech attacking the government for its savage cuts, Martin asked to meet with her. He had actually inquired about joining the Council, a national citizens' organization, in its early days (Mel Hurtig suggested it probably wasn't for him), and the two knew each other well from the 1980s when she had been active in the Liberal Party. Barlow tried to make Martin understand the impact of his cuts, but with no success. "He seemed truly baffled at my position," she remembers, "and we went around and around all evening. I said, 'Paul, do you know what is happening to women's shelters and daycare centres and programs for immigrants from your budget cuts?' 'No,' he answered. 'I haven't had time for that, and those are provincial decisions now. I can't be responsible for it all. I just did what I had to do.'"[1] For Martin, the downloading of responsibilities to the provinces was the equivalent of selling off unwanted divisions of Canada Steamship Lines—any problems that resulted were not his responsibility.

## CANADA ON THE CHOPPING BLOCK

While the CEO could not trouble himself with the impacts of down-sizing and restructuring, those results were very real. Paul Martin's watershed 1995-8 budget was so counter-revolutionary that it literally sowed the seeds for the eventual rollback of the egalitarian state fash-ioned in Canada over a period of four decades. Even if Martin could argue that he "did what had to be done" regarding the deficit, he offered no justification for dismantling two generations of nation-building. He judged, correctly at the time, that the nation's preoccupation with the deficit would keep attention off what had just happened to the country. Since Martin tabled the '95 budget, hundreds of cuts have come and gone virtually unreported. Many more were implemented over years, and only when tragedy struck were Canadians even aware that there was a problem. The cuts that did manage to attract some brief media atten-tion did so only because those involved cared enough to risk their careers by criticizing the government.

A story in the *National Post* in February 2003 reported, "Arctic research is in precipitous decline. As the costs of studying the North have risen, so has its global importance. But federal funding has fallen to less than half its former level.... U of A biologist David Hik said that the current level of investment in Arctic research by the Canadian Government is 'downright embarrassing.'"[2] The year 2003 also saw British Columbia and Alberta experience one of their worst years ever for avalanche deaths. The media focused on the tragedies themselves, which buried another important aspect of the story. Mr. Israelson, the director of the Canadian Avalanche Association, says Canada is the only country in the world with snow and mountains that receives no gov-ernment funding for avalanche research: "Primarily, our support comes from the private sector and public donations. That's not good enough."[3]

Again in 2003, the House of Commons Standing Committee on Fisheries and Oceans (SCOFO) tabled its long-awaited report on the "Canadian Coast Guard: Marine Communications and Traffic Services (MCTS)." Its study was a damning indictment in which committee members summarized the organization's main problems as "overworked MCTS officers; restrictions and deficiencies in training; old and unreliable equipment; the neglect of international commitments; uncertainty, apprehension, and frustration among staff; reduced levels of service; and compromised security of our borders." The committee's report praised the dedication of a small group of Coast Guard officers who had the courage to testify, saying they played "an invaluable role, as eyes and ears of other government agencies, in protecting the integrity of Canada's maritime borders and its sovereignty."[4]

These are just a handful of literally hundreds of such examples throughout the entire federal government and its agencies. They are, of course, in addition to the larger, sweeping issues that have resulted from Martin's budget cuts and restructuring initiative. Working people saw their quality of life stagnate in the 1990s thanks to Martin's "labour flexibility" programs, which are among the most harsh in the industrialized world. Poverty dramatically increased in Canada as a huge transfer of wealth from working- and middle-class people to the rich took place, in part as a result of new tax structures. The federal government nearly eliminated its previous role in protecting the environment and Canada's cultural institutions, and federal contributions to a huge range of scientific research projects simply ended because they didn't lead directly to business opportunities. Economic sectors of the country such as farming have been devastated in the wake of the free trade imperative, while urban and national infrastructures—water treatment being the most obvious example—are in an advanced state of decay due to a lack of any serious federal commitments. Universities have been commercialized as a result of being forced to seek corporate funding to survive, and medicare is being increasingly privatized as another "useful crisis" takes its toll on our public space. Canada's health protection branch, once a vigorous regulator of the products Canadians consume, has been slowly transformed into a corporate sales promotion agency. Indeed, virtually every department of the federal government now has a trade "branch" with virtual veto power over the departments' mandates and legislative agendas.

None of these measures were necessary. When the Liberals assumed power, Canada was in one of the worst fiscal situations of any of the industrialized countries, and many critics of Paul Martin wrongly dismissed the deficit as a political red herring. However, the question is and was did Canada have to suffer the deep cuts implemented by Martin to get rid of the deficit? Jim Stanford persuasively argues that had Martin simply frozen government spending, his goals would have been easily achieved.

The government, says Stanford, actually "…out-performed its own deficit reduction timetable by two full years—reducing the deficit to just 1 per cent of GDP in fiscal 1996 and then attaining a balanced budget a year later."[5] But what value did this accelerated reduction have compared to the destruction it entailed? Many other countries managed to eliminate their deficits by the late 1990s—more gradually than Canada, but without radical cuts to social expenditures.

Stanford shows that had program spending simply been frozen at $118.7 billion until 1999, the Red Book's five year timetable, the deficit would have declined from 4.8 per cent of GDP in 1994, to less than 1 per cent in 1997 and 1998, and to zero—a balanced budget—in 1999. The cost of getting us to exactly the same fiscal goal two years ealier was $41 billion in cuts to social programs and government services over five years. The explanation for how the deficit could have been eliminated without cuts lies in the $41 billion figure. Had it been spent, "…GDP growth during the period of spending cutbacks would have been strengthened by the amount of the spending cutback."[6] Stanford's analysis reinforces the suspicion that Martin had priorities other than the deficit in mind.

As much out of necessity as philosophy, Canada's founders and builders chose a model that emphasized cooperation, for only through cooperation could a small nation on the North American continent survive as a sovereign entity. Canada became a more communitarian culture in which citizens and political parties of all stripes chose to do many things collectively. It developed a highly practical model that focused on survival of the collective in the interests of both individuals and communities. Paul Martin's nine years in finance did not simply moderate these efforts at nation-building; his tenure nearly declared them null and void.

## PROMOTING THE FREE TRADE IMPERATIVE

Burned into the memory of Canada's corporate elite was the period between the late 1960s and the early 1980s, a period of low unemployment when it was a labour-seller's market: ordinary workers, even those without unions, had economic leverage and could demand real increases in pay and benefits. Politically, workers had never before received a higher level of state intervention in the economy. Big business was determined to stop labour from gaining this kind of power again.

Following the signing of the Free Trade Agreement (FTA), Bay Street became preoccupied with Canada's "competitiveness" with the US. Canada's corporate executives were determined to create a "level playing field," and their efforts to drive down wages and reduce social programs to match those found in the US confirmed what free trade critics had argued all along: the level playing field was an American one. The Canadian corporate elite really seemed to believe their own rhetoric in the battle over free trade. Tom d'Aquino, Bay Street's spokesperson, ridiculed free trade opponents, portraying anyone who didn't take up the challenge of competing with the US as an economic sissy with no faith in Canada.

It turned out that Canadian business, notorious among some commentators for being risk-averse and "thinking small," was simply not up to the task. One of the people who recognized this reality was, ironically, Martin's economic guru, Peter Nicholson. At the 1991 Aylmer Conference, Nicholson told delegates, "Many of those who supported the FTA believed its primary long-term effect would be to cause Canadian firms to pull up their socks and do whatever was needed to compete in the North American market. What perhaps was overlooked is that many Canadian companies ... might adjust to the FTA not by standing and fighting but instead by simply moving across the border.... It appears that too many enterprising Canadian companies are taking this path of least resistance."[7]

Signs that Canadian business had failed to compete were starkly obvious before the Liberals were even elected: if radical and rapid changes weren't made to ratchet up Canada's "competitiveness" with the US by ratcheting down egalitarian government, Canada might very well see some of its significant economic sectors effectively disappear. It was certainly too late to go back; Bay Street had taken the leap of faith into free trade. Not only was free trade going to be central to Canada's industrial strategy, it was going to be Canada's only industrial strategy. As the authors of *Double Vision* put it, "Over time, trade policy would pretty well subsume industrial policy.... The denizens of Jurassic Park, as the trade bureaucracy was known to its rivals, became one of the most powerful ministries in Ottawa."[8]

Paul Martin's most important crusade was not against the deficit, it was against a robust, democratic, and interventionist government—from his perspective, a government that led to an uncompetitive economy. Cutting the deficit was an end in itself, but more important, it was a classic "useful" crisis without which Martin would have been virtually powerless to implement "the redefinition of government." What was the new definition of government? Martin stated it in his 1995 budget speech: "It is to provide a framework for the private sector to create jobs through responsible policies on inflation, on taxation, regulation, trade, and the labour market. It is to see an aggressive trade strategy as central to Canada's industrial strategy."[9] As dictated by this new definition, one of Paul Martin's most important tasks would be demonstrating to Canadian workers that their easy ride was over. It was time to get "flexible."

## CREATING THE "FLEXIBLE" WORKFORCE

In the 1990s, speeches given by Paul Martin, Jean Chrétien, and other Liberal economic ministers—even social Liberals like Lloyd Axworthy—were replete with the term "flexible workforce." The Purple Book, the Liberal document on economic policy written by Martin and Peter Nicholson with the help of Terrie O'Leary, Martin's most trusted assistant, elaborated the term more clearly. While the book recognized the popularity of programs that guaranteed "income security—including Unemployment Insurance, Workers' Compensation and various forms of social assistance," the authors also discovered that such programs were now "understood" [though they didn't say by whom] "to harbour features that can discourage active search for work."[10]

This discovery gave rise to another innocuous-sounding phrase from the corporate economist lexicon: "labour market disincentives." According to the Purple Book's description of income-security programs, these initiatives were so generous that they actually encouraged people to quit their jobs or, at the very least, encouraged them not to look very hard for work if they became unemployed. It followed that if governments wanted to increase employment, they would have to reduce the "disincentive" to work by curbing generous social programs.

But it wasn't just these social programs that were a problem; so were the rules governing how employers treated their workers. As labour standards are largely a provincial matter, the Purple Book took aim at this level of government, too: "Added to these [federal] disincentives has been a growing body of labour market regulation … designed to increase employment security and augmented by a body of legal precedent which has strengthened safeguards against arbitrary dismissal."[11] It wasn't just the provincial governments that were to blame for these disincentives, but the courts, too. The Purple Book's criticism of these safeguards implied that governments should find a way to allow these employers to arbitrarily dismiss their workers.

Three of Paul Martin's key policy initiatives—the NAIRU inflation targets, the tightening of Unemployment Insurance (UI) regulations, and the elimination of the Canada Assistance Plan (CAP)—were directly aimed at ridding the country of its "labour market rigidities," or "disincentives." The principal one was the application of NAIRU, or the non-accelerating inflation rate of unemployment, as a rationale and guideline in the fight against inflation. However, while it was being applied by the finance department, there was virtually no threat of inflation given that the economy was operating at no more than 90 per cent capacity.

In other words, before there was any threat of upward pressure on wages and inflation, the economy would have had to grow by several percentage points. Unemployment in the US was running at about half of Canada's rate and there was still no sign of the wage-driven inflation that Paul Martin claimed he feared. Yet in 1997, Bank of Canada Governor Gordon Theissen raised interest rates four times because unemployment threatened to fall below 9 per cent. Asked whether he still supported NAIRU, Martin replied, "Yes, I do."[12]

Did Martin and the finance department really believe in the value of extremely low inflation? By all accounts they did, even though by 1997 they were among a small minority of those who still subscribed to NAIRU principles. Even the International Monetary Fund (IMF) expressed serious doubts about the theory. In a study by Michael Sarel published in May 1997, the IMF maintained that while high levels of inflation did hurt an economy, low levels—*anything below 8 per cent*—could actually help an economy grow, or at worst, have no effect at all. Two other mainstream studies conducted at about the same time came to the same conclusion. One of them, by Montreal economists Steve Ambler and Emanuela Cardia, found the Bank of Canada's claim that very low inflation spurred economic growth was simply not supported by the evidence. Likewise, Harvard economics professor Robert Barro examined the relationship between inflation and economic growth in more than one hundred countries over twenty-five years and found very minor benefits to low inflation.[13]

While the social and economic benefits of low inflation are debatable, there is one enormous benefit to keeping unemployment high and inflation low: it pacifies labour. While Canadian workers were seeing their real incomes actually decline during the 1990s before regaining 1989 levels in 1999, American workers saw their real per capita income increase a full 14 per cent for the decade. In 1997, for example, Canadian men working full-time, full-year jobs earned an average of $42,626 compared to $42,635 in 1975 (expressed in constant 1997 dollars). When examined from this perspective—the hundreds of billions of dollars saved by Canadian business in labour costs—it is not difficult to comprehend why Paul Martin's Bay Street-inspired budgets were so determined to "fight inflation."

## GUTTING UNEMPLOYMENT INSURANCE

The second front in the assault on workers' share of the economic pie was Paul Martin's further erosion of UI, an attack he launched in his very first budget. The Tories had already made serious cuts to UI, and the Liberals were onside with this important business priority right from the start. The corporate complaints about "labour market disincentives" were little more than ideological slogans, as no scientific study has ever proven that Canada's UI system seriously discouraged people from seeking employment. It may well have discouraged employers from abusing the rights of their employees, or threatening to fire them without cause. There was evidence, too, that employers laid people off because they knew those workers would stick around, supported by UI, and be available for work when needed.

The Liberals' cuts to UI would wear down the system to such an extent that it would end up even meaner and leaner than the system in the US. Before the Tories started their cuts, some 77 per cent of those contributing to UI were eligible for benefits. By 1998, fewer than 39 per cent of people paying into UI received benefits when they became unemployed, thanks to tightened eligibility rules, lowered benefits, and shortened periods of compensation.

One of the results of the radical changes to UI (as Mel Hurtig says, "ridiculously ... renamed Employment Insurance," or EI) was that it became a cash source for Paul Martin and allowed him to make his budgets look better than they were. In 1998 alone, employers and employees contributed $19.6 billion to UI coffers while the government allowed only $11.8 billion to be paid out. In that same year, 925,000 unemployed workers received nothing from the program they had been paying into. By 2000, Paul Martin and the finance department, ignoring criticism from virtually all quarters, including the Auditor General, had pocketed nearly $40 billion from the UI fund. In effect, they applied a special tax on workers and employers in a sleight-of-hand effort to make the fiscal situation look better than it was. The budget surplus of 1999–2000, for example, would not have existed at all had it not been for Paul Martin's raiding the UI fund of $6.5 billion in excess contributions.[14]

The cuts to UI had absolutely no impact on the level of joblessness. If there are no jobs and if it is government policy to deliberately keep unemployment at 8 to 10 per cent, even motivated and desperate individuals can't find work, and the structure of the UI program becomes irrelevant. Like NAIRU, the intended impact of UI cuts was the suppression of workers' economic leverage and any subsequent demand for pay increases, and the lowering of their expectations in terms of the kind of treatment they could get from employers. This objective was largely met. With 1.5 million workers unemployed, those who managed to keep their jobs would think twice about asking for a wage increase, or often accept employers' demands for wage or benefit rollbacks. Even unionized workers found themselves in this situation. The results were predictable: the 1990s were characterized by employers using this high rate of unemployment to extract more and more labour from their employees without compensation.

Paul Martin's final blow against "labour rigidities in the market" was the elimination of the Canada Assistance Plan, which disappeared in Lloyd Axworthy's social policy review. The disappearance of CAP's coordinating function and its effective ban on workfare, as well as the huge cuts implemented through the Canada Health and Social Transfer (CHST), were a signal to provinces to reduce and redesign their own welfare programs. These changes made it even more difficult for workers to seek a pay raise or to raise complaints with a labour standards branch about their working conditions.

Social assistance has been cut to the bone, as provinces have followed Ottawa's lead in reducing the social safety net for low-income earners. Workers who ten or fifteen years ago would have qualified for nearly a year of UI while they looked for work are now faced with no UI and welfare rates that are so inadequate that thousands of people, many of them formerly middle class, have ended up in shelters and on the street.

For millions of Canadians, the conditions of work and the impact of those conditions on families are now so difficult that a Health Canada study has called the pace of work in Canada "completely unsustainable." "The National Work-Life Conflict Study," released in July 2002 and prepared by Dr. Chris Higgins of the University of Western Ontario and Dr. Linda Duxbury of Carleton University, states that a decade ago, approximately 38 per cent of the workforce was "highly stressed"; by 2002 the number had reached 55 per cent. The details make for disturbing reading. The pressure put on workers as a direct result of Paul Martin's desire to create and enforce 'labour flexibility' has taken them back to conditions not experienced since the 1930s. The forty-hour work week is rapidly becoming a thing of the past for many, with one in four employees currently working more than fifty hours a week and unpaid overtime increasing dramatically in the 1990s. The report, which surveyed over 31,000 Canadian workers, goes on to state:

> The resulting effect of this long-hours culture is immense and multi-faceted. For the worker, there is the increase in stress and burnout caused by the increased workload. Workers are getting sick.... For the individual family, there is the delay in having chil-

dren, the decrease in family size, and the relinquishing of the care and guidance of children to day cares and extended school programs. On the society level there is an overall increase in numbers of "latch key kids," those children who come home from school to empty homes.

On the individual level workers' health is suffering. Family life is limited or non-existent.... On a national level, birth rates are falling, influencing just about everything from local school and hospital viability to the capacity of the future labour force to fulfil what is expected of it. The "workaholic" ethic has huge short- and long-term negative effects.[15]

This erosion in the quality of life is the price of "labour flexibility."

## CREATING A CLASS SOCIETY

By the end of the 1990s, the shape and character of Paul Martin's redesigned Canada was unmistakable in its dramatic social and economic inequalities and class divisions. These inequalities were meticulously documented by Armine Yalnizyan in the "The Growing Gap: A report on the growing inequality between the rich and poor in Canada," a study published in 1997. In 1973, at the height of the postwar social contract era, the wealthiest 10 per cent of Canadians with children under the age of eighteen made twenty-one times the income of the poorest 10 per cent. By 1996, the wealthiest 10 per cent made 314 times the income of the poorest 10 per cent. While no comparable study has looked at the figures for the late 1990s, Martin's additional cuts to UI and his record on tax breaks to high-income Canadians mean that the situation has almost certainly worsened.

While the poor were getting dramatically poorer, the middle class was slowly disappearing. Says Yalnizyan, "By 1996 the earnings bracket that used to account for 60 per cent of the population held only 44 per cent of Canadian families with dependent children. The change was most accentuated in the very middle, those earning between $31,666 and $55,992 (in 1996 dollars). In 1973, 40 per cent of families earned in this range."[16] Middle-class families that do exist now have almost no cushion if they face unemployment. The personal savings rate is plummeting, while personal debt is rising. According to StatsCan's Phillip Cross, the average savings rate was 17.8 per cent in 1982. It dropped to 10 per cent in 1993 and to 5.4 per cent in June 1996. In the first three months of 1997, it sank almost out of sight to 1.7 per cent.[17]

The impoverishment of Canadian families in the market economy has had a disproportionate impact on children. Since 1989, when free trade began and when Parliament voted unanimously to eradicate child poverty by 2000, the number of poor children in Canada has grown by 60 per cent, and the number of children living in families earning less than $20,000 has increased by 65 per cent. The result is that Canada has the shameful distinction of being ranked 17th out of 23 industrialized countries in successfully addressing the issue of child poverty.

At the other end of the social scale, wealthy Canadians have increased their share of the total wealth at an unprecedented rate. According to a StatsCan study released in March 2001, the top 20 per cent of families saw their net worth increase 39 per cent to $403,500 between 1984 and 1999. However, there was virtually no change for families in the lowest 20 per cent.[18] According to an Ernst and Young survey, in the 1990s, the number of millionaires in Canada tripled to 220,000 and was expected to triple again by 2005. Corporate CEO salaries increased, on average, 15 per cent each year throughout the 1990s. In a single year, 1999, compensation for the highest-paid one hundred CEOs increased by an average of 112 per cent. Increases in executive compensation were recorded regardless of how well the companies in question did.[19]

Canada's record in dealing with poverty has been vigorously attacked by international agencies that track poverty throughout the world. In December 1998, the United Nations Economic and Social Council Committee on Economic, Social and Cultural Rights heard testimony from Canadian officials on the level of poverty in Canada. The committee was already disappointed in Canada's performance based on a report submitted by another UN agency that ranked Canada 10th on the human poverty index for industrialized countries.[20] The committee was further troubled when Canadian delegates refused to answer for the country's record of homelessness and poverty, instead giving vague answers or saying data was not available.

Both observers and UN officials were left stunned by the performance. Mel Hurtig, in *Pay the Rent or Feed the Kids*, recounts a Canadian

Press story that covered the event: "The Canadian [government] delegation left committee members shaking their heads in disbelief at the vagueness of Canadian replies to specific and pointed questions about homelessness, reductions in welfare payments, living conditions in First Nations communities and other social problems."[21] The *Toronto Star* characterized Canadian officials' testimony as "brazen self-justification, half-truths, bafflegab.... It was a shameful performance."[22]

The committee members used language that was scarcely less critical, accusing government delegates of "stonewalling," "waffling," "avoiding the glaring facts," and of giving smug responses. The result of the hearing was reflected in the UN's report a month later, which condemned Canada's human rights record: "To hear about these things from a country like Canada with so many resources ... is really quite shocking." The committee's report was a devastating critique of Paul Martin's policies, as it noted that the serious decline in conditions began in 1994: "Since 1994 [the Canadian government] has not paid sufficient attention to the adverse consequences for the enjoyment of economic, social, and cultural rights, especially for the most vulnerable Canadians."[23]

The report was the most damning of any the committee had issued on an industrial country over a period of many years. It went on to attack in detail these disturbing facts about Canada: half of single mothers and their children live in poverty; mass unemployment seems to be tolerated; women face obstacles to escaping domestic violence because of cuts to social assistance; and employees working under workfare programs lack protection of their fundamental rights, a violation of a UN article regarding discrimination.[24]

The committee recommended that the federal government establish a national program that "includes universal entitlements and national standards, specifying a legally enforceable right to adequate assistance"—in other words, reinstate the CAP, but with enforceable guidelines. The UN committee also recommended that the government reverse the changes to Canada's UI program and pass legislation to prevent provincial governments from "clawing back" federal benefits for the poor from their own welfare programs. Finally, it called on the federal government to provide proper housing for low-income people.[25]

All of the UN's recommendations addressed actions that had been taken by the Liberal government as the result of Paul Martin's budgets.

## UNDERMINING RURAL COMMUNITIES

For over a century, the foundation of agriculture in Canada was the family farm, but starting with the Mulroney government and accelerating rapidly under the Liberals after 1995, the face of agriculture has been almost totally transformed. The family farm no longer features prominently in federal agriculture policy, though huge transnational corporations certainly do. In "The Structural Adjustment of Canadian Agriculture," a study released in 2003, Darrin Qualman and Nettie Wiebe of the National Farmers Union describe the transformation of agriculture in this period as essentially based on the IMF's structural adjustment formula—virtually the same formula applied to agriculture in developing nations. Key components of this structural adjustment program include: "rapid export expansion and a focus on production for export; dramatic cuts in government spending; deregulation; measures to attract and safeguard foreign investment; privatization of government industries and utilities; and removal of subsidies and price controls. Each of these elements of the IMF's often downplayed role as a promoter of free trade in agriculture have been applied in Canada."[26]

The Canadian government repeatedly boasts about the enormous increases in agricultural exports, leading many Canadians to believe that farmers must be benefiting from such an increase. Yet Qualman and Wiebe found that "despite a tripling of agri-food exports since 1989, and a seven-fold increase since 1974, farmers' realized net incomes have remained stagnant."[27] The principle reason for this development is the rapid consolidation and concentration of ownership in transnational agri-business corporations. After twenty years of mergers and buyouts, there are just a handful of companies at both the input end (machinery and chemicals) and the output end (buyers of products). These corporations are so huge that they can virtually dictate the price at both ends.

On the trade front, Canada has been engaged in what some have referred to as "trading naked"—that is, eagerly liberalizing its agricultural industry without regard to strategy or tactics when negotiating with trading partners. According to the Qualman and Wiebe report, "The Canadian federal government has cut its spending on agriculture by 48% in the past ten years: from $6.1 billion in 1991/92 to approximately $3.3 billion for 2001/02.... And this despite a grinding farm income crisis and drought in many regions."[28]

Canada has been nearly alone among Organization for Economic Cooperation and Development (OECD) countries in making these dramatic cuts to farm support. Not only have the European Union and the US declined to reduce their supports, they have increased them in the interests of their farmers despite their alleged commitment to "free trade." And while all such subsidies distort world prices and harm third-world farmers, the situation is not likely to change soon. Canada's subsidies were minimal compared to the EU's and US's, but only Canada threw away its only bargaining chips and penalized its own farmers based solely on free trade ideology. As a result of federal policies, farm debt had increased to $40.8 billion by 2001, an increase of 50 per cent in just five years. This debt almost exactly equals annual net farm income, which has now dropped to levels not seen since the 1930s. In just five years, between 1996 and 2001, Canada lost 11 per cent of its farmers, the fastest decline ever.[29]

The impact of the federal government's agriculture policies can also be measured in an escalation in suicides, family violence, mental illness, chronic depression, and the most rapid increase in rural depopulation in a thirty-year period already characterized by this trend. A host of small towns on the prairies are simply no longer viable as young people leave, schools close, and the tax base disappears. "In many villages, the centres of community social life—the churches, halls, arenas, clubs, and schools—have disappeared altogether," say Qualman and Wiebe. "The loss of cultural diversity and vigour in the countryside parallels the loss of biodiversity and may pose similar inherent dangers to the long-term sustainability of human survival."[30]

Nowhere are the tragic consequences of "economic rationalism" more stark or more permanent than in small-town Canada. These consequences are a direct result of government policy or inaction. On the 2003 leadership campaign trail, Paul Martin has claimed that he wants to address the issue of "western alienation," yet he has treated the prairie family farm as one of those company sidelines that no longer holds the interest of his government.

## SACRIFICING THE ENVIRONMENT

Elizabeth May, the executive director of the Sierra Club of Canada, describes the state of Environment Canada in the 1990s as "extremely grim. I recall writing in 1998—on the fifth anniversary of Brian Mulroney's resignation—that the Chrétien government was now *officially* far, far worse than the Tories. We thought everything Mulroney did, while flawed, represented a floor for the Liberals, below which they wouldn't go. Instead it was a ceiling. I said the Liberals went through the floor and are now digging into the basement." It was more than just cutbacks, says May. "The three things that contributed to environment policy being so appalling during the '90s were: one, the Program Review and the cuts that resulted; two, harmonization with the provinces; and three, the restructuring of the federal cabinet."[31]

Mulroney had actually been planning to invest billions in the department's new Green Plan. Kim Campbell began to reverse that process, but Martin's Program Review hit the plan the hardest. According to May, "It was so bad that really basic programs were just eliminated: closing science centres, stopping the monitoring of acid rain, slashing money for enforcement of existing regulations. Then the government would pass new regulations with no money allocated for implementation or enforcement."[32]

The other major blow to the department was the new committee structure of Cabinet. Throughout the Mulroney years, the Planning and Priorities Committee always included the environment minister. Under the Liberals, environment was assigned to the Economic Policy Committee, not the Social Policy Committee. As a result, "every recommendation for environmental policy had to run this nasty gauntlet of all the economic ministries' bureaucrats—industry, trade, agriculture—who were overtly hostile to any new measures," says May. Still, May gives Martin a mixed review: "Some of the very few good things we did get in that period came as a result of Paul Martin," she says. "One was the Green Infrastructure Fund for the Federation of Canadian Municipalities (FCM). It was a $250 million pot of money administered by the FCM and has been used very well. This was not achieved through the environment department, but from Martin personally."[33]

At the same time, Martin was directly responsible for the Program Review's number-crunching, and had the power to make less severe cuts to an area of government he had been championing just a year and half earlier. Indeed, that he was able to deliver some progressive items "personally" simply reinforces the suspicion that he could have chosen to make the cuts less severe. Or, perhaps, he could have prevented the wholesale downloading of responsibility for environmental protection to the provinces. Most of them had neither the resources nor the experienced staff to take up the slack. Instead, the environment department became one of the clearest examples of the decentralization imperative that Martin pursued throughout his time as finance minister.

Martin's 30 per cent cut to the department—1,400 employees and $235 million—ensured that Canada would be even more business-friendly than it had been before. According to Maude Barlow, Canada has an extremely dubious record for environmental regulation enforcement. In 1995, Ottawa caught just 169 corporate and government violations in the entire country, and laid minuscule charges. And this was before Martin's cuts even took effect. Compare this performance with that of the right-wing Conservative government of Ontario, which caught and charged 400 potential perpetrators, took the cases to court, and won 345 convictions.[34]

By the time Paul Martin reduced the department's budget, it had already become so ineffective that few people believed it could get much worse. Even if it did, the government made sure no one would know about it: it stopped publishing *The State of Canada's Environment*, the only comprehensive account of every aspect of Canada's environment. Even the pro-business *Ottawa Citizen* questioned the cuts to the environment department, stating, "The department has little influence on anything you eat, drink or breathe. And it doesn't enforce its own laws. Now it proposes reducing its role further, shifting more responsibilities to the provinces, private businesses and universities ..."[35]

The impact of the federal government's decision to shrink the environment department was not long coming. One of the alarm bells came from an unlikely source: a report by NAFTA's Commission for Environmental Cooperation titled, "The North American Mosaic: The State of the Environment Report." It raised serious questions about the direct impact of increased and unregulated trade on the environment: "On balance, we have an ever-growing ecological foot print. North Americans, mainly US and Canadian citizens, typically use more energy and natural resources, and generate more wastes than citizens of other countries. The health of an environment that sustains 394 million people and an economy worth nine trillion US dollars a year is at risk.... North Americans are faced with the paradox that many activities on which the North American economy is based impoverish the environment on which our well-being ultimately depends." The report detailed the loss of natural forests, the destruction of fisheries, increasing chemical and air pollution, and an agricultural sector too dependent on chemicals and irrigation. The report's conclusion stated, "By 'spending' natural capital without replenishing it, or by damaging processes and living systems that cannot be fixed by technology, we are living off our capital rather than the interest."[36] The Liberal government did not act on a single issue raised in the NAFTA commission's report.

The free trade imperative does not stop with NAFTA; trade routinely trumps other values in Canada's international dealings. For example, Canada is a member of a group of six countries, including the US, that was blocking a 150-nation consensus on the need to deal with the implications for environmental biodiversity posed by genetically engineered seeds. According to Michelle Swenarchuk of the Canadian Environmental Law Association, "Canada's goal [at an international conference in Montreal] was to prevent international regulation of food and feed. [Canada] parroted the US line and even *spoke for* the US on some topics. The Canadian negotiators, just as the end was in sight, almost derailed the protocol by holding out into the middle of the night. As one Asian delegate said to me, 'Canada used to be such a positive influence. What has happened?'"[37]

## INSTITUTING CORPORATE U

While Paul Martin's 1995 budget eliminated the Established Program Financing (EPF) scheme that funded universities and medicare, he also cut billions from the total budget, effectively declaring that public universities were on their own if they wanted monies to meet future needs. Canadian universities were suddenly faced with provincial governments that were $1.4 billion short in their post-secondary budgets. As the 1990s wore on, universities began hiring presidents and appointing boards of governors almost exclusively for their fundraising abilities, which meant that a potential administrators' most important qualification was status in the corporate world. A situation that originated in desperation with the unsavoury task of begging for money from corporations eventually evolved into one in which the people who actually ran the educational institutions were themselves supportive of a new, dominant role for corporations.

These corporate representatives were not reluctant fundraisers; they were, for the most part, eager promoters of so-called "partnerships" with the corporate world, a commercial fifth column that would take on the task of redefining the role of universities to suit the very specific needs of corporations. According to political economist Duncan Cameron, "The university president is no longer someone who takes a leadership role and speaks out on matters concerning society. They lunch, they raise money, and the terms of the relationship are quite clear: money for services rendered."[38]

Here are just a few examples that illustrate how the corporate elite now preside over many of Canada's universities. In 1999, the University of Toronto Board of Governors was chaired by the president of the Bank of Montreal with help from the publishers of the *Toronto Sun*, *The Globe and Mail*, and *Maclean*'s magazine, as well as executives from KPMG and Price Waterhouse. McGill University is run by the CEOs of Noranda, the Royal Bank, Canadian National Railway, and Bell Canada, and executives from the Bank of Montreal, the Bank of Nova Scotia, Ernst & Young, and Canadian Pacific. To make the whole structure even more integrated, many of these corporate members of university boards also sit on numerous corporate lobby groups, such as the Canadian Council of Chief Executives (CCCE) (formerly the Business Council on National Issues, or BCNI), the Corporate Higher Education Forum, and the Canadian Advanced Technology Association. To ensure the members of this corporate university family reinforce each other, many university presidents sit on the boards of the corporations that run their universities.[39]

Within a year of Martin's "useful deficit crisis," one of the high-tech industry's most ambitious initiatives in influencing the direction of universities was launched. The Consortium for Software Engineering Research was a five-year industry-federal government initiative to funnel $18 million to universities for software research. According to Canadian Centre for Policy Alternatives education specialist Erika Shaker, "it marked a substantial change from past relationships because its goals directly corresponded to corporate demands."[40]

Shaker cites other examples of the good deals corporations get when they are recruited by pro-business university presidents and departments. In one, McGill University got a $250,000 loan of high-end audio equipment from Sony Classical Productions in exchange for giving the company representation on the curriculum committee in the Faculty of Music. The agreement between Sony and McGill ensures that the university will "appoint a designated member of Sony to be a voting member of the university's ... committee ... for creating and/or approving the curriculum of the university regarding music and sound recording."[41] Just for *lending* musical equipment, an international corporation was given influence over the development and direction of the music curriculum at one of Canada's top public universities.

These stories repeat themselves across the country and in virtually every public university. Too often, these partnerships resemble little more than university officials handing over public resources and institutional credibility to corporations whose connections and affinities are much closer to the corporate world than they are to traditional university values and goals. According to education researcher Denise Doherty Delorme, the result of this partnership has been an incredibly rapid corporatization of universities: "The corporatization of post-secondary education, in the simplest of terms, means the transformation of the education system into an education corporation. Corporatization is the acceptance of corporate control over infrastructure, research and teaching, through private/public partnerships and secret arrangements. Corporatization allows for corporate-style management practices and a market orientation in the design and pricing of educational programs."[42]

Understanding the important role of public universities to a viable nation is not rocket science: they are open to everyone, funded by society, and governed in the broad public interest. They are intended to be a haven for the most vigorous exchange of ideas about the human project between students and professors, and among advanced researchers. Yet the corporatization of Canadian universities, and their redesign in the interests of narrow corporate interests, gradually erodes their original purpose. The current trend puts Canada at the forefront of neo-liberal states in this commercial restructuring of a key democratic institution.

The federal government's cuts went beyond general university funding. Between 1995 and 1997, Paul Martin also slashed funding to the government's science and technology budget by $1.3 billion. Even before this substantial cut, the Tories had brought Canada well below other developed countries in such funding by reducing support to just 1.5 per cent of GDP compared to the US at 2.7 per cent, the UK at 2.2 per cent, and Sweden at 3.1 per cent. That billion-dollar cut did show up elsewhere, however—in the newly formed Canadian Foundation for Innovation (CFI). Bowing to the prescription of the CCCE/BCNI, which recommended to the government "that university funding be aligned to support competitiveness," in 1997, Parliament effectively transferred $800 million that should have gone to basic public research agencies to the corporate sector for distribution. The CFI will not fund any project that cannot prove it will lead to direct financial returns to the private sector. The foundation's board has twenty-three members from corporations and industry; just seven members are from public universities. In 1999, the Liberals added another $200 million to this corporate research fund.[43]

## CORPORATIZING HEALTH PROTECTION

Corporate influence and control has infiltrated almost every dimension of democratic governance and citizen protection in Canada. While Paul Martin did not have his hand on every lever of government, nor did he design every scheme to harness government to the interests of the private sector, his imprimatur is on the government's evolution. No matter what a department or agency or institution was doing before 1995, it would have to redesign itself to fit the new imperative. Perhaps the most alarming example of this transformation, because it has such an immediate impact on the actual physical health of Canadians, was what happened at Health Canada's Health Protection Branch and at the Canadian Food Inspection Agency.

Throughout the late 1990s, Canadians began hearing alarming stories from senior scientists working for various branches of government assigned to protect Canadians' health. Some government scientists started going public with charges that they were being harassed, threatened, and demoted because they wouldn't support the approval of new drugs. Others were afraid to speak up about a problem because the laws they were enforcing didn't protect them from being sued by the companies they might criticize. That any government scientist would go public at all was remarkable; public employees, when they do feel it necessary to expose an issue, most often protect themselves by anonymously sending a brown envelope to the media or a politician in the Opposition with the hope that they will make the information public.

It was the Health Protection Branch (HPB) that generated by far the most controversy. Senior government employees, hired to make sure no drugs made it to market before it was absolutely certain that they were safe, alerted the public to what they maintained was corporate interference in their work. One of the first cases arose in 1996, when Michele Brill-Edwards resigned from her job as a drug reviewer at the federal HPB because of what she considered to be undue industry influence in the drug approval process. She left in a dispute over a controversial heart drug called nifedipine, claiming that her superiors in the HPB ignored independent research showing the drug could actually cause heart attacks, rather than prevent them, if used over a long period of time.

The department played hardball in all of these cases, including Brill-Edwards's. When she sought a public inquiry into the decision-making processes at Health Canada, Assistant Deputy Minister Joe Losos tried to intimidate her by requesting to see her confidential personnel files. Losos's actions were rebuked by Federal Privacy Commissioner Bruce Phillips, as they were in violation of the federal Privacy Act.

Perhaps the highest-profile case at the HPB involved the bureau of veterinary medicine and a drug known as bovine growth hormone, or BGH. The drug, which increases milk production in dairy cattle, was being boosted by food biotechnology transnational Monsanto. The five scientists assigned to evaluate BGH had serious concerns about its long-term effects, which had not been thoroughly studied. However, when they refused to approve the drug, they were put under relentless pressure by their superiors.

One of the five scientists, Dr. Chiv Chopra, went before a Public Service Staff Relations Board for a hearing in September 1998. According to an article in *Maclean's* magazine, one of Chopra's managers "threatened to ship him and his colleagues to other departments where they would 'never be heard of again' if they didn't hurry their evaluations" of BGH.[44] The five scientists responded by filing a grievance claiming management harassed and pressured them to approve drugs they considered to be unsafe. Another member of the group, Dr. Margaret Haydon, a drug researcher with fifteen years' experience, told the tribunal that managers pressured her to approve another growth hormone, Revalor-H, a product marketed by Hoechst Canada. She resisted because she felt the company had not provided enough data about the drug's safety. Haydon was told that she might be sued if Hoechst was unhappy with her recommendations.

The Senate Standing Committee on Agriculture and Forestry took an interest in the scientists' case and gave them a chance to tell their story. *Maclean's* reported that the story sounded "at times like a paranoia-driven *X-Files* fantasy. Stolen scientific files, critical data gone missing, an alleged bribe by a giant multinational drug company—all intended, the scientists claim, to pressure them into approving bovine growth hormone..."[45]

The scientists were so fearful of their superiors that they demanded, and got, written assurances against future reprisals before they testified in front of the Senate committee. Dr. Haydon told the senators "that officials from Monsanto offered her department one million dollars in research funding in 1990—an offer she interpreted as an attempted bribe to obtain approval of growth hormone."[46] Adding to the sense that this was a story involving some "rogue corporation" rather than a staid and stodgy government department, Haydon also testified that her files on BGH had gone missing from her Ottawa office in 1994. A week after the scientists' testimony, the senators were informed by one of their own research staff that Health Canada employees were busy shredding documents about the BGH case.

Partly as a result of the tremendous negative publicity around the Brill-Edwards case and the BGH story, Health Canada began a restructuring process of its department in 1998. Brill-Edwards is not convinced things will improve, however, and says it was just an excuse for more deregulation: "There is no question that what is going on at the HPB does not really protect citizens.... The government just wants to water down the legislation." Health Canada officials did away with the health minister's power to instigate criminal charges to keep food and drug manufacturers in line. "If it cannot enforce one act of Parliament," the former HPB scientist says, referring to the Food and Drugs Act, "it is sheer folly to rejig eleven acts and hope to give them teeth."[47]

It is interesting to note that the man who was in charge of restructuring at Health Canada in 1998 was none other than David Dodge, Paul Martin's former deputy minister and the man who helped Martin envisage the entire "redesigning of government." His crusade had not slowed on the way to the health department. Asked about the changes he planned, Dodge stated, "The regulatory approach is an old-fashioned way to deal with risk.... We have to operate in the face of uncertainty. The [current] process is now geared to not making decisions. Risk management," says Dodge, "is about maximizing benefits and minimizing risks."[48]

According to *Maclean*'s magazine, critics of the Health Protection Branch (HPB) said they could "pinpoint the root cause of the agency's problems: the deficit-conscious Chrétien government's decision to review the funding of all programs after its election in November 1993."[49] That assessment, of course, did not give credit where credit was due: the funding review was designed and executed by Paul Martin, Marcel Massé, and David Dodge. Federal spending on the HPB was cut from $63 million in 1993-94 to $22 million in 1998.[50]

The department's effort to deal with the shortage of funding not only made the problem worse, it created new ones. The solution was to have pharmaceutical companies pay to have their new drugs reviewed. In 1998, a full $40 million, or 70 per cent of the agency's drug review budget, came from corporate pockets. Some consider that very reliance a cause for concern. This effort at recovering costs from the companies themselves actually turned the pharmaceutical corporations into HPB "clients" who had high expectations that they would get what they paid for. "The drug companies have become all-powerful," says Tom Barr, a retired veterinary-drug reviewer. "The implication is always, 'We paid you money, so why isn't our drug on the market?'"[51]

While the corruption of the HPB mandate certainly began well before the Liberals took power in 1993, Brill-Edwards maintains that the Chrétien-Martin government made a major contribution: "The final, and current, phase of deregulation is the dismantling of the structures of the regulatory agency, the physical components of the agency, and the emasculation of the laws that govern the regulatory process. The Bureau of Drug Research, for example, has been dismantled, so there are no more public drug research labs. On the food side, half the labs were literally destroyed."[52]

Brill-Edwards resigned her government position in 1996 because she felt she could no longer do her job. "Corporate interests have simply taken over within the health protection services of the government," she says. "At first I believed, naïvely I guess, that it was simply a localized problem, a problem of personalities. But then I finally realized—after spending some months in Geneva—that this sort of thing was going on in many other countries. It wasn't a question of personalities or ineptness, it was systemic. The whole system was serving the interests of corporations, not citizens."[53]

When it comes to the health of Canadians, the Health Protection Branch is not the only branch of government that has been transformed by corporate interests. In 1997, a new health protection agency, the Canadian Food Inspection Agency (CFIA), was established. Its primary responsibility was to protect the health of Canadians, but in a move unprecedented in any such agency in Canada or the US, it was also given a mandate to work in partnership with business to promote trade and the agricultural industry. By enshrining these dual, and contradictory, mandates in the legislation that set up the CFIA, the government institutionalized a conflict of interest that poses potentially disastrous consequences for the health of Canadians.

In the very first major health crisis the agency faced, it abandoned its health safety mandate in favour of responding to the wishes of the company responsible for a massive outbreak of salmonella, one that caused serious illness in over eight hundred children across the country. In March 1998, cases of salmonella started showing up in Newfoundland and in Ontario. At first, all the agencies involved—Health Canada (which establishes standards), the CFIA (which, under the agriculture department, enforces the standards in the food industry), and the Ontario and Newfoundland health ministries—agreed that the first priority was to stop the spread of the disease by identifying the source. Within days they had done just that: it was a snack food called Lunchmate, made by Schneiders.

When the detective work shifted to finding out which of Schneider's suppliers was responsible for the salmonella poisoning, things got messy. The supplier was identified as an Ontario subsidiary of the transnational Parmalat, the largest dairy corporation in the world. According to a major investigative story on the outbreak by the *Toronto Star*'s Laura Eggertson, the CFIA's mandate prevented officials from naming names.

While Ontario officials had legislation that allowed them to do whatever was necessary to warn the public, CFIA employees did not. "Unlike Ontario officials, who operate under legislation that protects them from personal liability," wrote Eggertson, "federal bureaucrats at the Canadian Food Inspection Agency don't have that security under any of the thirteen laws they administer. Because of the inspection agency's secondary role in promoting trade, [CFIA inspector Doreen] Moore had to balance her actions with the possible effect on the food producer's profits."[54]

As a result of intervention by Parmalat's vice-president with CFIA Manager of Food Inspection Blake Ireland, the agency did not pursue its investigation. Dr. Chuck LeBer, the lead investigator for the Ontario health ministry, stated, "We have no inspection reports from the CFIA on anything. These are their plants. I believe that we were forced to inspect by total political abdication of CFIA responsibility."[55]

There are many other stories that reveal the federal government's willingness to bypass the health interests of Canadians for the interests of companies. In 1999, the CFIA failed to issue a public warning about a botulism outbreak in cattle slaughtered at a Maritime meat plant, "even though federal officials knew 2,300 kilograms of meat from some infected animals had likely made it to dinner tables..."[56] Then, in 2001, the Canadian government went ahead and approved a new line of genetically modified potatoes, even though its own scientists at the CFIA said the endorsement was based on "extremely poor" field tests they feared would undermine the credibility of Canada's regulatory regime. And, in 2003, the government approved testing of genetically modified wheat—a Monsanto product—despite almost total opposition from farmers who feared that the resulting cross-contamination would ruin their global market for non-genetically modified wheat.

In fact, there are so many stories about the Health Protection Branch abandoning its responsibilities to protect Canadians' health that in the first half of 2003, the CBC-TV program *Marketplace* featured a new case almost every month. When such severe cuts are made to federal departments, it is inevitable that they become unable to properly serve the public interest. Still, there have been no changes to policy or legislation that address concerns regarding public health protection.

## CANADA: THE UNRECOGNIZABLE COUNTRY

Brian Mulroney made a promise to Canadians *after* he was elected: "Give me twenty years and you will not recognize this country." Mulroney was given only nine years to do the job, but Paul Martin had nine years to finish it, and today we truly do not recognize our country. Mulroney's efforts made him one of the most unpopular prime ministers in Canadian history. He gained that status, in part, thanks to the social and economic upheaval caused by free trade (which cost Canadians 276,000 industrial jobs), the GST (which shifted $15 billion in taxes from corporations to citizens), and large cuts to medicare and other social programs. However, his reputation was also a result of the common perception that he simply didn't respect Canadian values.

Paul Martin isn't Brian Mulroney, and the contrast in their popular standing would be hard to match, but the impacts of Martin's policies were every bit as devastating as Mulroney's for millions of Canadians and their families. Perhaps Paul Martin has not been forced to account for these results because Canadians associate those destructive policies so strongly with Mulroney, that they cannot credit the notion that Paul Martin picked up where the Tory prime minister left off. Nonetheless, when the Liberals took power, it wasn't so much the changing of a political regime as it was a changing of a corporate CEO.

The transition was as smooth as silk. Martin accepted the logic of Mulroney's policies and followed them to their inevitable conclusion, either finishing off what Mulroney had started or taking new steps in the direction charted by his friend and business colleague. The results, as chronicled in this chapter, are indisputable. Despite all the promises in the Red Book and his record in the Opposition, Paul Martin oversaw the continued undermining of the Canadian public sector. Whether it is workers' rights, poverty, the environment, education, or health care that is in question, Martin's record is demonstrably worse than Brian Mulroney's.

Paul Martin will maintain, as he did to Maude Barlow, that he only did what he had to do. Martin will sometimes acknowledge that preparing the 1995 budget and implementing it was not a pleasant process. On October 9, 1996, he told the Commons Finance Committee, "Free trade and globalization have forced a painful process of adjustment on the whole country. Among those who are without jobs, there has been despair. And among those who have jobs, there has been fear."[57] But he justified the pain by promising a better country at the end of the process. Paul Martin, CEO, claims he changed the country for the better: "But today [the end of 1996], it is possible to say we are emerging from these shadows. What our three budgets have done is to begin the process of restoring policy sovereignty to Canada, giving us the room, the capacity to make new choices freed from the need to ever have to look back over our shoulder again. Cleaning up the nation's balance sheet need not paralyze the nation's government."[58]

Policy sovereignty. The capacity for new choices. Never looking back. These were the promised gains for the acknowledged pain. But did Paul Martin deliver?

# 5

# JUDGING PAUL MARTIN

As CEO of Power Corporation, it was Paul Martin's job to put out fires: fix problem companies by cutting out unnecessary parts of their operations. To paraphrase Al "Chainsaw" Dunlap, the famous corporate "doctor," Martin was making bad companies good and good companies better. The making of Martin's 1995 budget resembled the restructuring of his own company, Canada Steamship Lines; in both cases he got rid of what he considered non-essential operations and focused on what he believed each organization did best. The Canadian economy, as managed by the federal government, was in bad shape. So Martin set out to "redesign the role of the government in the economy to fit the size of our pocketbook and the priorities of our people." That role was to "provide a framework for the private sector to create jobs through responsible policies on inflation, on taxation, regulation, trade, and the labour market."

Laying the question of how Martin's plan affected people and communities aside, another question remains. Did Paul Martin succeed on his own terms? Was the company better after Paul Martin did everything he set out to do? Was it more efficient—that is, more productive? Did the private sector invest more productive capital in the economy, the major point of the exercise? Did the economy create more jobs as a result of his "labour flexibility," trade, and taxation policies? Martin's program of restructuring, which faithfully followed the neo-liberal handbook, was sold on the basis of "short-term pain for long-term gain." It is fair to ask Mr. Martin if the gain was worth the pain.

Beyond a cost-benefit analysis of Paul Martin's nine years as finance minister, it is also necessary to assess what he claimed he would do in this role and how he portrayed himself in it. Paul Martin wants to be prime minister, and Canadians have an enormous amount of evidence by which to judge his fitness for the job. More than possibly any other candidate in history, he has had a significant hand in shaping the country before even holding its highest office. He has addressed Canadians directly in nine budget speeches, setting out his goals and outlining the values they were meant to reflect. How did he actually deal with Canadians when presenting his many budgets? In his key statements as finance minister, was he forthright and candid about his intentions? Simply put, did what he say jibe with what he did?

## PAUL MARTIN'S CONFLICTING MESSAGES

When Paul Martin got up in the House of Commons on March 6, 1996, to deliver his third budget, the second phase of the cuts he had announced in 1995 were about to take effect. Calling for six more years of reduced spending *regardless of economic growth*, Martin told Parliament, "The attack on the deficit is irrevocable and irreversible."[1] If Canadians listened to other parts of the speech, however, they might have concluded that Paul Martin had recanted and was returning to the old Liberal agenda of nation-building. Of his budget measures, Martin said, "They reflect our desire to put in place the strongest economic framework possible for sustained growth and jobs. They act on our obligation to preserve our great social programs for the next century, programs such as medicare and our pension system."[2]

Martin's speech was full of optimistic language about meeting challenges, setting goals, and "going forward together." He ended the speech with this statement:

Let us act, not as special interests, but as stewards of the national interest, knowing that the destiny of our children is in our hands.

Let us follow in the footsteps of those who came before, who saw challenge as a rallying cry to move forward, never as an excuse to give up.

And let it be said by those who come after us that we set the goals, that we met them together, that we propelled Canada forward into a new millennium—still and always among the front ranks of nations.[3]

There was a glaring disconnect between the words that Martin was speaking—and what he was actually doing. The impact of his budget cuts on economic growth had been heavy. The real GDP growth rate had been rising steadily from the recession of the early 1990s, from 1 per cent in 1992 to 4.8 per cent in 1994, but Martin's '95 budget cuts caused that economic growth to stop as if it had hit a brick wall. Just the first phase of Martin's three-year plan saw the economy's growth rate drop to 2.5 per cent for 1995 and then to 1.6 per cent in 1996—a trend that suggested Canada was headed for a recession. Even the government's own figures suggested the staggering cost of the Martin's cuts. Human Resources Development Canada estimated the cost of this induced unemployment in Canada would amount to $77 billion in 1996—or nearly 13 per cent of the country's total GDP. None of these facts was presented as part of Martin's claim that he was "propelling Canada forward into a new millennium."

As for Martin's reminder that "the destiny of our children is in our hands," the government did not announce a single additional dollar in new programs to reduce the level of child poverty in Canada, even though the United Nations had declared 1996 the International Year for the Eradication of Poverty. Instead, 1996 was the year that Martin's decision to eliminate the Canada Assistance Plan (CAP) in favour of the Canada Health and Social Transfer (CHST) would come into effect, a policy initiative that would exacerbate poverty and inequality by downloading costs to the provinces and allowing them to restructure their welfare systems.

Though the fiscal impact of Martin's actions was included in his speech, it was disconnected from the optimistic language: "This budget, together with our last two, will contribute $26.1 billion in savings to secure our 2 per cent deficit target for 1997-98, and a further $28.9 billion of savings for the following year, 1998-99, to continue the downward deficit track, and to give the debt-to-GDP ratio the downward thrust it needs."[4]

Of course, Martin's budget speech can be dismissed as the usual sales job that any finance minister engages in. As an indicator of goals and values, however, Martin's speech does a good job of outlining his view of the economy and its role in the lives of the country's citizens. When asked about the economy's purpose, undoubtedly the majority of Canadians would answer that it is a means to an end: its growth should serve the society and the community by allowing individuals to be productive and enjoy the fruits of their labour.

The neo-liberal approach to the economy turns this understanding on its head by claiming that a nation's wealth is measured not by how many people are engaged in productive work, but by stock market value. Newspaper headlines in Canada revealed as much in the mid-1990s. A July 20, 1995, *Toronto Star* headline about US economic growth declared, "Good news puts stocks in a tailspin." "Growth a potential peril," worried the *Financial Post* on September 15, 1995, and a month later figured, "What we really need now is a serious jolt of despair." The *Globe and Mail* had a headline on July 6, 1996, that announced, "Good news on employment sinks Dow."[5]

Paul Martin's take on the economy did not stray far from this view. On November 15, 1996, he told CBC Radio's *Morningside* host Peter Gzowski, "There have never been a better set of economic indicators than now." Though Gzowski, unfortunately, didn't ask which indicators Martin was referring to, here are some of them for the time of the interview:

- Unemployment rate: 10 per cent
- Labour force participation rate: 65 per cent, down from 67.5 per cent in 1989
- Real per capita GDP, third quarter, 1996: down 0.2 per cent since 1989
- Real hourly wages: up $0.05 since 1989
- Poverty rate: 18 per cent, up from 14.3 per cent in 1989
- Child poverty rate: 21 per cent, up from 15.3 per cent in 1989

None of these statistics would have troubled Martin as far as the health of the economy was concerned, because all of them except the poverty numbers (poverty is not considered an economic indicator) were right in line with his goal of labour flexibility. It is very likely there were other indicators on Martin's mind as well: government spending was dramatically down, and falling, and inflation was below 2 per cent.

One man's ceiling is another man's floor. The indicators a government pays attention to are determined by its perception of the economy's purpose. Martin offered insight into the Liberal government's relationship to the economy when he said, "The government's reforms [to UI and social programs] are aimed at making sure we never repeat the experience of the late 1980s." What was that experience? According to Jim Stanford, author of *Paper Boom*, "Between 1985 and 1990 employment grew by 2.3 per cent a year, the labour force participation rate rose, real per capita GDP climbed 8 per cent, and the poverty rate fell by 2.3 percentage points." But inflation, the obsession of Martin's finance department, increased from 4 per cent to 4.8 per cent in the same period.[6]

While the mainstream media didn't inform most Canadians that Martin's cuts were on the verge of dragging Canada back into a recession, the inflation fighters at the Bank of Canada didn't need a news flash. Having kept a chokehold on the economy for eight years, the Bank suddenly lost some of its taste for permanent recession. It lowered interest rates and effectively countered some of the impact from the fiscal restraint of Martin's budget cuts. The response was nearly immediate: economic growth picked up again, unemployment declined, consumer demand increased, and government revenue began to climb. By budget time in 1997, Paul Martin's war on the deficit was virtually over. He told Parliament:

But now, Mr. Speaker, having done what we had to do, we can see that the worst is behind us, that brighter days lie ahead. The era of cuts is ending. The finances of the nation are finally being brought under control. We are at the point where we are now able to forge a new destiny for ourselves.... [Now we] build on a shared vision of the kind of country we want for our children.

Let us never come to believe that there is such a thing as a tolerable level of child poverty or that a growing gap between the rich and the poor is ever acceptable.

And let us speak loudly and clearly to those who believe that we cannot afford medicare anymore. Let us say that if there was ever a time in our history when we cannot afford not to have medicare, it is now-and let us go on to strengthen it, for all time.

It is time to say that this will not be a good country for any of us until it is a good country for all of us. It is time to make this nation a place of great hopes once again.[7]

Every politician tries to put the best face on the situation they are dealing with and on the policies they are implementing. As a result, Canadians will have to judge Paul Martin's expansive language for themselves. What did he mean by declaring he wanted "to forge a new destiny"? After all, the budget Martin had just introduced contained an additional two billion dollars in cuts on top of the ones already scheduled in his '95 budget.

One must remember that this was a budget speech, not an impromptu defence of his policies. These speeches were, according to the authors of *Double Vision*, written, rewritten, and practiced for weeks. Every word was carefully chosen. So when the finance minister's speech attacked "those who believe that we cannot afford medicare anymore," to whom was he referring? As finance minister, Paul Martin had cut more from that program than any other federal politician. He further declared, "...if there was ever a time in our history when we cannot afford not to have medicare, it is now—*and let us go on to strengthen it, for all time* [italics added]." What could Paul Martin have meant, considering the budget he was laying out—and every budget he would table until his last day as finance minister—denied additional long-term medicare funding? Even in the year 2000, when he estimated a five-year budget surplus amounting to $193 billion, there was no announcement of an additional commitment to medicare.

Martin may have believed that "this will not be a good country for any of us until it is a good country for all of us." In reality, increasing inequality meant that the country was progressively becoming a good place for fewer and fewer Canadians. As Martin spoke, millions of

Canadians were falling through the cracks, and the gap between rich and poor was opening more quickly than it had at any time since the 1930s.

As he had in his 1996 budget speech, Martin voiced concern for impoverished children, appealing that there was no such thing as "a tolerable level of child poverty." Yet, in each year since the Liberals had taken office, the level of child poverty had increased in spite of their pledge in 1989, backed by the other political parties, to eliminate child poverty by the year 2000. As Martin spoke these words, 5,222,000 Canadians were living in poverty, up 30 per cent from 1989. Poverty would continue to increase throughout the 1990s, even as the economy grew—an almost unprecedented development.

If Martin could claim some genuine, if moderate, progress on this front, it was his introduction of the Canada Child Tax Benefit (CCTB) in the 1997 budget. He boasted that it put $600 million in "new money" to fight child poverty. He did not remind Parliament, however, that with the introduction of the CHST a year earlier, he had cut far more than that from the government's welfare transfers to the provinces. Social policy analysts quickly pointed out that most of Martin's "new" money just went into the general revenue accounts of the provincial governments. Sixty per cent of the poor families who received the new money were on social assistance and would have the whole CCTB benefit clawed back by provincial governments.

## "FORGING A NEW DESTINY"

In his 1996 budget, Paul Martin promised Canadians that the government would lead the way in "forging a new destiny," a promise he restated in 1997. However, he managed to hide much of the government's real financial situation with what economist Jim Stanford calls "deliberately conservative assumptions, new program spending that isn't actually spent and other accounting gimmicks."[8] For example, in 1997 Martin beat his own deficit forecast by a stunning $17 billion. Normally a finance minister would determine spending for the coming year based on the projected revenue for the current year. By underestimating the revenue (in this case, a large surplus), Martin could claim there was no extra money to allocate. Then, at the end of the budget year, when the huge surplus was "discovered," he simply applied it to the debt and started over again. Through this manipulation of the numbers, Martin managed to ensure that virtually none of his first surpluses went to new spending.

In his first four budgets, Paul Martin overestimated federal deficits by a cumulative $37 billion, his errors growing in size with each passing year. By 1998, even the mainstream media were reporting on this sleight of hand, and Canadians were starting to get impatient. The government was forced to acknowledge the strong public sentiment for restoring social programs and came up with a formula that reflected its polling. Martin pledged to divide any surplus on a 50:50 basis, with 50 per cent going to program spending and 50 per cent going to a combination of tax cuts and debt reduction.

Despite his pledge, Martin was determined to avoid any new spending. By assuming slower growth than most economists estimated for 1998, forecasting lower revenues and higher debt service charges, and presuming high Unemployment Insurance (UI) payouts (despite falling unemployment and more restrictive UI rules), Martin effectively hid what other economists were estimating would be an $8 billion surplus for the year. In fact, the surplus was virtually eliminated for the purpose of formulating the budget. As a result, the highly touted 50:50 formula became moot. Virtually 100 per cent of the surplus at the end of 1998 would be applied to debt reduction. In a paper for the Canadian Centre for Policy Alternatives, Jim Stanford wrote, "In addition to his $3 billion annual contingency fund, Mr. Martin has another $2–4 billion in disguised surplus hiding in his fiscal 1998 projections. His revenue forecast is especially, and manipulatively, well-padded: Final tax revenue for 1998 will likely exceed the figure presented in the 1999 budget by at least $2 billion. And for fiscal 1999 there is even more padding: at least an extra $6-8 billion in disguised surplus monies. Mr. Martin is counting on virtually no increase at all in total tax revenues between 1998 and 1999. His debt service cost is forecast to *rise* even as the government pays off $10 billion in market debt per year and interest rates languish."[9]

The result for 1999? According to Stanford, "The federal government's actual debt repayment will [be close] to $10 billion in 1999.... New program spending ... will not exceed $4 billion, and tax cuts will equal some $2.5 billion. Instead of the 50:50 rule promised to Canadians in the last election, the 1999 budget suggests something like a 25:75 rule."[10] While Martin appeared to be listening to Canadians, it was, once again, the IMF which revealed finance department thinking. In late 1999, the agency's assessment of Canada's economic policies criticized the 50:50 formula. The IMF claimed, "Debt reduction and income tax reform should be the top priorities in allocating the prospective fiscal surpluses. While some additional moderate spending initiatives in the areas of education and health care would be useful, debt reduction and reform of income taxation are likely to produce more significant long-term benefits for the economy."[11]

Paying down large chunks of the debt out of current government revenue has long been considered a questionable practice by many economists, especially if the objective is economic growth—which Martin claimed it was. An examination of the much larger post-World War II debt demonstrates that very little was paid directly on Canada's huge debt; the country simply grew itself out of debt.

In short, a government committed to increased social spending and full employment eventually solves its debt problem "naturally" over time. This was exactly the time that Canada should have been spending to counterbalance continuing global financial instability. If the government didn't want to spend, paying down the debt was a perfect solution to avoid having to do so, and in his 1998 budget Martin had established a new mission that would help him to evade any new spending. On February 24, 1998, Martin told the House of Commons, "This budget will demonstrate that we have left the era of chronic deficits behind, that we are now on an irrevocable course to reduce the debt."[12]

## PAUL MARTIN'S SURPLUS CRISIS

Paul Martin was sticking to his plan, but executing it was getting more and more difficult. Martin had relished the deficit crisis, for it allowed him to do what he wanted to do. Now he had a surplus crisis, and it wasn't quite so useful. In 1999, he felt he had to compromise. In his budget speech on February 16, Martin announced an addition of $11.5 billion to the CHST over five years, starting with $2 billion and increasing to $2.5 billion by the third year. It was a small compromise, given the surplus he had to work with. Yet Martin refused to make the funding long-term: it was a five-year program only. He seemed determined to preserve his cuts, stating even as he announced the money for the CHST, "Program spending as a percentage of the economy will decline from 12.6 per cent this year to 12 per cent by 2000–01, its lowest level in 50 years."[13]

Tax cuts and debt reduction continued to dominate in 1999: "With the budget in balance, Canadians have a right—and we have a responsibility—to ensure that more money is left in their pockets. This is one key to raising the standard of living and increasing disposable incomes for all Canadian families."[14] Martin boasted not only of the $9.7 billion in debt payments the government had made in the previous year, but of a further payment of $10 billion scheduled for 1999–2000. He also mentioned the tax cuts in his previous budget, which totalled $7 billion over three years.

However, there was minimal popular support for tax cuts in 1999; it was a non-issue. Polls suggested unanimously that people wanted Martin to restore social programs. That would not happen. Later in the year, on November 2, 1999, he told the House of Commons Standing Committee on Finance, "We must not return to the old ways of the old days, when every priority was declared equal; when every problem was met with yet another program; when government often overreached, over-promised and underperformed. Those days should be behind us forever. We have come too far and accomplished too much to do otherwise. Government should act only where it can make a difference. *After all, we are not here to spend the surplus* [italics added]."[15]

Paul Martin proved again and again that he could make a bold statement without worrying about how much it contradicted other, equally bold statements. In spite of repeatedly breaking his 50:50 pledge, he did change his colourful budget prose in 1999: "There is so much we must continue to build. There is so much that lies ahead to accomplish. There are barriers we must bring down—of circumstance and of privilege-and new bridges to be built that we can all cross together. Our goal must be to forge a new alliance—a free market and a fair society supporting one another.... Some may say this is too ambitious. We say there is no ambition too great for this country.... The 21st century belongs to Canada."[16] Students of Canadian history will recall that Wilfred Laurier used the exact same words to refer to Canada's place in the 20th century.

The year 2000 was an election year, and by the time the Liberals had begun drafting their Red Book III, Paul Martin's pledge to bring down barriers "of circumstance and of privilege" and to "meet the challenge of an aging population and our obligations to the young" seemed a distant memory. In its place was an election promise of the biggest tax cuts in Canadian history: $100 billion to be spread over five years. The surplus crisis was to be dealt with in the same manner Martin had dealt with spending cuts—with a high-risk venture that would allow him to sidestep major new program spending for the rest of his tenure as finance minister.

According to economist Armine Yalnizyan, 77 per cent of the personal income tax cuts Martin introduced would go to those earning over $65,000; 19 per cent would go to those earning between $30,000 and $65,000; and just 4 per cent would go to those earning less than $30,000. About 8 per cent of Canadians earn $65,000 or more. Looking at the two extreme ends of the income scale, the top and bottom 5 per cent of income earners, the tax cuts would provide and extra $8 a year for those earning less than $10,000, while those earning over $150,000 would get a tax break of $2,441.[17] These tax breaks for the wealthy looked like reparation in the class war. In the 1960s and 1970s, workers had seized a bigger share of the economic pie; in his 2000 budget, Paul Martin gave it back to its rightful owners. Corporate tax cuts were almost as generous, with the banks getting a $500 million gift despite record profits and the corporate income-tax rate scheduled to drop to 21 per cent by 2004 (compared to the US rate of 34 per cent).

Though the huge surplus numbers forced Martin to finally commit to increased spending, his Spring 2000 budget and his November update leading into the election again ignored his promise of a 50:50 split. The five-year surplus total was an enormous $193 billion. Martin and his finance officials revealed that the breakdown would be $100.5 billion (52 per cent) for tax cuts; $49.9 billion (25.8 per cent) for spending; and a likely total of $42.9 billion (22.2 per cent) in debt reduction—a repeat of the 25:75 ratio from 1999.[18]

This time around it had been the provinces that forced Martin to restore funding to the CHST. Angered by the 1995 cuts and frustrated by their own limited taxing abilities, they put relentless pressure on Martin to loosen the purse strings. In an agreement signed with provincial ministers in September 2000, Martin allocated $23.4 billion for health ($18.9 billion through the CHST), early childhood development ($2.2 billion through the CHST), and new health technology and information ($2.3 billion). Significant spending was also applied to defence ($2.75 billion), and a gradual doubling of the parental-leave benefits provided through Employment Insurance ($3.5 billion) over five years.

Even when Paul Martin announced new spending, it often didn't happen. The Millenium Scholarship Fund, announced in 1998, generated an enormous amount of hype, but the criteria for qualifying for a loan meant little of the $3 billion, ten-year fund has been used. Fewer than 10 per cent of students who need a loan actually get access to the money. While it was the first major new federal spending plan instituted under Paul Martin's reign, there was still no restoration of long-term stable funding for medicare, and no retreat from the CHST lump-sum formula, which signalled that the principle of universality was not to be reinstated.

## SURPLUS REVENUE? DON'T COLLECT IT

Paul Martin's zeal for tax cuts and his enthusiasm for paying down the debt in current dollars were not the only indications that there was a burgeoning surplus crisis, as less and less effort seemed to be put into finding cases of tax avoidance and even tax fraud. In the fall of 2002, CBC reporter Anthony Germaine broke one of the biggest tax fraud stories in Canadian history. It involved the Goods and Services Tax (GST) and quite possibly cost the Canadian government, and Canadian citizens, tens of millions of dollars.

The fraud was absurdly simple to carry off. The criminals used existing companies or simply created phony new ones (often car dealerships), and then claimed that they had made major sales of goods abroad, usually to the US. As American companies or customers don't have to pay the GST, the Canadian company would then apply for a GST rebate and the Canada Customs and Revenue Agency (CCRA) would send out the rebate cheques.

In the early years of the new tax, the CCRA had actually set up a special forty-member team to investigate GST fraud. Despite its success in tracking down fifty people who had defrauded the government for about $30 million ($20 million was recovered), the team was suddenly disbanded in 1995. After months of investigation by the CBC and other media outlets, it still isn't clear who ordered the team's dissolution. However, the CCRA is a creature of the finance department, and key decisions about changes to its legislation and regulations have to be approved by finance officials. According to the CBC news Web site, "Internal memos suggest there was considerable opposition to the move [to disband], that some within Revenue Canada recognized a need for a centralized and specialized intelligence unit involved in enforcement and fraud detection."[19]

Did Paul Martin know about or have any role in making the 1995 decision to disband the investigative unit that was tracking down GST fraud? Did he know the CCRA was imploring his department to change their legislation so the fraud could be stopped? Those questions will likely never be answered. Yet Martin was in charge of a department that, despite repeated requests, chose not to act in order to prevent millions from being stolen from the public purse every year.

The revenue was there for the taking. Audits for GST non-compliance (as opposed to fraud) net a very high return on investment. In 1997–8 alone, auditing just 1 per cent of GST claims netted the government about $355 million. With nearly a 1,200 per cent rate of return, why is the frequency of audits not increased to 5 per cent or 10 per cent? In 1993 both the Auditor General and a Commons Committee were pressuring the Tory government to implement a more vigorous program to detect illegal tax shelters. In 1994, Martin bowed to this same pressure. The result was a 25 per cent increase in income tax reassessments in 1995–6 alone, two thirds against corporations.[20]

But finance since than seems to have faltered. In a March 2003 ruling with enormous consequences, the Supreme Court of Canada decided the federal government was so negligent in pursuing tax arrears within a reasonable period of time that the revenue department received a $1.26 billion setback, nullifying hundreds of decisions on taxes owed to the government.[21]

The finance department seems determined to ignore tax evasion and the revenue it could recover by stopping it. In March 2002, a *Financial Post* story noted, "Canadian securities regulators admitted yesterday that they were surprised by the number of offshore accounts used as a base for stock trading.... Thirteen thousand client accounts have been opened in offshore money havens."[22] While this activity will never be stopped completely, the finance department has the power to change regulations and demand that Canadian banks reveal which of their clients have such accounts. So far little has been done to stem this loss of tax revenue.[23] It is not surprising that the finance department under Paul Martin did virtually nothing to correct this situation. When CBC-TV's *Disclosure* investigated offshore tax haven practices, it could not find any indication that Martin took any initiative at the international level to challenge tax-avoidance practices in flags of convenience shipping.

## WORDS VERSUS DEEDS

It is clear that there was a large gap between what Martin said and what he did during his time in office. While Martin isn't the first politician to have behaved this way, Canadians still need to judge him based on this gap. However, we ultimately need to ask a simpler question about Paul Martin: Did he make the country better? Did his policies, his promise of long-term gain for short-term pain, deliver what he promised they would?

Paul Martin set out his prescription for making the "company" better in his 1995 budget, a prescription that would change the role of government. The government wanted, said Martin, "to provide a framework for the private sector to create jobs through responsible policies on inflation, on taxation, regulation, trade, and the labour market. It is to see an aggressive trade strategy as central to Canada's industrial strategy ... It is to do only what government can do best."[24]

Those were the policies—and the goals were stated just as clearly: Canada would pursue free trade as a singular industrial development policy, create the right conditions to attract new foreign investment, and increase economic productivity, all to facilitate private-sector job creation and a higher standard of living for Canadians. This was Paul Martin's promise. He had nine years to deliver. But did he?

Canada has always been a trading nation. For decades trade has provided jobs for millions of Canadians and their families, and revenue for the government. But with the signing of the free trade agreement (FTA) in 1989 (and NAFTA in 1994), Canadian governments declared it wasn't just any sort of trade that would displace the domestic economy as the government's most important objective, but so-called "free trade." Making free trade the country's top priority was a high-risk strategy, and there was no way of predicting its outcome.

Nonetheless, the Liberal-appointed MacDonald Commission recommended in 1983 that Canada take a "leap of faith" and negotiate a deal with the US. Paul Martin didn't sign the free trade agreement; as such, the deal is not part of his legacy. But free trade itself is. Martin declared himself a free trade advocate as far back as 1988, but criticized the particular deal Mulroney was promoting. Ironically, his criticism was that the deal undermined industrial development. When Martin and the Liberals came into power, they took an even greater leap of ideological faith than Mulroney had when they systematically downsized the departments of industry, regional development, agriculture, and natural resources, and then voluntarily did the same to other industrial development tools that were still allowed under free trade. This downsizing went far beyond what even Mulroney seemed to have planned.

Canada had to pay an enormous signing bonus to get the free trade agreements. When the federal governments signed the FTA and NAFTA, they agreed to do what literally no other country in the world ever had: they gave up forever (barring the abrogation of the agreements) the legislative and regulatory authority to protect and conserve the country's energy resources for its own needs. In effect, Canada abandoned the part of its national sovereignty that allows it to determine energy policy based on the current and future needs of Canadian consumers, both individual and industrial.

What did Canada say it wanted in exchange for giving up one of its greatest competitive advantages over the US? Canada's only stated goal for the free trade deals was unrestricted access to the US market. Yet we have been subject to continuous trade harassment on softwood lumber, wheat, marketing boards, and magazines. Moreover, while Canadian governments have transformed the country in order to accomplish increased trade with the US, in doing so they have missed out on the growth of trade with Asian countries, according to the Bank of Canada. Canada's share of the Japanese and European Union markets shrank in this period. While 85 per cent of Canadian exports now go to the US, up from 75 per cent before free trade, the Canadian Centre for Policy Alternatives' Bruce Campbell says, "Canada's share of US imports (18.5 per cent) is about where it was at the outset of free trade. Thus, Canada has become even more vulnerable to US trade sanctions, without having improved its share of the US market."[25]

Most Canadians assume the doubling of trade between Canada and the US in the 1990s was a result of the two free trade deals, including NAFTA, implemented by the Liberal government. However, according to a study by Industry Canada, "the impact of [free trade] after controlling for other variables on Canadian exports to the US was modest, [just] 9 per cent.... These results strongly suggest that the strong US economic expansion and the real exchange rate were mainly responsible for the large expansion of Canadian exports to the US in the 1990s."[26] In other words, our cheap dollar and the US economic boom in the 1990s accounted for 91 per cent of the increase.

In fact, almost 40 per cent of the total increase in Canadian exports to the US in the free trade era has been accounted for by just two industrial sectors: energy and automotive. Our energy exports to the US were already conducted on an essentially tariff-free basis prior to the FTA, and increased energy sales to the US was an American objective of the deal, not a Canadian one. Still, free trade proponents like Paul Martin and his fellow business Liberals will argue that we have still increased trade exponentially since 1989, and it now accounts for 40 per cent of the Canadian economy. Theirs is a compelling argument: in exchange for Martin restructuring the economy and redesigning the national government, Canada received unprecedented increases in trade. Unfortunately, that argument doesn't hold up.

In reality, nowhere near 40 per cent of Canada's GDP is accounted for by trade. According to Jim Stanford, "It's true that the total gross value of exports and imports exceeds 80 per cent of our GDP. But that doesn't mean that 80 per cent of our economic output is exported. These trade figures double-count and triple-count the value of many manufactured products which now flow back and forth across the Canada-US border in the course of their final processing. In reality ... over 80 per cent of our total economic output is produced in Canada, and consumed in Canada—by Canadians, for Canadians, never crossing a national boundary."[27]

Paul Martin did not refer to even one of these facts in his budget speeches to the House of Commons over the nine years he sat as finance minister. The failure of the free trade strategy to dramatically improve the Canadian economy, a path that led to a net loss of some 275,000 of the best Canadian industrial jobs by 1997, was best left unexplored by the man who declared free trade to be the key to Canada's future.

It is also interesting to note just how many companies benefit from Canada's policy of focusing almost exclusively on trade. While over forty-one thousand enterprises recorded merchandise exports in 2001, a relative handful of companies, many of them foreign-owned, accounted for most of the value. According to StatsCan, "In 2001, 4 per cent of all exporting establishments accounted for 82 per cent of the total value of merchandise exports. The fifty largest exporting enterprises accounted for almost one-half of all merchandise exports."[28]

## FOREIGN INVESTMENT OR FOREIGN TAKEOVER?

No theme was referred to more often by Finance Minister Paul Martin than the need to attract foreign investment. Typical were his October 9, 1996, comments to the House of Commons Finance Committee. He repeated four times that the goal of his budget cuts was to establish the conditions for more investment: "An improving debt-to-GDP ratio means an improving economy ... [and] more investment-greater economic growth. It means more jobs." What were the consequences of failing to cut spending? Claimed Martin, "Goods not purchased, investments not made, and jobs not created.... It was simply that a terrible price would be paid if we did nothing—a price measured in high interest rates, lost investment, lost income, lost jobs."[29]

Foreign direct investment (FDI) became such an obsession with Bay Street, the financial media, and the Liberal government that it often seemed to be the singular objective of all government activity—and the single measure of success. If fighting inflation and the deficit, cutting spending, and implementing tax cuts were really key to attracting capital investment for new productive capacity in Canada, then the 1990s should have been a record-busting decade for such investment, both domestic and foreign, as the business world had gotten exactly what it wanted from Martin on all these fronts.

Inflation was below 2 per cent for the last two-thirds of the decade; the deficit was virtually gone by 1997; the social supports for labour were weaker than at any time in the previous twenty-five years; and by the time Paul Martin left the finance department, there was a tax regime in place that had corporate income taxes 50 per cent lower than those in the US (23 per cent in Canada versus 34 per cent in the US, which also has two extra tax brackets for the very wealthy). Despite Martin's success in achieving these critical elements in his plan to attract foreign investment, Canada's investment record in the 1990s was the worst it had been in five decades.

There was a lack of new productive investment in spite of aggressive efforts to change the "business climate." The Fraser Institute gave Paul Martin high marks for his efforts, placing Canada in the top ten countries in terms of its openness, the government's protection of property rights, and its minimal "interference" in the economy. In a paper he prepared for the Canadian Autoworkers, economist Jim Stanford combined five risk factors to determine the overall business climate in Canada and revealed that in 1997, investment risk reached its lowest level in the thirty-seven-year period the study examined.[30]

Not only was investing in Canada low-risk, it was also low cost. Canada won the competitiveness sweepstakes with the US hands down. Since 1997, the international business consulting firm KPMG has done yearly in-depth comparisons of the cost of doing business in eight countries in North America, Europe, and Japan. In every year, including 2002, Canada has taken the number one spot—and by a wide margin over the US. According to KPMG, "Canada is the overall cost leader for 2002 with a ... 14.5 per cent cost advantage over the United States." Canada beat the US in virtually every industrial sector and in all major business cost categories: labour, employee benefits (largely due to medicare), investment, electricity, telecommunications costs, and taxes.[31]

Instead of attracting more foreign investment to Canada, the free trade deals seem to have done just the opposite. More Canadian capital has left Canada than has entered it seeking investment. Says Stanford, "Canada's foreign direct investment position shifted from an aggregate inward net stock equal to 6 per cent of our GDP in 1988, to an aggregate outward net stock also equal to 6 per cent of GDP in 2001. Between 1988, when the first free trade deal was negotiated and 2001, outflows of direct investment exceeded inflows by $100 billion.[32] Moreover, as important as the imbalance of investment capital is how that capital was used. Had Paul Martin pursued a growth policy throughout his tenure as finance minister, many of those Canadian investment dollars might have stayed in Canada and been used for new, productive investment in the domestic economy. What the country got instead was mostly US foreign investment—and hardly any of it was productive.

In 1998, the Investment Review Division of Industry Canada prepared a report that looked at FDI in Canada. In 1997, FDI reached $21.2 billion—the second-highest total on record. However, according to the study, fully 97.5 per cent of that total was devoted to acquisitions of Canadian companies. And 1997 was not an aberration. On average, between June 1985 and June 1997, 93.4 per cent of FDI went to acquisitions—that is, corporate buyouts of Canadian companies. That rate has actually accelerated since 1997 due to the federal government's decision that year to stop defending the Canadian dollar. The most recent figures show the average percentage of FDI going to takeovers between 1985 and the end of 2001 was even higher, at 96.5 per cent.[33]

In his book *The Vanishing Country: Is It Too Late to Save Canada?*, Mel Hurtig examines the impact of foreign ownership on Canada's economy. One impact is that more and more decisions are made in the US. As Canadian companies are acquired by US corporations, the head offices of those companies almost invariably move south of the border. Corporate functions once undertaken in Canada by Canadians are now performed by absentee managers. The result is that in addition to having little influence over decisions about Canadian operations, Canadian companies are being managed according to the harsher culture of American capitalism.

Those becoming increasingly alarmed about the disappearance of Canadian head offices include several public figures who were among the most prominent promoters of free trade in the great debate of 1988. Former Alberta Premier Peter Lougheed stated in late 1999, "People will fall from their chairs to hear me say this, but maybe right now we need to return to the Foreign Investment Review Agency. We need to be more interventionist, the passive approach isn't working. If the present trend continues, we are going to look at out country in three years and say, 'What have we got left?'" Ray Protti, president of the Canadian Bankers' Association, said, "An independent, self-confident nation requires a dynamic economy and dynamism requires not just subsidiaries but head offices."[34] While numerous business luminaries have raised the alarm about the loss of head offices, Paul Martin has yet to address the issue.

A further impact of foreign ownership, says Hurtig, has been the "hollowing out" of the Canadian economy. "Canada is now in 30th place in the UN list of high-development countries when it comes to high technology exports as a percentage of total goods exports," writes Hurtig. "In terms of patents awarded to residents on a comparative population basis, Canada now stands 20th on the list of the top 37 technology leaders and potential leaders.... In the UN list of high human-development countries Canada is 15th in terms of research and development expenditures as a percentage of GNP, and 20th in business spending on R&D as a total of R&D expenditures. When it comes to the number of scientists and engineers in R&D per one-hundred thousand people Canada is down in 14th place."[35]

So if the business climate was so conducive to investment—the best it had been in four decades—why didn't it happen? Using econometric modelling, Jim Stanford deconstructed the decline in investment starting with the advent of neo-liberal policies in 1980. By far the most important factor, which explained 43 per cent of the decline, was the slowdown in economic growth; higher real interest rates accounted for a further 33 per cent, and declining business profitability explained 11 per cent. According to Stanford's study, the statistics on the decline of private investment in the 1990s make it clear that not only did Martin's policies fail to increase investment, they were the dominant reason for the decrease. Once again, it is necessary to re-examine Martin's claims for a better economy in the light of concrete results.

## PRODUCTIVITY: GOING BACKWARDS

Another indicator of the role of investment in a modern industrialized economy is the capital:labour ratio, a figure that captures the extent to which the value of each employee's labour is magnified by the use of capital equipment. Ultimately, the notion of productivity is rooted in this economic measurement. Productivity, like foreign investment, was another recurring theme in Paul Martin's speeches. His 1995 speech to the Canadian-American Business Council in Washington characterized this emphasis on productivity: "In the 1970s, '80s and early '90s, we let productivity lag. And we saw government spending and debt surge. But today the country is responding with aggressive, concrete policies—policies to keep inflation low, and boost productivity."[36]

If we are to judge Paul Martin's economic policies by any measure, productivity would be one of the most relevant, as it is the main determinant of the standard of living. If the value of each worker's labour does not increase, then the total wealth per capita of the country cannot increase.

As the 1990s progressed, Canada's productivity gap with the US increased. According to Jim Stanford, "Real GDP per worker employed grew 50 per cent faster in the US than in Canada during the first decade of the FTA, in both the manufacturing sector and in the economy as a whole.... It is recognized that the relatively less developed structure of Canada's economy (with a greater reliance on resource industries, and disproportionately small high-value, new-technology industries) is an important factor in Canada's relatively poor productivity performance."[37] Throughout the 1990s, the US invested near record amounts in new machinery and management systems, causing a huge spurt in productivity and leaving the Canadian corporate sector in the dust. According to Andrew Duffy, writing in the *Ottawa Citizen*, "Canada's average worker produced $60,163 US worth of goods and services [in 2002], versus $75,573 US for the average American. That gap continued to grow even as Canada's rate of economic expansion outpaced that of the US over the past five years."[38]

"Astonishingly," says Stanford, "the capital:labour ratio has not increased at all during most of the 1990s; in fact, it has declined slightly."[39] In other words, our economy actually became less capital-intensive in the 1990s, the first time that has happened in the post-war period. Even when the Canadian economy began to grow again post-1997, the nature of the growth exposed Canada's dismal record on productivity in the second half of the 1990s. In 1998, the economy grew by 3 per cent, but job growth in 1998 was 2.5 per cent. The productivity growth implied by these numbers is about two-tenths of 1 per cent. Most European countries and Japan had near-zero population growth, so even 2 per cent growth meant improved living standards. Due to immigration, however, Canada's population grows 1.5 per cent each year, meaning that our slow economic growth represents virtually no improvement in living standards.

Also noteworthy is that the new jobs available to Canadians were not, for the most part, good jobs. Most were part-time with mostly marginal earnings in low-value occupations such as retail. The amount added to total earnings would have been much higher had those jobs been in high-tech or traditional industrial sectors. According to the Organization for Economic Cooperation and Development (OECD), in 1998 Canada had the second-highest number of low-paid jobs of all the twenty-nine industrialized countries, with fully 25 per cent of full-time jobs falling into this category.[40]

As Jim Stanford points out, it is ironic that the free trade agreements Canada signed, with their many restrictions on how governments can implement industrial policies, "have made it harder than ever for Canadian governments to take pro-active measures to develop ... high-value industries."[41] The relationship of free trade to productivity is revealed through an examination of where the increase, small as it was, came from. Productivity increased overall by 9 per cent between 1991 and 1998, but in the auto sector it increased a full 80 per cent over that period, effectively dragging the rest of the stagnant economy up with it. The auto industry accounted for $20.24 billion, or 60 per cent, of Canada's overall trade surplus in goods in 1999, suggesting that without that sector's contribution to growth, productivity may well have been in the negatives for the whole of the 1990s.

The auto industry provides a unique baseline by which to judge both the free trade agreement and Paul Martin's radical restructuring of Canada to create the perfect business climate. The automotive industry is the single most powerful driver of the economy because it was built on the foundation of a *managed* trade agreement, the Auto Pact, under which each country was guaranteed to benefit equitably from the North American production of automobiles. If free trade is superior to this kind of managed trade, where are the examples of similarly strong industries nurtured by liberalized regimes and measures to make labour more "flexible"?

The uncomfortable fact Paul Martin and the Liberal government do not want to recognize is that their efforts to create an integrated North American economy have had only one major effect: large transnational and US corporations no longer have to establish production facilities in Canada. The US has been getting the most benefit from productive investment and new investment in technology, and has taken a hugely disproportionate share of the high-tech industries, treating Canada as if it were the 51st state, to be supplied by US facilities. Jayson Myers, chief economist of the Canadian Manufacturers and Exporters, has stated the obvious: "Canada has always been faced with this problem of how do you keep investment here when American production facilities are so large?"[42]

Paul Martin's policies were intended to "boost productivity," primarily by keeping inflation low but also by reducing costs to corporations—through labour flexibility, tax cuts, the draining universities of their public interest research funding and handing it over to corporations—so they could invest in new technology. It was all a wasted effort, resulting in a decrease in productivity.

## DID PAUL MARTIN DELIVER?

In 2002, the year Paul Martin was forced out as finance minister, Canada created a staggering number of new jobs: the total of 560,000 was an all-time record. Though the quality of these jobs was low, the half million people who got them were no doubt happy for the work.[43] Furthermore, for two of the last three years, Canada led the G7 industrialized countries in economic growth. Yet, the reasons for that growth had nothing to do with the federal government's economic policies. With all its eggs in the free trade basket and all its economic policy initiatives aimed at creating a US-modelled "level playing field," Canada did not have any proactive economic policies other than a moderately expansionary monetary policy implemented by the Bank of Canada when it realized Martin's budget cuts were driving the country toward a recession. The easing of interest rates and the moderate amount of new spending in Martin's final two budgets relaxed the chokehold he had kept on the economy. The result was a release of pent-up consumer demand, especially for big-ticket items like houses and cars. The economy finally grew when Martin abandoned his war on inflation and the deficit. Even so, the country has never come close to matching the 5.5 per cent growth it had in 1994 before Martin started down his restructuring path.

Interestingly, a similar growth pattern to Canada's emerged in New Zealand, a country that also launched a free-market counter-revolution (though New Zealand's plan was even more radical than Canada's). At the height of New Zealand's restructuring, from 1985 to 1992, average economic growth in the OECD countries totalled 20 per cent, compared to New Zealand's negative 1 per cent. A burst of catch-up growth in the 5 to 6 per cent range from 1993 to 1995 petered out and steadily declined until it dipped into negative territory again in 1998, when New Zealand posted the fourth-worst growth in the OECD. Currently, Canada may be experiencing the same catch-up phenomenon. It is also worth noting that New Zealand foreshadowed Canada's experience in other ways: most foreign investment in this period went into buying up New Zealand's corporate assets; most new jobs created in the mid-1990s were low paying and part-time; and productivity growth fell to one-quarter of Australia's (Australia being New Zealand's historic competitor).[44]

Nonetheless, personal incomes are slowly beginning to rise, and in 2002 the average Canadian saw a 2.9 per cent increase in disposable income. As of 2003, Canada is the only G7 country with both a federal budget surplus and a surplus in the trade balance of its goods and services. Yet the structural weaknesses of the economy, exacerbated by Paul Martin's policies, suggest that such growth will not continue at this pace. Canada lacks the large pool of skilled labour needed to respond to new investment; in any case, Canadian companies—those that are left after the 1990s asset loss—still show no signs of major investment in the new machinery that would increase productivity. By June 2003, Canada experienced a quarter of negative growth and the new finance minister, John Manley, warned that the country's growth would be just over 2 per cent—not the forecasted 3.2 per cent.

It didn't have to be this way. A different set of policies implemented at the beginning of Martin's reign to reverse the Mulroney neo-liberal formula could have resulted in a stronger economy, not a weaker one. Throughout the decade that Paul Martin redesigned and ran the Canadian economy—or, rather, refused to run it—there were many voices critical of his approach, including mainstream economists. Left-wing criticism of Martin's budgets came from dozens of public-interest groups across the country, from environmentalists to anti-poverty organizations, but because the voices were isolated, they were regularly dismissed by a hostile media as "special interests."

Martin, however, was challenged every year at budget time with a comprehensive alternative budget. From 1995 to 2000, the Canadian Centre for Policy Alternatives, a labour-sponsored think-tank, partnered with Manitoba social justice coalition Choices to put together the Alternative Federal Budget (AFB). Its relatively modest goal was to show that Paul Martin's stated deficit goals could be accomplished without cutting social programs. Every year the AFB project took Martin's deficit targets and achieved them without a single spending cut.

With the government facing surpluses in 1999, the AFB proposed "an additional public investment in medicare of $2 billion in 1999, and $4 billion per year over five years. The budget also dedicates $2 billion for a public home care program and $500 million for the phasing in of a National Pharmacare plan." These were modest proposals by almost any standard given the growing surpluses that Martin had to work with. Under the AFB's growth-oriented budget, the unemployment rate would have fallen below 6 per cent by 2001, and the poverty rate would have fallen from 18 per cent to 12 per cent in four years. "This is accomplished at the same time as the budget is balanced and the overall federal tax-to-GDP ratio remains constant." The AFB called for increased core program spending by $12 billion in 1999, and a repeal of EI cuts, allowing for $6 billion in additional payments.[45]

All the AFB budgets were validated by Informetrica, one of the most respected independent economic forecasting firms in the country. They needn't have bothered. Paul Martin wasn't interested in whether or not the AFB budget worked for citizens while still bringing down the deficit. He wasn't looking for a plan. He already had one.

## JUDGING PAUL MARTIN

In his second budget, Paul Martin set out to radically change the role of the Canadian government in the country's economy. Gone were the days when the government identified particular sectors of the economy or regions of the country for special attention and nurturing, Martin told an audience in Jackson's Hole, Wyoming in 1995. All government departments previously engaged in this traditional industrial strategy were systematically gutted, their budgets cut by an average of 60 per cent and their roles similarly reduced. Martin was also a key player in restructuring those departments that did remain active, enlisting them in the government's singular economic and industrial strategy: trade promotion. From post-secondary education to health protection to the environment, traditional department mandates were subjected to a trade-policy filter intended to remake the entire government into a trade promotion agency.

The theory behind this radical restructuring was simple: if Canada made every effort to promote trade, then private capital and the market, on their own, would deliver the goods. At the time, very few observers seemed to realize just how radical this approach was. In fact, it was a high-risk gamble. Fifteen years of this experiment—nine guided by Paul Martin—is surely enough time in which to judge it, and based on the criteria established by Paul Martin himself, the gamble failed. After all that time, Canada is no further ahead in terms of new productive foreign investment, the number of companies with head offices in Canada, increased productivity, or Canadians' standard of living. In fact, it has fallen behind.

Despite Paul Martin's reputation for having rescued the economy, the evidence shows that the 1990s represented Canada's worst economic decade of the century excepting the 1930s. The 1990s were harrowing in terms of unemployment, increased poverty, the gap between rich and poor, the erosion of the middle class, the weakening of the country's physical infrastructure, and more. If Martin had been running a large corporation, he would currently be unemployed—like Al "Chainsaw" Dunlap, whose disastrous "restructurings" of former corporate icons like Sunbeam and Scott Paper have made him an outcast who can't get a job.

Martin shares yet other characteristics with the modern CEO. To start, his focus is extremely short-term. Like his contemporaries, who are preoccupied with short-term share value, CEO Martin has no discernible long-term plan for the country's economy. His obsession with reducing the "company's" costs has allowed him to severely damage some of its most important functions. All companies need healthy, educated workers motivated by something other than fear. Public services like universities, research and development, and medicare are instrumental in providing the company with productive workers. These formerly robust dimensions of the federal government's role contributed enormously to the strength of the Canadian economy and to the competitiveness of its indigenous corporations. However, Martin remained blinded by a rigid ideology that had nothing to do with the realities in the country he was effectively directing. Like Chainsaw Al, Martin seemed quite capable of ruining the company in the process of saving it.

In spite of these actual policies and their detrimental effects on Canadians, Paul Martin's budget speeches were full of shining declarations about building the country, eliminating child poverty, and ensuring the healthy future of medicare "for all time." These declarations can only be described as disingenuous. His repeated efforts to underestimate government surpluses and his broken promises to use 50 per cent of any surplus to restore social programs were manipulations of Canadian citizens. Together, Paul Martin's words and deeds reveal an attempt to mislead Canadians about his intentions and the state of Canada's finances.

Based on his record, then, does Paul Martin deserve the trust of Canadians?

# 6

# WHERE WILL PAUL MARTIN TAKE US?

It is impossible to predict with any certainty where Paul Martin will take the country if he is, as expected, elected prime minister sometime in 2004. Political conditions, public sentiment, and outside forces can converge incredibly quickly and make a mockery of conventional wisdom. Where will Paul Martin take Canada? We can't answer this question based on factors we can't foresee; we are left to answer based on what we already know—which is a great deal about Paul Martin and where he has already taken the country.

Earlier in the book I made the observation that Brian Mulroney and Paul Martin, in the eighteen years they consecutively directed Canada's national government, kept Mulroney's promise: Canada is truly unrecognizable. The changes that have taken place in the last two decades are as profound and transformative as any the country has ever experienced. On the surface we still have democracy: we still have the Parliament Buildings, we still have elections, and, ostensibly, we still get to choose which parties and leaders will govern us. However, despite these trappings of democratic choice, the parties and leaders who have governed us for the last twenty years have presented the country at large with no choices at all. Never in Canadian history has there been a more flawless exchange of the corporate baton than in 1993; the governing party changed, but the interests being served were identical. Not since the 1920s have governments so shamelessly administered on behalf of "investors," a euphemism for Canada's—and the world's—largest corporations.

Our government in Ottawa is charged with defending the interests of the nation. Yet, under the direction of Paul Martin, the word "nation" was rarely heard. Canada is now an economy. In that seemingly innocuous shift in language is a world of difference. As finance minister, Paul Martin was so disconnected from the people he was governing that it did not even occur to him to express regret when he effectively fired fifty thousand Canadians and cut billions from their services. In fact, the quintessential CEO *boasted* about it. How can this be? Canadian philosopher and activist Ursula Franklin says we have been "occupied":

> We are being occupied by the marketeers just as the French and Norwegians were occupied by the Germans. We have, as they did, puppet governments who run the country for the benefit of the occupiers. We have, as they did, collaborators. We, like the French and Norwegians of the time, have to protect our families and on many occasions have to work with the occupiers.... We are, as they were, threatened by deliberate willfulness, by people who have only contempt for those they occupy and who see their mission to turn over our territory to their masters.[1]

Will Paul Martin again lead a "government of occupation?" When he was finance minister, his policies were determined not by his personal values, but by historical context. It was a period of history in which extreme free-market ideas dominated the political discourse, and a pro-business Liberal Party was tightly integrated socially and economically into a corporate elite that in turn occupied the most powerful boardrooms in the nation. Since Martin left Chrétien's cabinet, the Liberal Party has not changed, the elite consensus has wobbled a bit but is still intact, and it is difficult to imagine Paul Martin changing course.

As citizens, Canadians have the right, and arguably the duty, to pick leaders specifically for their times. The next prime minister will assume the leadership of Canada at one of the most dangerous times in recent world history. US President George W. Bush has set the United States on an unpredictable course by rejecting multilateralism and embracing the notion of the New American Century. How will Paul Martin "run the company" in response to the major changes in the US conglomerate with whom we do so much business?

Canadians will judge Paul Martin partly by the success or failure of policies he has already implemented—that is, by what the country looks like after his lengthy time as finance minister. But, as citizens, we also intuitively judge politicians when we ponder where they are likely to take us. We assess their political judgement, their ethical makeup, and the substance of their vision. Paul Martin is no different. While we don't know with any certainty what Canada will face in the next decade, we do know that we will need exceptional national leadership to guide us.

## AN UNSEEMLY ACCUMULATION OF POWER

The obstacles Canada will inevitably face in the next few years will require a depth of leadership ability and political judgment that would challenge any political leader. Deciding if Paul Martin has what it takes to guide Canada, and projecting where he will lead the country, relates as much to his use of political power as it does to his vision for the country. The disconnect between Paul Martin's stated social values and his adherence to pro-business policies is not the only issue on which he seems inconsistent. Paul Martin is almost universally well-liked, and while he himself does not project an image of a politician wielding power ruthlessly, the same cannot be said of those long associated with him during his time as finance minister and during his leadership campaign. Paul Martin's leadership bid—which literally no one believes Martin can lose—has been characterized by a degree of excess not matched in recent history, if ever. The aggressive campaign raises the question of how Martin actually views the political process: is getting elected a task he feels he should undertake personally, or is it a task he can handle like a CEO through delegation—assign the job and forget about it?

The first aspect of Martin's campaign that needs careful examination is its funding. Paul Martin has raised so much money—$6 million by July 2003, not counting what has been collecting in his trust fund since 1998—that some have suggested by the time this process is finished,

Martin could have as much as $9 million in his war chest. By normal Canadian standards, this is enough financing to run and win at least four national leadership races. To put it another way, it is almost as much as each of the country's two dominant parties spent on the 1993 federal election.

Not only has Martin now set the bar for leadership races unbelievably high, but he steadfastly refuses to reveal who has donated to his trust fund until thirty days before the November 2003 leadership contest. While Americans are trying to reform their election financing out of this kind of pattern, Paul Martin is fashioning Canadian politics in its image.

The fundraising, which began in public in July 2002, has a simple and lucrative template: invite up to one hundred people willing to pay $1,000 each for a get-together at which they meet and greet the next prime minister. The economic class of the attendees is exclusive. Ms. Felicia Salomon, a long-time Liberal Party supporter, told the *Hill Times* that the evening she organized for eighty-five to ninety contributors "was a chance for 'ordinary people' to meet Mr. Martin." Her event was "a small, informal setting" designed for "the insurance industry and smaller or mid-sized corporations." According to Ottawa lobbyist James Deacey, five or six of these get-togethers bring in a total of $500,000 each month.[2]

The size of the Martin leadership campaign is unprecedented. Corporate executives are prominent among fundraising organizers and hosts. Izzy Sharp, chairman of the Four Seasons hotel chain, hosted one event in Ottawa; Barry Sherman, the CEO of Apotex, Canada's pre-eminent generic drug corporation, and his Chief Operating Officer Jack Kay, hosted another in Toronto the same week. There are twelve Martin fundraising committees across the country, each made up of ten to twenty-five members; additionally, Martin had between twenty and twenty-five paid staffers working in campaign offices in Ottawa, Toronto, Montreal, and Vancouver as early as December 2002, one full year before the leadership convention. While Martin was engaged in this intensive organizing, his main rivals hadn't even declared. Others, like Allan Rock, dropped out of the race, intimidated by the sheer size and scope of the Martin campaign.

The amount of money being raised was just a part of the Martin campaign's efforts to overwhelm its opponents. It seemed that it was not enough for him to win; he had to take every inch of ground, every rid-ing association, every section of the party in a no-holds-barred effort. Did Paul Martin provide his campaign team with some guidelines or limits? If he didn't direct the team to actively overwhelm his opponents, then he clearly didn't stop them, either, when what was happening became obvi-ous. Martin faced a barrage of criticism from MPs and party activists across the country for his tactics and 'take-no-prisoners approach.'

Throughout the first half of 2002, a controversy raged throughout the party about the availability of membership cards. Each province has its own rules, but in several key provinces, including Ontario and British Columbia, there are tight restrictions on how many blank mem-bership cards can be handed out at any one time to party organizers. In those provinces, only members of the party executive have access to an unlimited number of cards. Everyone else, including the supporters of other candidates, can only get five cards at a time. This rule came about as a result of changes implemented by provincial executives which were controlled by Martin loyalists.

After the rule change, the newspapers were full of stories accusing Martin's team of unethical conduct. "Organizers for Mr. Martin's rivals say his forces are using an unprecedented tactic: gaining overwhelming control over the party machinery—riding and provincial-wing execu-tives—and using it to set membership rules that favour the front-runner."[3] Even cabinet ministers were not immune to the tactics of Martin's team. Herb Dhaliwal, Minister of Fisheries and not a Martin supporter, discovered that the executive of his own riding association, run by members partial to Martin, had deliberately chosen a date for the delegate selection meeting when he was to be out of the country on government business. MPs, party activists, and even party members with no affiliation to any candidate have charged Martin and his team with damaging the party's image—and the party itself.

Yet, Martin's responses to the stream of criticism and the media accounts of dirty politics were strangely remote and almost aloof—as if the situation had nothing to do with him. Martin made no mention of having met with his organizers to set guidelines or limits for the cam-paign. Faced with the huge question of cutthroat campaign tactics, all Martin could think to say was, "The fact is that anybody who wants to sell a membership can sell a membership."[4] The question demanded a substantive answer from a political leader, but Paul Martin had nothing of substance to say. People were looking for Martin to show some sign of good judgment, some understanding about why people were upset—or at least an acknowledgement that there was a problem. They got nothing of the sort.

The result of the campaign juggernaut was revealed when Martin officially filed his nomination papers, which were signed by an incredible 259 of the party's 299 riding presidents (2 ridings had vacancies). The *Globe and Mail* reported, "The list included the presidents of every Hamilton constituency association except the one from Sheila Copps's riding and every Ottawa riding except John Manley's."[5] In addition, Martin had every provincial youth president on his list of nominators, as well as the president of the Liberal Women's Commission.

Two questions arise from Paul Martin's leadership campaign. The obvious one is tied to Martin's political judgment regarding what many commentators characterized as overkill in the pursuit of victory. The campaign looked more like a hostile corporate takeover than a genuine party contest—even for a party known for nasty campaigns. The longer-term question relates to the payback corporate donors will expect for their contributions. Why would a savvy and extremely popular politician like Paul Martin go so deep into political debt when he already has so much political capital? On both scores serious questions linger about a key aspect of Martin's political leadership: his personal and political judgment.

## SELLING PAUL MARTIN

The tendency for Paul Martin to conduct himself as a CEO permeates everything he has ever done and continues to do. This confusion between the narrow, bottom-line principles of business and the need for ethical substance in politics also revealed itself in how Martin carried out the budget process. Martin relied heavily on his long-time leadership team for both budget-making and budget-selling. This team was consolidated in an Ottawa lobbying firm called the Earnscliffe Group.

Founded by some of Brian Mulroney's closest associates, Earnscliffe was sold to a handful of Paul Martin's most trusted friends and loyal political supporters when the Tories lost the 1993 election. The core group included David Herle, who had worked for Martin at Canada Steamship Lines; Terrie O'Leary, Herle's common-law partner and one of Martin's closest political confidantes, and his former executive assistant; and Mike Robinson, a lobbyist, former financial officer for the Liberal Party, campaign chair for Martin in 1990, and the man who will lead Martin's transition team in 2004. Over the years, other Martin associates were added to the Earnscliffe roster, including Scott Reid, who worked as Martin's communications chief from the mid-1990s to 2001, and Elly Alboim, the former and very influential chief of the CBC's Ottawa bureau.

The common denominator for those in the Earnscliffe Group was their absolute loyalty to Paul Martin and their dedication to getting him elected as leader of the party. The charge that Earnscliffe was actually working for Martin, advancing his political career more than it was working for the finance department, dogged the company for the nine years it received contracts from finance. According to the *Globe and Mail*'s Hugh Winsor, "Mr. Herle and Mr. Alboim were clearly providing political advice to Mr. Martin, although their invoices were paid by the department bureaucrats. Mr. Herle is still providing political advice to Mr. Martin and his firm is contributing his services to the Martin leadership campaign."[6]

By contracting out substantive parts of the budget-making process to a private lobbying and consulting firm run by his future campaign team, Paul Martin raises serious questions about his understanding of the democratic process, and therefore about his political ethics. Did his budget include the priorities and wishes of actual citizens, or were his budget consultations just public relations exercises? Did the progressive language of his budgets reflect his values or were his declarations simply crafted as sound bites?

As this book documents, Martin's optimistic budget statements simply did not jibe with the policies he was implementing. How would Paul Martin explain the discrepancies between his declarations and his deeds? Is there any reason to believe this pattern of contradictory behaviour, which persisted throughout his nine years as finance minister, will not repeat itself when he is prime minister?

Paul Martin and his loyalists at Earnscliffe virtually revolutionized the way the finance department was run and the way budgets were packaged and sold to the public. The old days of sitting down with finance bureaucrats, cranking out the numbers to be delivered in the House of Commons, and then allowing Parliament, public interest groups, and the business community to judge the budget were no more. By means of mini-leaks, formal statements, and broad hints about things to come months before the budget was actually brought down, Martin created a new phenomenon in the world of government finance: the no-surprise budget.

The strategy worked wonders for Martin and the finance department. The mini-leaks and hints could be attacked—and were—but the attacks did not have the same force or moral authority afforded to an attack on the actual budget. After all, the budget wasn't real until it was delivered in the House. So all the hints and leaks had another effect: they drew fire before the real battle was engaged, forcing enemies to play their hands before the budget was actually announced, which allowed Martin and his spin doctors more time to fine-tune their public relations job of selling finance policies.

More important, by the time the budget was actually brought down in Parliament, everyone from Bay Street to labour unions to social organizations to ordinary Canadians had already absorbed its main features; the actual delivery was almost an anticlimax. And as far as the media was concerned, attacks on the actual budget speech were old news, having been made already, piecemeal, over several months. Consequently, most Canadians simply acquiesced to what they already knew was coming. Those opposing the budget were placed in the impossible position of protesting either too early or too late. The financial affairs of the country had never been stage-managed in such a way before, and it was that managing that put a coat of Teflon on Paul Martin.

The role of Earnscliffe in both constructing and selling Paul Martin's budgets was the seminal piece in Martin's ability to reinvent the federal government. The firm's model for massaging the public and the media was first tested on Martin's 1995 budget. The process is described in detail by the authors of *Double Vision: The Inside Story of the Liberals in Power*. The morning of budget day, February 27, 1995, Earnscliffe worked with two focus groups set up to watch the budget speech and react to it. Members of the groups had a dial called a "perception analyzer" that they continuously twirled as they watched to indicate the parts of the speech they found favourable or unfavourable.

After the results were analyzed, Martin refined his subsequent interviews and speeches according to what had worked and what hadn't. As the authors of *Double Vision* put it, "It was like insider trading on the information highway."[7] Practitioners boast that this kind of public opinion monitoring and shaping can get people to accept things that they normally wouldn't. Initially used in product promotion, Martin and his future leadership team integrated the corporate marketing model into politics and used it to convince Canadians that the finance department's policies were exactly what the country needed.

The key figures who sold Finance Minister Martin and his budgets to the public continue to be key figures, either working directly on Martin's leadership campaign or helping to plan his transition agenda. Collectively, they have earned the nickname "The Board," a term that fits well with Martin's corporate CEO persona.

If Paul Martin wins the Liberal leadership and the anticipated spring election as most predict he will, these Earnscliffe loyalists will likely end up in key advisory positions, ensuring that Paul Martin's Teflon coating will remain unscratched. Instead of a prime minister who leads openly and transparently, Martin's history with Earnscliffe suggests that we will see a leader carefully managed and guarded by his public relations crew, and a government that has all the features of a transnational corporation in substance, style, and ethics.

## PAUL MARTIN'S VISION: CREEPING CORPORATISM

Perhaps more than anything else, citizens want to know where their prime minister is going to lead them. They want to know about the candidate's vision for the country, and what role the government will take in guiding it. If Paul Martin continues to implement his past vision for the country, we have ample evidence that shows exactly where we are headed: we will have a government modelling itself on, and facilitating, corporations. Paul Martin's use of his Earnscliffe team in massaging public sentiment to garner support for his budgets was just part of the corporatization of the democratic process. His team had almost as much authority over what went in the budget as finance officials did.

Hiring Earnscliffe to do so much of the work for which the department itself was supposedly responsible was one of the most controversial aspects of Martin's tenure as finance minister. At the time, even other lobbying firms were critical of the obvious conflict of interest inherent in this situation, where a private company with intimate knowledge of budgets months before they came down was also lobbying the finance department for corporations with a direct interest in those budgets.

The influence and the privileged position of the Earnscliffe Group has attracted determined criticism from those who track threats to democratic principles, including the abuse of process by lobbyists. Most prominent among these monitors is Democracy Watch. "You cannot have democratic government when lobbyists are working for politicians or political parties," says Democracy Watch Coordinator Duff Conacher. "Lobbyists represent private interests and politicians are legally required to uphold the public interest and tying the two together creates a clear conflict that is destructive to the public interest." Making reference the Lobbyists' Code of Conduct, Conacher describes how the work Earnscliffe did for Paul Martin and the finance department is a clear conflict. "The ethics rules clearly draw a line that requires lobbyists to choose between being a lobbyist and working for a political party or politician," he says.

The watchdog group specifically identified Earnscliffe's Mike Robinson for breach of conflict rules, citing that he represented sixteen private clients lobbying the Department of Finance while he was working for Martin and that department. It also cites two other Earnscliffe employees, Richard Mahoney and Dennis Dawson, who worked for finance and Paul Martin while simultaneously representing a combined twelve private clients lobbying the finance department. Despite what seems an obvious appearance of conflict, Ethics Counsellor Howard Wilson ruled there was none: "I conclude that the mere fact that these two legitimate activities are being pursued by a lobbyist does not, in and of itself, breach the Lobbyists' Code of Conduct."[8]

On December 18, 2002, Democracy Watch launched a court action against the Ethics Counsellor, in part challenging his ruling on the Earnscliffe situation. "We believe the Ethics Counsellor is himself in a conflict of interest when reviewing conflict of interest situations involving lobbyists and politicians, or lobbyists with ties to the Liberal Party, and we expect the court will agree," read the group's press release.[9] Conacher expects that it will be two years before the case is decided.

Despite this strong evidence of a philosophy that the corporation's interests rule above all, Paul Martin's statements on the campaign trail and in media interviews are full of calls for change. He told *Time* magazine, "We don't need managing. We need building."[10] Yet, the restructured government that Martin designed and put in place does not lend itself to building. To begin a new building era in Canada based on the values of the country's citizens would mean undoing much of the work that Paul Martin put into creating a corporate state. As a result, his optimistic declaration about building brings to mind his budget speeches, whose hopeful language rarely matched the consequences they meted out.

Paul Martin, with the assistance of Marcel Massé, was a pioneer in fashioning the corporate state and remaking government in the interests of private capital. One example of a government department restructured to meet Martin's corporate objective is Industry Canada. This department once worked with local communities and encouraged the dispersion of new productive private investment across the country. Now one of Industry Canada's objectives is to promote the privatization of municipal services through public-private partnerships (P3s). The department gives private corporations advice on how to take over local public services and make a profit from them.

In a section of the department's Web site called "The Political Office Division," the government gives this advice: "This section looks at the need for a [P3] project champion to take the project from the idea stage to implementation. The most likely candidates are politicians which head a unit responsible for a project, such as the mayor of a municipality. A secondary, but extremely important, audience will be senior bureaucrats responsible for implementing a project.... A project champion who is determined to drive the process forward and to find solutions to obstacles is a pre-requisite for a successful partnership."[11]

By what democratic mandate does the federal government now openly interfere in municipal politics to sell off public facilities on behalf of international corporations (who do most of the bidding for these projects)? This Martin-inspired evolution of the corporate state shows up everywhere, from the dual mandate of the agency that looks after both our food safety and the promotion of products, to the grants for cultural institutions that favour "entertainment exports" over a strengthening of Canadian culture. The blurring of the lines between corporate and public interests is almost complete. It should come as no surprise, then, that ex-CEO Martin closely followed the advice of the Business Council on National Issues (BCNI, now Canadian Council of Corporate Executives [CCCE]), which provided the Chrétien-Martin government with ten objectives for transforming Canada. Whether it was targeting social programs to "those most in need," in effect "doing more with less"; radically changing Unemployment Insurance rules so the program did not "act as a disincentive to work"; making "non-inflationary growth" a tenet of economic policy; eliminating the deficit by 1998–9; or minimizing government to "create a more decentralized federation,"[12] the BCNI's list of demands is a virtual summary of what Paul Martin accomplished in his nine years as finance minister.

The BCNI/CCCE has been a key player in the corporatization of the federal government for nearly twenty years. The genius of the BCNI was explained by its former president, William Archibald. Rather than waiting for a national crisis to emerge, the BCNI would anticipate "emerging public policy areas and develop approaches and solutions ... that they can put forward early in the process so that they have a chance of being considered."[13] In effect, the BCNI established itself as a parallel government in the 1980s. The research that went into its presentations was of much higher quality than previous business lobbying. The BCNI structured itself through a series of task forces working on separate policy areas. At its most sophisticated, the council actually presented the Trudeau government not just with policy papers, but with the actual wording of the legislation needed to implement that policy. The logic of the BCNI's approach reached its peak in the Mulroney years, when its policy prescriptions and draft legislation began to be adopted virtually word for word.[14]

For Paul Martin to take Canada on a course of building rather than managing, he would need to fundamentally change the relationship with the current CCCE and its policy prescriptions, reversing the path the federal government has been traversing for two decades. "Building" implies using the state to help fashion the nation. In assessing Paul Martin's pledge to build Canada, his tenure as finance minister must be taken into account. Paul Martin and the Liberals advanced the corporate state far beyond where Brian Mulroney had left it. It is difficult to imagine Martin dismantling his own work in this arena—particularly when he has stated clearly that this is the work of which he is most proud.

## DEEP INTEGRATION: ANOTHER LEAP OF FAITH

Given the enormous importance of the FTA and NAFTA in shaping Canada's social and economic policies, it is critical to assess where Paul Martin is likely to take the country in terms of increased integration into the US economy. Paul Martin was not responsible for signing either of these agreements, but in the period leading up to the 1993 election, he played an instrumental role in re-establishing the Liberal's traditional pro–free trade position. According to the authors of *Double Vision*, "Roy MacLaren, Paul Martin and ... John Manley conspired to pull the party back toward the centre on free trade. [MacLaren] would later laud them in a speech as a small band of insurgents who view free trade as not just a practical necessity but a guiding ideal."[15] Even though he did not have the trade file in cabinet, Martin used his status as the most powerful cabinet member other than Jean Chrétien to make free trade the core of the government's industrial and foreign affairs policy.

The free trade imperative has redrawn the economic and governance map of Canada by creating an enormous pressure to assimilate our country—not just our economy—into the United States. As a result of NAFTA's thrust to create a "level playing field," we have diminished our social programs, our labour protection laws, our ability to promote new industries through subsidies, our authority to protect and preserve our natural resources, and even our prerogative to create new programs if we choose to do so. The federal government has passed only two significant pieces of environmental legislation since NAFTA was signed—both were overturned by NAFTA challenges. In June 2003, the Maritime premiers asked the federal trade department to assess whether or not an east-coast public auto insurance program would violate NAFTA.

Paul Martin has never denied being a free trader; even during the 1988 election he made it clear that he objected only to the particular deal being proposed by Brian Mulroney. While Martin has suggested that he is conflicted between his fiscal conservatism and his attraction to his father's social-liberal legacy, here there is no conflict: Paul Martin Sr., in the long tradition of the Liberal Party, was a vigorous advocate of free trade. In few other policy areas is it easier to predict where Paul Martin is likely to take the country. Moreover, when it comes to continentalism, the BCNI/CCCE, the organization Martin has always looked to for policy direction, has already offered up its plan. It's called deep integration, or DI.

The deep integration plan was launched in the spring of 2002 with an article for the C.D. Howe Institute written by economist Wendy Dobson, a former finance department official under Paul Martin. She presented her blueprint as a "Big Idea," but far from being something new, imaginative, or visionary, this Big Idea was designed, said Dobson, to get the attention of the Americans, who would otherwise continue to ignore us. She wrote, "Canada should anticipate change and initiate a Big Idea that *serves the major interests of its partner*, while channelling action in ways that best serve its own interests [italics added]." Dobson claimed a key component of the Big Idea should be the handing over of Canada's energy resources as a sort of initial sacrifice: "Instead of waiting to be told what's expected of us, Canadian governments and industry should prepare for this possibility in a proactive way." Other sacrifices would include joint continental defence, aligned immigration policies, border security, and—Dobson throws it in as almost an afterthought—our water. The plan to ensure American energy security, said Dobson, "could also provide a model for dealing with demand pressures on other ... natural resources such as water." Canada would also have to "modify" our cultural policies and give up the Wheat Board and orderly marketing.[16]

The deep integrationists—or, as the Canadian Centre for Policy Alternatives' Bruce Campbell refers to them, deep assimilationists—believe the US will eventually focus pressure on Canada in two areas: resources and security. They reason we should offer up what they want before that pressure reaches the breaking point, and we should do so in the context of trading for guaranteed access to the US market for our goods and services. The form of that access would be a customs union whereby all customs regulations and tariffs would be completely harmonized, and Canada would no longer be subject to the US's arbitrary trade remedy laws. Over the long term, the border would be dismantled entirely through a harmonized immigration and refugee policy. Further down the road, the assimilationists would press for adoption of the US dollar as Canada's currency.

Unlimited US access to all of Canada's energy resources—gas, oil, and electricity—is directly related to US security needs. Unregulated access to the first two of the three is already effectively in place through NAFTA, and enormous pressure is already being applied by the US on the last. After his aggressive criticism of Canada's "failure" to support the US-led war on Iraq in the spring of 2003, US Ambassador Paul Cellucci quickly dismissed the resulting hard feelings, using a "business is business" approach that focused on energy: "I know that [Canadian] resources are vast," said Cellucci in April. "And part of what the president's national energy policy is about is a complete integration of [the] North American energy market. We need to have reliable sources of energy, reliable transmission of energy in North America, so we're not dependent on Venezuela ... and the Middle East."[17] The message was unmistakable: give us your energy and all will be forgiven.

The second piece of the puzzle is US security needs. To meet those needs, the DI plan would have Canada further integrate border controls and offer up the effective integration of Canadian and US armed forces, combined with a massive increase in military spending. To reinforce this latter position, the DIs enlisted prominent University of Toronto historian Jack Granatstein to produce a paper on the role the Canadian military would assume in this new relationship. Granatstein's formula is simple: Canada should simply go along with whatever the Americans ask them to do, except that we should be offering this cooperation before we are asked for it. Canada's cooperation would include support for both the US missile defence system and plans for an integrated command for homeland security. Granatstein even acknowledges that Canada would have no real say in the decisions; effectively, we would place our armed forces under US command.[18]

For Granatstein, the whole notion of any difference between the US and Canada is just an irritation: "The superpower neighbour has global responsibilities and burdens, and it often tires of Canadian caution, endless remonstrances, and prickly independence when what it wants and needs is support."[19] Both Dobson and Granatstein write about Canada as if the country has no history, no distinct values, no traditions, no accomplishments, and no real sovereignty. James Laxer suggests this approach is very similar to what the US called "Finlandization" in the 1970s—the process by which Finland anticipated the Soviet Union's every need and developed policy accordingly.

Even though the DI initiative is the creation of some of the most powerful economic and political institutions and figures in Canada—the business think-tanks, free-enterprise foundations, and a formidable collection of CEOs, former politicians, journalists, and consultants—it is only an idea until it is acted upon. In Wendy Dobson's view, "A strategic package like this one needs champions, preferably in a framework agreement between the US president and the Canadian prime minister. But one leader is distracted by a potential war; the other by his domestic political troubles. Thus, the initiative must be spearheaded by the private sector—in the auto, energy and transportation industries—and among border states, provinces and cities. (The new Canadian Council of Chief Executives could be the catalyst.)"[20]

In fact, CCCE head Tom d'Aquino was already fully engaged in the initiative; indeed, it is almost certain that it came from the CCCE in the first place, as hinted at by d'Aquino himself. His speech to the CCCE's 2003 annual meeting revealed ideas and language virtually identical to Dobson's. Discussing "security and prosperity" in North America, he said, "Well before September 11, the council had committed itself to working with Canadians and Americans to update the Canada-United States partnership. You will remember that in our Canada Global Leadership Initiative in 2000 we said that 'the bilateral trade, investment, regulatory, security, and institutional relationship did not reflect the advanced level of integration between the two countries.' The events of September 11 provided a powerful catalyst. Homeland security and economic security quickly became cross-border rallying cries. At the council, we did not waste a moment."[21]

D'Aquino's vision is of a severely truncated Canadian nation as part of "North America." D'Aquino even suggests the adoption of a North American identity card and the eventual signing of a comprehensive North American Treaty. Perhaps his most radical contribution to the DI theme is his suggestion for a series of supranational bodies to make decisions in four critical areas: "reinventing the border; maximizing economic efficiencies; building on resource security; and sharing in continental and global security."[22] D'Aquino proposes autonomous decision-making authority, completely separate from Parliament or Congress, for all of these bilateral issues.

The process of signalling the advance of the DI initiative may have already started. One Liberal insider, who chooses to remain anonymous, sees Brian Mulroney in the position of fence-mender with the Bush administration, soothing the Americans' anger at Chrétien and asking them to hold their fire. Mulroney is a friend of Martin's; he shares Martin's views about Canada-US relations and free trade, and most important of all, he is close to both Bushes. He is allegedly playing the role of informal ambassador, placating Washington until a new Liberal leadership takes over.

What can we expect of Paul Martin with respect to the CCCE's deep integration initiative? Will he be the "champion" Dobson and d'Aquino need to take the next steps toward fuller implementation of DI? Responding to d'Aquino's speech, Martin stated, "There's going to be a border between our two countries, and there ought to be. We are different countries with different interests and different needs."[23] No candidate for the prime ministership would commit political suicide by suggesting the Canada-US border be erased. Yet, there is lots of room for maneuvering within the huge policy terrain of deep integration. On the day that Paul Martin formally announced his leadership campaign, he made it clear that one of his priorities was repairing relations with the US. Part of that repair job was delivering on one of the deep integrationists' most cherished goals: a North American defence perimeter. According to CTV's Craig Oliver, "I think that is something that we would see very quickly on in a Martin government if there is one—a dramatic change in our relationship with the United States, and it sounds to me as if he is ready to talk to the Americans about a perimeter border."[24] The most dramatic declaration of support for DI was Martin's sudden commitment to the Bush administration's Star Wars II missile defence system, made at the same time he promised to give the Canadian military a major funding boost.

The closest Martin has come to speaking the specific language of deep integration was at one in a series of invitation-only town-hall meetings he appeared at across the country. "I have heard it argued that

Americans are preoccupied with physical security while Canadians are preoccupied with economic security," he said. "I believe the distinction is false. There is no real choice to be made. Canada must be prepared to act in our national self-interest. To do that, we have to advance the mutual objective of a safe and secure North America."[25]

It is impossible to predict how hard Martin will push deep integration simply because it is such a complex proposition fraught with a variety of unknowns—the principal one being that the Americans have shown little interest in it. They are especially unlikely to talk about any bilateral political institutions that dilute American political sovereignty. Still, the DI initiative takes this reluctance into account and suggests that Canada give the US what it wants. In short, deep integrationists want Canada to take another "leap of faith."

Paul Martin will find it extremely difficult to turn his back on the initiative for a number of reasons. First and foremost, he is a dyed-in-the-wool free trader. Second, like Mulroney and Chrétien, and as a true CEO, he will simply never make a major policy decision without ensuring that the CCCE is onside. Finally, Martin himself is now personally beholden to his large corporate donors, and his party will be even more so after the next election. As a result, when it comes to DI, it is really a question of how far he goes and how quickly. A customs union is far into the future, as is dollarization, but perimeter defence, harmonized immigration, Star Wars II, huge increases in military spending, and a continental energy deal are virtual certainties and likely to take shape in Martin's first term. American access to Canadian water is also a distinct possibility.

This further assimilation into the United States will come at a time when the American economy is in the worst shape it has been in decades. The US has a staggering federal debt, and this year it will add a deficit of nearly $500 billion (the Canadian equivalent would be $75 billion); US balance of payments deficits are unsustainable; dozens of US states are literally in bankruptcy, selling state buildings to pay their employees; personal debt is at an all-time high as Americans borrow to maintain their standard of living; and the stock market is in the midst of yet another overvaluation. The US dollar is falling in the wake of these perils and as a result, oil-producing countries that hold hundreds of billions of these declining dollars are contemplating a switch to the Euro. The final outcome could be the US's catastrophic spiral downward. Paul

Martin's commitment to continentalism means we could be even more closely tied to this country on the verge of potential disaster.

## A NEW VISION?

In his interview with *Time* magazine, which chose him as Canadian Newsmaker of the Year in 2002, Paul Martin stated, "The challenge of politics today is probably closer to my dad's time than it was in the '70s or '80s. We don't need managing. We need building. That's why I think the next decade is going to be the most exciting decade in which you or I have lived."[26] That phrase, which Martin has repeated several times, builds high expectations for his leadership. However, he has never elaborated on a vision that matches such optimism. For Canadians who watched Martin dismantle the country's post-war social contract, this notion of building and an exciting future comes as a pleasant surprise. No one can say with any certainty that he won't make it happen. The problem is that Martin did not have to wait until he was Liberal leader to build such a future. What better time than the year 2000 to change course and begin the building process? That year, Martin had a five-year, $193 billion surplus to use as he saw fit, and Jean Chrétien, anxious to leave a legacy, clearly would have supported him—as he always had. Martin's stature in the financial community would have muted any criticism from that quarter. The markets would have given a brief shudder, then looked at Canada's excellent fiscal situation and moved on.

If Paul Martin didn't adopt a plan to build the country when he had the chance, it's easy to be skeptical when he says we now need building, not managing. Paul Martin often seems to use words in ways that raise far more questions than they answer. What would an "exciting" decade look like? An image of a poverty-free country springs to mind, as does one characterized by improved medicare, affordable and universal child care, an end to child poverty, education and career opportunities for young people, a protected environment, and a host of other communitarian goals. For the economy an exciting decade would include sustained increases in productivity; new productive investment that adds value to our natural resources; a turnaround in the huge number of low-paying jobs; low inflation; *and* low unemployment.

## THE CANADA THE LEADERSHIP CAMPAIGN PROMISES

After months of preparations and studious efforts at avoiding the media, Paul Martin finally launched his campaign in April 2003. The launch was most notable for its absence of policy statements, and it did not get much more substantive in the weeks following as the Martin campaign team hosted a series of tightly controlled town-hall meetings nation-wide. The team seemed to have chosen Martin's sound bites, and the one repeated the most was intended to subtly distance Martin from the government—the government that he had effectively run. "I am proud of what we have done as a government," he said. "But in recent times a kind of complacency, a certain drift, has set in. We've lost some of the great energy and enthusiasm that Canadians are looking for. In my view, new times require new approaches."[27]

Martin went on in the florid language that became such a trademark of his budget speeches: "This leadership race is about the future and the changes we need to make as a country. It is about embracing new ideas and charting a new course. I want to lead a new government with a renewed sense of purpose, a sharper focus and a clearer plan—a government unafraid to change and eager to turn the page and look to the future."[28] This statement would be difficult to satirize. It is completely devoid of content. A "renewed sense of purpose," given Martin's history, could mean anything from an even more determined effort to corporatize the national government to opening up medicare to private competition to abandoning the federal role in environmental protection altogether.

Throughout the months of May and June, Martin continued to avoid any substantive policy statements, preferring to participate in the "town-hall" meetings where his legendary listening skills were put to good use. According to journalist Adam Radwanski, "Mr. Martin has perfected the art of the non-response, leaving himself 'very open to' or 'very interested in' almost everything without actually committing to anything.... By my count, he was 'open to,' would 'like to see' or outright supportive of twelve of the fifteen ideas raised on Tuesday night. But for all the policies that allegedly intrigued him, Mr. Martin seems excited by few of them."[29]

Some policy ideas got repeated often enough that they seemed to stick. Martin said he was committed to shortening hospital waiting lists, but refused to say whether or not he would actually police provincial performance by measuring those waiting lists. He talked about dealing with western alienation, but despite that repeated pledge did not say what he thought might be its root cause (elimination of farm subsidies and the resulting crisis on the family farm, for instance). He said he was determined to give backbenchers in his government more power, something observers are skeptical about given the Martin's advisors' penchant for controlling every detail of his political agenda and how it is sold.

In the fall of 2002, those hoping for some positive signs from Martin on the social-policy front thought they might be rewarded on the occasion of a conference celebrating the tenth anniversary of the Caledon Institute, one of most respected social-policy think-tanks in Canada. Yet Martin, in spite of having many important social-policy advocates and thinkers in his audience, used the occasion to put forward an extremely modest set of goals. According to John Andersen of the Canadian Council on Social Development, "Martin stated three very specific areas he wanted to act on: people with disabilities, aboriginal issues, and community economic development. When pressed on other larger issues, Martin said, 'You know, I can only do so much even if I have a couple of terms, and I want to pick a small number of issues that I can really have an impact on.'"[30]

Martin could not elaborate on his thoughts about any of these issues, but when Andersen suggested Canada could follow the US lead with a National People with Disabilities Act, "Martin said he was interested but worried that it might overstep the provinces' authority." In short, it would conflict with his decentralization imperative. There was no commitment on any of the big items such as medicare, restoration of funding for universities, or the reinstatement of the Canada Assistance Plan. "He didn't actually say he would decrease social spending further," said Andersen. "But he implied that necessary increases in defence spending meant he could only do so much."[31] As for any initiatives in the huge fields of economic and industrial development, the only commitment was Martin's vague reference to community economic development.

Martin's policies continued to be put forward in dribs and drabs with no discernable pattern except for one: none of his statements suggested he was going to move the federal government back into its previous activist role. He talked about Senate reform and he talked about cities, but in the context of giving municipalities a share of gas-tax revenue rather than leading the way in infrastructure renewal. He told a meeting of mayors, "Canada's municipalities need billions of dollars just to keep their infrastructure working," but he made no commitment. He encouraged the premiers to keep to their promise of setting up a Health Council, but made no commitment to the medicare spending increases announced by Jean Chrétien. On his Web site he promised a home care program, but it is clear that the program would rely heavily on volunteer caregivers who would get tax breaks.[32] He promised to restore the $25 million John Manley cut from the Canadian Television Fund, but this small amount will just take Canadian television production back to the crisis situation it was in before the cut. And Martin continued to waffle on a commitment to the Kyoto Protocol.

Those concerned about international development issues might have hoped for some commitments from Martin. As finance minister, he got involved with international financial institutions and their relationship to the Third World. Martin's highest-profile initiative was his role in the formation of the G20. But, according to John Dillon, a long-time activist for reforms to the World Bank and the International Monetary Fund (IMF), Martin's principal task was to assist the US in solving the problem of creating a viable body that would lend legitimacy to the G7. At a G7 meeting in Prague, Martin explained how the G20 happened. "He told us it was the initiative of Larry Summers [Bill Clinton's treasury secretary], and that he and Summers devised the plan to set it up," says Dillon. "But if Summers had assumed the chair of the G20, it would have really looked like the US was manipulating the whole thing. So Martin took it instead, made it look like a credible multilateral body."[33]

On the debt cancellation front, Martin's initiative was similarly criticized. While he was "the first finance minister to back 100 per cent bilateral debt relief, the actual cost of doing that was very minimal because Canada was a very small creditor," says Dillon. "But it was very clever politically.... He pulled the rug out from under us with an inexpensive move, but one consistent with our demands."[34] Also noteworthy is that while Martin has expressed an interest in a Tobin tax on international financial speculation, he wouldn't risk backing it at the G7.[35]

Perhaps the best test of Martin's commitment to the Third World relates to foreign aid. As finance minister Martin slashed Canada's contribution to aid by twenty per cent, but in his campaign he has made no commitment to increasing that level, saying only that he will strategically "target" current aid to fewer countries. On debt reduction and the Tobin tax he has made no commitments.

We can genuinely hope that Paul Martin really meant what he told *Time* magazine, that we need building, not managing, and that the next decade will be an exciting one for Canada. It is simply too early to tell what Paul Martin will do if he becomes the next Liberal prime minister in 2004. Still, the sum of all these statements does not add up to a coherent vision of the country. Nothing he has said suggests any backing away from the key policies he introduced as finance minister: a pattern of paying down the debt rather than restoring social programs; a "labour flexibility" program that has made Canada a relatively low-wage country with the second-lowest wage levels in the OECD; and the provision of tax cuts for the wealthiest Canadians and large corporations. If Paul Martin is planning to change any of these, his core policies, he hasn't said as much.

We can hold out hope that Paul Martin will, after he wins the leadership contest, listen to what Canadians say they want and begin to restore the nation. Still, it is hard to fend off a powerful sense of déjà vu when listening to Paul Martin's social-liberal policy statements, for they sound a great deal like the promises in the Liberals' Red Book. Martin co-wrote that 1993 policy book, and within six months was down to business, telling his staff to "Screw the Red Book."[36] His also broke his other promise, to shift direction when he had burgeoning surpluses—the 50:50 pledge. Moreover, there is a note of hypocrisy in several of Martin's pledges, as they promise to fix things that Martin himself broke—but with no acknowledgement of the role he played in breaking them.

If Paul Martin really were contemplating a change in policy direction, it might show up in the people he is enlisting to help him with policy development. However, his decision to bring back his economic guru, Peter Nicholson, does not bode well for such a change. The former vice-president of the Bank of Nova Scotia is returning from two years at the Organization for Economic Cooperation and Development (OECD) to work with Paul Martin on his policies once again. The OECD is widely regarded as the one of the most conservative global organizations in terms of its promotion of free-market policies characterized by privatization, deregulation, program cuts, and free trade. It was the source of the infamous MAI, the (defeated) Multilateral Agreement on Investment, the most radical corporate rights treaty ever proposed. It seems unlikely that Nicholson, who was instrumental in convincing Martin to dump the Red Book promises and beat the deficit through spending cuts, has changed his views.

It seems highly probable that Paul Martin, de facto prime minister for nine years, is ready to pick up right where he left off.

# 7

# KEEPING OUR EYES ON THE PRIZE

**P**aul Martin is the serial seducer of Canadian politics, the man it is impossible not to like. When you meet him in an airport lounge or a hotel lobby, he gives every indication that he really believes he has something to learn from you. He has an intellectual curiosity that captivates the smartest and most wary political animals—and even some of his most vociferous critics. His charisma makes people feel good, about themselves and about him. Give Paul Martin an interesting, progressive idea about how to make Canada a better place to live, and through the sheer force of his undivided attention, you will walk away thinking he is actually going to consider implementing it.

## EXCEPT THAT HE VIRTUALLY NEVER DOES

And that is the problem for those hoping that Paul Martin will change his course and rebuild the country as prime minister. When he gets down to business, all of those charm-filled moments and engaging conversations just fade away. Martin's ability to engage is based partly in his abilities as a problem solver; his curiosity has led people to think he was looking for solutions. Paul Martin wasn't looking for solutions, however. He already had them, and they were absolutely consistent with the policy handbook of the Washington Consensus. In his entire nine-year tenure as finance minister, Paul Martin deviated barely a centimetre from this market imperative.

Paul Martin's market agenda didn't stop at the doors of the finance department. By virtue of the peculiar set of circumstances he found himself in, with Jean Chrétien backing him almost unconditionally, he was able to act as though he was the prime minister. Along with cabinet colleague Marcel Massé, the long-time professional bureaucrat who knew the machinery of government better than almost anyone, Paul Martin designed and implemented a revolutionary transformation of the Canadian state. His watershed 1995 budget led to the rewriting of the mandates of almost every government department. By his own assessment, it was not deficit reduction that he was most proud of: "The very redefinition of government itself ... is the main achievement of this budget.... This budget overhauls not only how government works, but what government does."[1]

This book has tried to demonstrate that things could have been done differently in Canada, that we didn't have to travel the road down which Paul Martin took us. But the question of whether Paul Martin could have done things differently is much more complex. Furthermore, it is perhaps the most important question we can ask in trying to predict what Paul Martin would do as prime minister. Finance Minister Martin was not acting in a historical vacuum; he was a Liberal Party finance minister at a time when market forces and corporate voices enjoyed a dominance unprecedented in this century. In an era of increasing corporatism, of the merger of corporate and government interests, Paul Martin could not have acted differently. Martin's personal values, whatever they might have been, could not withstand the imperatives of the context in which he found himself. He really did what he had to do—history and circumstance dictated it. And they will again.

In imagining Paul Martin as prime minister, Canadians will choose between two very different men: Paul Martin the citizen and Paul Martin the CEO. While the former Paul Martin has spoken of his social values, the latter Paul Martin implemented the largest cuts to social programs in Canada's history; he decentralized the country to such an extent that by the time he was finished, our federal government had a radically reduced role in actually shaping the economy or the nation; he took Brian Mulroney's agenda for the country and completed it, transforming the mandate of government into little more than a huge business development bureau; he combined "labour flexibility" policies with large tax cuts for the rich, making Canada more unequal than at any time since the Great Depression. He did all of this, and then boasted that his government had turned the country around.

Finance Minister Paul Martin wasn't a member of a policy-debating club; he was behaving like a CEO. In fact, Paul Martin's preoccupation was never about competing ideas or alternative policies; it was always about power. As this chapter will go on to explore, creating an equitable and dynamic nation is not a question of money—there is more than enough wealth in Canada, as Paul Martin's "surplus crisis" proved. It is not a question of changed values—if anything, the last twenty years have seen Canadians become more progressive, not less so. It is also not a question of requiring radical change—we can construct a better world with the democratic institutions we have and with economic policies that are tried and tested, just as many European countries have done.

## WHO DECIDES?

The development of the corporate state entails a revolutionary change; indeed, Canadian Council of Corporate Executives (CCCE) head Tom d'Aquino used that very term when I interviewed him in the early 1990s. The post-war social contract moderated our capitalist, or "market," economy through government intervention in that economy, with social programs, the redistribution of income, and extensive corporate regulation. Rising expectations drove the policy agenda. D'Aquino's revolution began when that social contract began to unravel in the early 1970s: profit levels hit new lows, and public expectations of their governments and employers hit historic highs. Conflict was both inevitable and unresolvable. The contract had expired.

One of the clearest expressions of that expired contract was a 1975 publication of the Trilateral Commission (TLC), a private global forum where men of influence could discuss the future of the world—and help determine it—away from the glare of parliaments and the media. Formed in 1973 by the most powerful CEOs, influential former government heads, and prominent academics from Japan, North America, and Europe, the TLC met each year and planned the future of the global economy and democracy. The commission's 1975 publication was titled *The Crisis of Democracy*. One of its co-authors, American Samuel Huntington, described the "crisis" as "an excess of democracy." It developed, said Huntington, out of rising expectations of "previously passive and unorganized groups ... to opportunities and privileges, [to] which they had not considered themselves entitled to before."[2] That notion of entitlement, of rights, to things like medicare, education, clean water, parks and libraries, labour standards, and human rights was to become the target of every corporate think-tank, business political party, and corporate media conglomerate. By the early 1980s, just as Paul Martin was purchasing Canada Steamship Lines, the corporate war on rising expectations was underway. Long before he became Liberal finance minister, Martin would become immersed in this new-consensus corporate culture.

The campaign to lower peoples' expectations was deliberate and carefully thought out. It followed the same pattern and even used much of the same language in Canada, Australia, Britain, and New Zealand. The first assault on our expectations was the classic "big lie" technique, the constant repetition of the notion that "There Is No Alternative": if we don't adopt free trade (and privatization and deregulation), we will be left behind. Next came what I have called the "debt terror" campaign, which Martin himself used very effectively in his goal of downsizing democracy. This was an especially manipulative crusade because it played on Canadians' better instincts by asking them to sacrifice for the good of the country by acquiescing to the slashing of social programs.

The assault on public-sector workers was continuous for over ten years. In hundreds of media stories, anyone working for the government or providing public services was referred to as a "bureaucrat": overpaid, underworked, inefficient, and basking in a secure luxury job. The campaign drove a wedge between citizens and those who provided them with the services they needed. When Paul Martin laid off fifty thousand public employees, there was little sympathy for them among most Canadians. Then, when services eroded (as they must when funding is cut), the corporate media used every hospital waiting-list story to amplify the problem and make governments appear wasteful, inept, and unresponsive.

As people began to have less faith in public services, the white knights of the market, the private service providers, rode in to save us. The marketplace—the paragon of efficiency, effectiveness, and cost-saving—was ready and willing to move in where public services had failed. Paul Martin contributed here, too, by capitalizing on the erosion of the public sector by using government to facilitate private capital. To lock in the cuts to public services, neo-liberal forces launched a relentless tax-cut campaign, their insurance against any future retreat from the neo-liberal agenda: if there is no revenue, there is no democracy.

## THE BIG DISCONNECT: VALUES VERSUS EXPECTATIONS

While the corporate campaign to lower expectations has been extremely successful, it has nonetheless failed to change people's core values. Canadians' resilience in maintaining the traditional values upon which the country was built and by which it flourished is a testament to the power of democratic ideas. Canadians hold onto their values because they give their lives meaning. They know what government should be doing if it is to work for them and not against them. They have not lost or changed their values; they have just lost faith that governments will do their jobs.

It seems that Canadians are starting to filter out the doom-and-gloom messages about what is, or rather, isn't, possible. They are now returning to their expectations and renewing their values. At no time in the past twenty years have Canadians been so conscious of what it is they believe, and the way they express these values gives the lie to the dismissal that their values are simply anti-American.

EKOS, the polling firm that does the most extensive values polling in Canada, put the following question to a large sample of Canadians: If you were prime minister for a day, and had to pick overall national goals for Canada to achieve by the year 2010, which of the following would you choose? Here is how Canadians responded:

- Best quality of life in the world: 66 per cent
- Best health care system in the world: 64 per cent
- Lowest incidence of child poverty in the world: 62 per cent
- Best-educated population in the world: 57 per cent
- Eliminate public debt: 50 per cent

- Lowest overall tax burden of major industrialized countries: 45 per cent
- Highest productivity level of major industrialized countries: 45 per cent
- Most innovative/high-tech country in the world: 35 per cent
- Highest standard of living of industrialized nations: 30 per cent[3]

In effect, the majority of Canadians turned Paul Martin's preferred policy agenda on its head.

According to EKOS's Frank Graves, "Our research has revealed a profound gap between the resonance of 'standard of living' and that of 'quality of life': In what we have labelled the 'Bay Street variant,' productivity is primarily linked to improving the material standard of living and involves ... tax cuts and minimal government. Formulated in these narrow, economistic terms, the issue finds little resonance with Canadians. In the people's variant of this agenda, or what we call the 'Main Street variant,' the issue is constructed around productivity for quality of life. This objective brings into play: [an] emphasis on human capital (e.g., health, education, skills, kids)." Indeed, says Graves, the survey results showed an "increased receptivity to the need for government to play a role in addressing problems in our collective life. We are also seeing a fairly strong rejection of trickle-down economics."[4]

In 2002, well known Canadian researcher Judith Maxwell led the Canadian Policy Research Network in an exploration of Canadian values. The initiative went beyond focus groups and polling; it conducted day-long dialogues on major issues around the discussion theme, "The Kind of Canada We Want." The research team compared the results to an identical 1995 dialogue. In 1995, investment in children was a core value, but by 2002 the investment theme "had strengthened and broadened to include the right of every child, youth, and adult to receive support to become a fully contributing citizen." Whereas in 1995 citizens emphasized "self-reliance and compassion leading to collective responsibility," the 2002 dialogues revealed a desire for "mutual responsibility for all actors in society." In 1995 there was much talk of waste and abuse, but today the focus is on a critique of "weak social program design, especially the program barriers to participation ... [and] a broader shift in perspective from recipient and critic, to more engaged citizen."[5]

Perhaps the most encouraging result of the dialogues was on the topic of democracy: "On democracy, the 1995 citizens were saying 'everyone should have a chance to participate in this kind of dialogue.' By 2002, they were stating their right and their responsibility to engage more actively in the policy process. Many recommended that governments get advice from program recipients." A surprise for the organizers was the high degree of awareness of the negative role played by the media. When asked about "why the media reflects such different perspectives from their own[,] [c]itizens questioned the extent to which citizens' views are truly reflected in the media ... [suggesting] that the media is manipulative and provides misinformation."[6]

None of these strong views seems to conflict with the values of Paul Martin the citizen. Unfortunately, it isn't Paul Martin the citizen who will be prime minister; it's Paul Martin the CEO. The values reflected in the CEO's policies mesh perfectly, not with the values of ordinary citizens, but with the values of Canada's economic and political elite, the shareholders of the new corporatized Canada. EKOS has been doing periodic polling for the federal government called "Rethinking Government" since the mid-1990s, and the pollsters conclude, "A chasm exists between those charged with governing (the decision-makers) and those being governed." Given twenty-two value choices for the role of government, the two groups' attitudes were diametrically opposed to each other. "Competitiveness" and "minimal government" ranked 1st and 3rd for the elites, and 20th and 22nd for the general public. The EKOS poll revealed, "Virtually all of the government roles related to equality, social justice, collective rights, full employment and regulation of business were low on the elite's preference list and high on the general public's."[7] Economist Robert Reich, President Bill Clinton's first labour secretary, referred to this development as the "secession of the successful," or the disengagement of the elite from the broader society and its interests. This disengagement is symbolized by the elite's feeling that it is now morally acceptable to avoid paying taxes. A book of advice on tax avoidance, called *Take Your Money and Run*, sold eighty thousand copies in Canada. What better symbol of the elite's disconnect with their own country than Paul Martin? The man who was in charge of raising money for the betterment of the country has been owner of a company known for chronic tax avoidance.

## POLITICS: THE ART OF THE POSSIBLE

Canadians have been persuaded by a fifteen-year propaganda assault that their expectations of democratic government—including vibrant communities, robust social programs, an end to child poverty, full employment, and participatory democracy—are unrealistic. Yet there are many developed countries that have followed alternative policies reflecting these same values held by Canadians, and their economies are growing quickly, with higher productivity, lower unemployment, and higher profits. According to neo-liberal dogma, Denmark, which has a highly export-oriented economy like Canada's, should be a failure. As an article in *The Economy* points out, "It has one of the highest tax 'burdens' in the OECD, and a very large public sector that employs more than one-third of all the country's workers. Income transfers are funded by high personal taxes, and Denmark has one of the most generous unemployment insurance programs in the world."[8] Yet Denmark's annual economic growth averaged a strong 3.1 per cent throughout the late 1990s.

In the Netherlands, the 1996 unemployment rate was 2.7 per cent. At the same time, Canada's real rate was over 10 per cent. Rather than create the "flexible" workforce and drive down living standards like Canada, the Netherlands did the opposite. Through the gradual implementation of a "work-time reduction" policy, half of the sectors in the economy, and about half of the workforce, had moved to a thirty-six-hour week by 1996. The Netherlands boasts the lowest annual average work hours per employed worker of any industrialized country—1,370 hours per year versus 1,996 in the US and 1,732 in Canada.[9]

Sweden has the highest standard of living in the world. It has a law that guarantees child care for all families and twelve months of parental leave for each child born. Parents are allowed up to sixty days of leave per year to care for sick family members, and by law they are allowed to work at three-quarter time until a child is eight years old. Sweden also has one of the highest tax rates in the industrialized world. Yet no one is claiming that Sweden is having trouble attracting productive investment or is experiencing a brain drain to countries with lower taxes. The key difference between Canada and many countries in Europe is political and cultural: quite simply, their economic and political elite have not seceded from the nation. In these other countries, the elite are prepared to pay higher taxes because they get something of value in return: an equitable society as the foundation for their nations and communities.

Canada is not Sweden, and it is naive in the current context to suggest that Canada will be able to easily or quickly replicate the richness of the commons in European countries. We are economically integrated into the United States and this situation places practical and cultural limits on what kind of society we can develop here, at least in the foreseeable future. Yet it is just as true that Canada need not adopt the policy of pre-emptive surrender implied by deep integration, a policy prescription Paul Martin has already begun to endorse. We don't have to give Canada up without a fight.

What would that fight to save the country look like? Economist Ricardo Grinspun says, "First of all, we have to maintain our policy space, and gradually expand it so that we can maintain and enhance a distinct kind of society in Canada, different from the US, based on a different social model."[10] The past twenty years have seen consecutive governments savage the domestic economy, which nearly 80 per cent of Canadians rely on, with the false hope that ever-increasing trade with the US will bring us prosperity. There is nothing stopping us from beginning to reverse that process. According to Grinspun, "The issue of strengthening the domestic economy is connected to the question of industrial policy. If we look at something like the Kyoto agreement, and the move to a more sustainable economy, that creates huge opportunities … for various types of knowledge-intensive investment and economic activity."[11]

Throughout the nine years that Paul Martin was finance minister, the Canadian Centre for Policy Alternatives (CCPA) and the Choices coalition put forward Alternative Federal Budgets (AFB) to demonstrate that Martin's policies of high interest rates and huge spending cuts were not only harming the country, but were completely unnecessary. Bruce Campbell, executive director of CCPA, suggested in a 2003 study titled "From Deep Integration to Reclaiming Sovereignty" that we "reassert and rebuild the capacity of government as an active manager of the economy, rather than as a bystander to the excesses and failures of the market. Strengthen the national economy and the national demand through a variety of macroeconomic, labour market, and industrial policy tools."[12] In other words, we need to revisit and embrace the policy tools that Paul Martin, and Brian Mulroney before him, discarded.

A government committed to reclaiming sovereignty would strategically target certain key policy areas. Instead of eroding the federal presence in medicare, as Paul Martin did, strengthening it would make medicare less vulnerable to NAFTA and privatization. In another important area, the federal government would pursue a vigorous environmental protection agenda. There is also nothing stopping Canada from implementing policies that add value to the natural-resource products we produce, nor from taking measures to further limit foreign ownership of those sectors of the economy critical to nation-building and independent economic policy: broadcasting, banking, and basic telecommunications. Though such policies have been abandoned by Paul Martin, it doesn't mean it is too late to use them again.

Canada has some extremely important cards to play in its "partnership" with the US. The very thing that threatens Canada most, continental integration, also gives us enormous leverage in the struggle; specifically, the US needs our energy. The only reason we haven't played this card already is because corporate powers that determine Canada's trade and foreign policy don't want it played. The energy sector is politically powerful in the CCCE and in Ottawa, and is also dominated by US corporations, which are an acknowledged instrument of American foreign policy (just as they are in every other country with oil and gas resources).

Marjorie Cohen, a Simon Fraser University economist and authority on energy and energy deregulation, says Canada is far from powerless on this issue. Energy provides Canada with powerful influence in trade fights with the US. There is no reason why Canada could not take dramatic retaliatory action every time the US uses its trade remedy laws against us. Canada could use the rules of NAFTA, which allow us to declare emergency measures in order to cut back on oil and/or gas exports, or we could simply decide that there will be no increases in gas exports—and no deal at all on electricity—until the US permanently settles all outstanding issues.

After Jean Chrétien refused to go to war against Iraq, CCCE chief Tom d'Aquino took one hundred corporate leaders to Washington and made abject apologies amidst (their own) dire warnings of US retaliation. But the notion that the US holds all the cards in the trading game is just not true. Closing the border would, for example, immediately incapacitate the fully integrated auto industry—not something President George W. Bush is about to do. *Globe and Mail* columnist Michael den Tandt commented, "For both economic and strategic reasons, the United States needs Canada in its corner…. Canada supplies 94 per cent of US natural gas imports, nearly 100 per cent of its electricity imports, 35 per cent of the uranium for its nuclear power generation, and 17 per cent of its crude oil imports."[13] Even the *Globe*'s Jeffrey Simpson, not known for his economic nationalism, was contemptuous of the business lobby's fear-mongering, calling the warnings about "terrible economic consequences … tripe that passed for analysis."[14]

## PAYING FOR THE CANADA WE WANT

Canadians know what they want. They want a return to an activist government, a restoration of the social programs that activist government can provide, and they want their money spent wisely and accountably. But can we afford it? There is simply no debate about our capacity to create the kind of country we want. Canada's GDP per capita has been steadily increasing for thirty years. In 1970, Canada's GDP per capita was $16,481. By 1999, it was $28,869, an increase of 75 per cent.[15] (Both figures are in constant 1992 dollars.) If we don't have free university tuition, universal child care, pharmacare, and vibrant cities, it is because the money that would pay for those things has been given away, bit by bit, to a small minority of Canadians over the past twenty years. The last instalment was Paul Martin's $100 billion tax cut—a staggering amount of money that could have changed the face of the country for the better. It isn't a question of having enough money; it is a question of who decides how we divide it up between Bay Street and Main Street.

Ed Finn, a researcher with the Canadian Centre for Policy Alternatives, looked at the question of government revenue in a 2002 study titled, "Where's the Money Coming From?" Here are some of the facts Finn discovered: The federal revenue voluntarily forgone through the many tax cuts made by Tory and Liberal governments since 1984 totals about $250 billion. Sixty-four per cent of those cuts went to the wealthiest 20 per cent of income earners. The capital gains tax exemption alone is providing an extra $12 billion to the most affluent Canadians. Yet there was no sound economic reason for cutting taxes in Canada. According to the

OECD, our effective average personal tax rate of 18 per cent is now lower than those of all other G8 nations except Japan. We now tax our wealthy and our corporations at rates far below those in the US. We have given up billions for nothing—the tax cuts have had literally no impact on investment. We need to increase those rates. For those who worry about a brain drain becoming a revenue drain, they should rest assured: every year Canada actually attracts three times as many university-trained people as it loses. Surveys show that of those who do go to the US, a small minority cite taxes as the reason for their move.[16]

Had Paul Martin been committed to finding revenue to fund the programs Canadians want, he would have listened to the Canada Customs and Revenue Agency (CCRA). The CCRA's research shows that four of the five largest and most profitable corporations in this country paid, on average, less than $25,000 annually in income tax from 1995 to 1998. The number of our largest corporations with revenues of more than $250 million that pay *no tax at all* in any given year ranges from 29 per cent to 41 per cent each year. In the 1998–9 tax year, the total corporate income tax actually collected was $21.6 billion. The revenue sacrificed due to corporate tax loopholes? About $22 billion.[17]

According to the Conference Board of Canada, a prestigious and conservative economic forecasting agency, "federal government surpluses are projected to rise steadily over the next two decades, reaching $85.5 billion in 2020.... Under current revenue and spending structures, the federal government is forecast to achieve multi-billion-dollar surpluses large enough to virtually eliminate its interest-bearing debt by 2019/20."[18] In other words, even without reinstating a fair income tax system for corporations and the wealthy, over the next two decades, Canada will have more than enough revenue to rebuild the country. This would be true even if the Board's numbers were off by half.

## KEEPING AN EYE ON THE PRIZE

Canadians, in the millions, are admirers of Paul Martin the citizen, that engaging individual who seems to share their values and shows interest in their ideas. What they will almost certainly get, however, is Paul Martin the CEO, the politician committed to a corporate policy agenda. They will vote for Dr. Jekyll, but they will get Mr. Hyde. They will get

Paul Martin, merchant-fleet magnate, who chose international shipping because flags of convenience were tax-free and offered cheap labour. They will get Paul Martin, CDC board member, whose response to his board's connection to the tainted-blood tragedy was that he "had no recollection." They will get Paul Martin, finance department CEO, who helped dismantle three generations' worth of nation-building in defiance of Canadians' wishes and unnecessary given alternative economic policy options. They will get the Paul Martin who is subject to upwards of $9 million in IOUs held by donors of the most powerful companies and wealthiest families in the country.

Paul Martin will be the leader of the Liberal Party at a time when Canadian corporations are aggressively pushing the same agenda they pushed when he was finance minister. The Liberals are often referred to as the "natural governing party" because they have been better than others in determining how to best represent the interests of big business in a market economy while still remaining legitimate in the eyes of ordinary citizens. If he is elected prime minister in 2004, Paul Martin's job will be to maintain that historic status for his party. Exactly how he will do this job is impossible to predict with any certainty. Whether he gets the job at all, however, will depend on what ordinary Canadians decide to do.


## HISTORY IS MADE BY THOSE WHO SHOW UP

In recent years, fewer and fewer Canadians have been showing up at election time. Fewer than 55 per cent of voting-age Canadians actually bothered to cast a ballot in the 2000 federal election. Still, there may be a silver lining in these disturbing numbers: America's revolutionary constitution reminds us that governments are artificial creations, "deriving their just powers from the consent of the governed." Perhaps the 45 per cent of Canadians who no longer bother to vote are actually withdrawing their consent to be governed by CEO Paul Martin and the decision-making elite that no longer govern in their interest. Unfortunately, that is not an effective way to challenge the legitimacy of Paul Martin's power, or to change his agenda. After the 2000 election, the elite still governed, and Paul Martin was still finance minister.

Among the millions who do not vote are thousands of the most politically conscious and committed young people in the country. The future of Canada will be determined by what young people do or do not do in the next ten years. If they stay away from the ballot box, the older, more conservative generations will keep shaping the country. History shows us that every period of progressive change in Canada, every surge in democratic engagement, increased expectations, and resistance to corporate power, has been driven by young people. Yet, a large number of young social-justice, anti-corporate, and pro-democracy activists continue to treat elections as an irrelevant farce, and purposely reject them as a part of their politics.

It is easy to understand why they feel as they do. The complicity of governments with corporations in designing the New World Order has turned what should be the expression of our collective will into an instrument of corporate greed. Arguing that the real source of political power is the corporation, activists have shifted their focus away from the nation-state. However, the past fifteen years of effort has shown that effectively challenging corporate globalization by confronting corporations directly has proven to be extremely difficult. These behemoths are essentially faceless, and hard to confront, precisely because they are "transnational." Exposing them does not take away their power, either. The scandals at Enron, WorldCom, and Arthur Andersen revealed the criminal rot at the heart of modern corporate culture, yet absolutely nothing has changed.

In their entirety, corporations are the creatures of government; they are not going to change until we change the laws that govern what they are and what they are allowed to do. Powerful as they are, corporations don't make those laws—governments do. It is a simple question of power. The only institution on the earth with enough organized, legitimate, and legal authority to challenge the power of corporations is the nation-state, the representatives of which are elected by the people.

Those who doubt the power of laws and government need only examine the incredible effort that corporations put into getting their parties elected and persuading citizens that ordinary people's dreams and aspirations can never be achieved through government. If corporations want laws that increase their power, they know they have to have governments that will pass those laws. In their struggle for a better world, activists from previous generations understood that principle, too, and fought and died for the right to vote. Just like current social activists, they held huge demonstrations, occupied factories at a time when strikes were illegal, and had violent and often deadly confrontations with police. But they also participated in elections. They participated so effectively, in fact, that they won the battles for medicare, public universities, labour standards, the right to form unions, and literally hundreds of other measures that made life easier for working people. The post-war social contract wasn't a gift of big business—it was won by fifteen years of struggle by ordinary Canadians for control over state power. The "historic compromise" represented by the social contract was just that: the elite gave up some power for fear of losing everything.

The good news is that millions of Canadians know that the Liberal government and Paul Martin will not govern in their interests or in the interests of Canada. Moreover, thousands of young activists have a sophisticated understanding of corporatism, or the melding of corporate and state interests into one. Yet, at the end of the day, all those who boycott the electoral part of the political process need to ask the question of who benefits from this boycott other than the Canadian Alliance, Paul Martin's Liberal government, and the 150 largest corporations that make up the CCCE.

Equally important are those millions of other Canadians who still vote, but do so based on their expectations and not their values. The wealthiest 20 per cent of Canadians, interestingly enough, do not vote this way. The vast majority of the wealthy actually vote, and they do so overwhelmingly in their own interests. It is a tragic irony that when other Canadians vote on the basis of their expectations, they, too, vote for the interests of the wealthy elite, effectively giving up the power of their ballot.

How did other generations of active citizens engage the voting process? They did it by involving themselves in electoral politics and convincing millions of people to vote according to their values. They did it by listening to their own hearts, by honouring their sense of right and wrong, by having faith in their own good sense about what made strong communities and viable nations. They did it by resisting the relentless campaigns in the 1930s and 1940s that tried to lower expectations and persuade ordinary people that social programs would "bankrupt the country."

In short, they kept their eyes on the prize: a Canada based on their values of equality, community, fairness, and genuine democracy. They showed up and voted their values. If Canadians put their values aside and elect Paul Martin Chief Executive Officer of Canada, he will almost certainly use his mandate to pick up exactly where he left off as finance minister: running the "company" in the interest of the shareholders, who have already voted to accept a buyout from America, Inc.

# NOTES

**INTRODUCTION**

1 Paul Martin, "Budget Speech," 27 February 1995, www.fin.gc.ca/budget95/speech/speeche.htm

2 Ibid.

3 Edward Greenspon and Anthony Wilson-Smith, *Double Vision: The Inside Story of the Liberals in Power* (Toronto: Doubleday, 1996), 133.

**CHAPTER 1**
**WHO IS PAUL MARTIN?**

1 James Laxer, interview with author.

2 Nancy Southam, "Paul Martin leaves big shadow behind," *Vancouver Sun,* 9 March 1982.

3 Kathryn Leger, "Power in Europe: Montreal's Desmarais family has forged ties with some of the continent's wealthiest dynasties," *Financial Post,* 12 July 1997.

4 Robert Chodos, Rae Murphy, and Eric Hamovitch, *Paul Martin: A Political Biography* (Toronto: James Lorimer & Co., 1998), 36–37.

5 Ibid., 43.

6 David Olive, "Paul Martin Takes the Watch," *Canadian Business,* April 1984.

7 Chodos et al., *Paul Martin,* 55.

8 Chodos et al., *Paul Martin,* 51.

9 Ian Jack, "Martin's CSL sails into union fight," *National Post,* 5 January 2002.

10 Will Hutton, "Capitalism Must Put Its House in Order," *Observer,* 24 November 2002.

11 Ibid.

12 "Anchors Away," Kathleen Coughlin and Mike Gordon, producers, *Disclosure,* CBC-TV, 1 April 2003.

13 Crumlin, interview.

14 "Anchors Away."

15 Paddy Crumlin, interview with author.

16 "CSL ship ignored safety code," MUA Web site, 20 February 2003.

17 "ITF unions support Australians in flagging out row," ITF media statement, 30 April 2002.

18 Paddy Crumlin, interview with author.

19 Buzz Hargrove, interview with author. The individual Hargrove mentions is almost certainly CSL Vice-President Pierre Prefontaine. Hargrove declined to name the Liberal MP.

20 Crumlin, interview.

21 Larry Zolf, "Sitting on the Story," CBC news viewpoint, 17 April 2003, www.cbc.ca/news/viewpoint/columns_zolf/zolf030417.html.

22 Memo from Tony Burman to all CBC news staff and contributors, "Subject: *Disclosure,* Paul Martin and Me," 21 March 2003, 16:21:59 P.M.

23 "Anchors Away."

24 Paul Martin, "Budget Speech," 6 March 1996, www.fin.gc.ca/budget96/speech/speeche.html.

25 "Anchors Away."

26 "Company fined $125,000 for dumping 92

litres of oil," *Alberni Valley Times* (BC), 26 Novemeber 2002. Staff story.

27 Tim Naumetz, "Martin ship sails into trouble," *Ottawa Citizen,* 4 March 2003.

28 Campbell Clark, "Martin left himself open to conflict," *Globe and Mail,* 18 February 2002. See also Glen McGregor, "Paul Martin's Business Linked to Suharto Family," *Vancouver Sun,* 17 February 2003.

29 Ibid.

30 Paul Martin, statement on Canada Steamship Lines given in the National Press Theatre, Ottawa, Ontario, 11 March 2003.

31 "Anchors Away."

32 Chodos et al., *Paul Martin,* 138.

33 Marci McDonald, *Yankee Doodle Dandy: Brian Mulroney and the American Agenda* (Toronto: Stoddart, 1995), 331.

34 Ibid.

35 Mike McCarthy (former vice-president of the Canadian Hemophilia Society), interview with author.

36 Andre Picard, *The Gift of Death: Confronting Canada's Tainted-Blood Tragedy* (Toronto: HarperCollins, 1995), 68

37 "Krever Commission Report" (Ottawa: Public Works and Government Services Canada, 1997).

38 Krever, 71.

39 Gerald McAuliffe, Joan Hollobon, and John Marshall, "Federal Regulations Violated: Contamination problems, danger of infection reported at Connaught," *Globe and Mail,* 27 February 1975.

40 Ibid.

41 Krever, 69.

42 Ibid., 988.

43 Ibid., 399.

44 Ibid., 391.

45 Ibid., 395.

46 Ibid., 396.

47 Ibid., 406.

48 Andre Picard, "Canada still lacks controls on plasma trade, inquiry told," *Globe and Mail,* 14 December 1995.

49 J. Furesz, M.D., Director of Bureau of Biologics, Federal Department of Health, "Memo to File: Telephone Conversation with Mr. James Gesling, FDA", October 30, 1974. Furesz notes that there had been a US investigation of Continental Pharma's distribution of plasma in the US and Canada, and that "The procedure started a few months ago when in New York the FBI found that this firm violated the law."

50 Picard, "Canada still lacks controls."

51 Mark Kennedy, "Martin's past back to haunt. What did he know about tainted blood?," *Ottawa Citizen,* 15 May 1999.

52 House of Commons Debates, 36th Parliament, 1st Session, Edited Hansard, Number 231, 26 May 1999.

53 Krever, 75.

54 Anne Shortell, "Under the Microscope," *Whig Standard,* 23 November 1991.

55 Mark Kennedy, "Tainted-blood sleuth firebombed: Intimidation campaign suspected as Arkansas clinic razed, Montreal office ransacked," *Ottawa Citizen,* 22 May 1999.

56 Dennis Bueckert, "Information commissioner reprimands Martin staff for withholding documents," Canadian Press, 25 March 25 2002.

57 Peter Newman, "The good and the ugly: Begin vs. Boyle," *Maclean's,* 30 September 1996.

58 "Opposition say Martin can't be prime minister and owner of CSL," CBC news online, 25 February 2003, www.cbc.ca.

59 Edward Greenspon and Anthony Wilson-Smith, *Double-Vision: The Inside Story of the Liberals in Power* (Toronto: Doublday, 1996), 59.

60 Olive, "Paul Martin Takes the Watch."

## CHAPTER 2
### HIDDEN AGENDA

1 Paul Martin, quoted in Robert Chodos, Rae Murphy, and Eric Hamovitch, *Paul Martin: A Political Biography* (Toronto: James Lorimer & Co., 1998), 77.

2 Paul Martin, quoted in Chodos et al., *Paul Martin,* 65.

3 Karen Mahon, interview with author.

4 Paul Martin, quoted in Chodos et al., *Paul Martin,* 81–83.

5 "The Government Has Given Up on Housing," Liberal Task Force On Housing News Release, 14 May 1990, resources. web.net/show.cfm?id=421&APP=housing.

6 Paul Martin, quoted in Chodos et al., *Paul Martin,* 72.

7 Michael Marzolini, quoted in Edward Greenspon and Anthony Wilson-Smith, *Double Vision: The Inside Story of the Liberals in Power* (Toronto: Doubleday, 1996), 62.

8 Tom Kent, interview with author.

9 Ibid.

10 Maude Barlow and Bruce Campbell, *Straight Through the Heart: How the Liberals Abandoned the Just Society* (Toronto: HarperCollins, 1995), 92.

11 Lester Thurow, quoted in Barlow and Campbell, *Heart,* 92.

12 Peter Nicholson, "Nowhere to Hide: The Economic Implications of Globalization for Canada," quoted in Barlow in Campbell, *Heart,* 93.

13 Ibid.

14 Jean Chrétien, quoted in Greenspon and Wilson-Smith, *Double Vision,* 98.

15 John MacLaren, quoted in Greenspon and Wilson-Smith, *Double Vision,* 99.

16 Barlow and Campbell, *Heart,* 129.

17 Arthur Kroeger, quoted in Greenspon and Wilson-Smith, *Double Vision,* 43.

18 Paul Martin, Pre-budget speech to the Commons, 1 February 1994.

19 Greenspon and Wilson-Smith, *Double Vision,* 155–56.

20 Doug Peters, interview with author.

21 Linda McQuaig, *Shooting the Hippo: Death by Deficit and Other Canadian Myths* (Toronto: Viking, 1995), 35.

22 Seth Klein, "Good Sense versus Common Sense: Canada's Debt Debate and Competing Hegemonic Projects" (Master's thesis, Simon Fraser University, 1996).

23 "One Part Poverty Reduction, Two Parts SAPs: A Recipe for Disaster" *Economic Justice Report* 10.4 (December 1999).

24 Pierre Fortin, interview with author.

25 Linda McQuaig, *The Cult of Impotence: Selling the Myth of Powerlessness in the Global Economy* (Toronto: Viking, 1998), 84.

26 Paul Martin, "Notes for an address by the Minister of Finance of Canada, Paul Martin, to the IMF Interim Committee," 8 October 1995, www.fin.gc.ca.

27 Murray Dobbin, *The Myth of the Good Corporate Citizen,* 2nd Ed. (Toronto: James Lorimer & Co., 2003), 226–27.

28 McQuaig, *Cult,* 92.

29 Ibid., 57.

30 Doug Peters, interview.

31 McQuaig, *Cult,* 87.

**CHAPTER 3**
**HARD RIGHT TURN**

1 Hugh Mackenzie, interview with author.

2 Peter C. Newman, *The Canadian Revolution: From Deference to Defiance* (Toronto: Viking, 1995), 192.

3 Murray Dobbin, *The Myth of the Good Corporate Citizen,* 2nd Ed. (Toronto: James Lorimer & Co., 2003), 220.

4 Maude Barlow and Bruce Campbell, *Straight through the Heart: How the Liberals Abandoned the Just Society* (Toronto:

HarperCollins, 1995), 78.

5 George Vasic, "Down the Slippery Slope of National Debt," *Canadian Business,* February 1991.

6 George Vasic and Pierre Fortin, quoted in Linda McQuaig, *Shooting the Hippo: Death by Deficit and Other Canadian Myths* (Toronto: Viking, 1995), 71, 80.

7 Murray McIlveen and Hideo Minmoto, "The Federal Government Deficit, 1975–1988-89' (unpublished paper, Statistics Canada, 1990).

8 "The Massive Federal Debt: How Did It Happen?" Dominion Bond Rating Service, February 1995.

9 Jean Chrétien, *Straight from the Heart,* quoted in Edward Greenspon and Anthony Wilson-Smith, *Double Vision: The Inside Story of the Liberals in Power* (Toronto: Doubleday, 1996), 162.

10 Ibid., 163.

11 Greenspon and Wilson-Smith, *Double Vision,* 164.

12 Doug Peters, interview with author.

13 Barlow and Campbell, *Heart,* 120.

14 Peters, interview.

15 Ibid.

16 Greenspon and Wilson-Smith, *Double Vision,* 7.

17 Duncan Cameron, interview with author.

18 Greenspon and Wilson-Smith, *Double Vision,* 161.

19 Greenspon and Wilson-Smith, *Double Vision,* 166.

20 Anne McLellan, quoted in Greenspon and Wilson-Smith, *Double Vision,* 166.

21 Marcel Massé, quoted in Jamie Swift, "The Debt Crisis: A Case of Global Usury," in *Conflicts of Interest,* ed. Jamie Swift and Brian Tomlinson (Toronto: Between the Lines, 1991), 97.

22 Greenspon and Wilson-Smith, *Double Vision,* 105.

23 Ibid., 133.

24 Ibid., 167.

25 Ibid., 211.

26 Paul Martin, "The Canadian Experience in Reducing Budget Deficits and Debt," (address presented to the Federal Reserve Bank of Kansas City, Jackson Hole, Wyoming, 1 September 1995).

27 Barlow and Campbell, *Heart,* 66–67.

28 Barlow and Campbell, *Heart,* 150–1.

29 Barlow and Campbell, *Heart,* 155.

30 For all references to the Goldman Sachs report, see William Dudley, quoted in Linda

McQuaig, *The Cult of Impotence: Selling the Myth of Powerlessness in the Global Economy,* (Toronto: Viking, 1998), 96–97.

31 Ibid., 91.

32 Letter from Paul Martin to Bob White of the Canadian Labour Congress, quoted in McQuaig, *Cult,* 93.

33 Barlow and Campbell, *Heart,* 139.

34 McQuaig, *Hippo,* 41–42.

35 Barlow and Campbell, *Heart,* 143.

36 For all reference to the February 1995 budget speech, see Paul Martin, "Budget Speech," 27 February 1995, www.fin.gc. ca/budget95/speech/speeche.html.

CHAPTER 4

PAUL MARTIN'S CANADA

1 Maude Barlow, *The Fight of My Life: Confessions of an Unrepentant Canadian* (Toronto: HarperCollins, 1998), 174.

2 Joseph Brean, "Frozen Out," *National Post,* February 15, 2003.

3 Rod Mickleburgh, "Weak snow layers need more study, experts say," *Globe and Mail,* 3 February 2003.

4 SCOFO, "Canadian Coast Guard: Marine Communications and Traffic Services (MCTS)," quoted in "CAW's Hargrove calls for immediate action to rescue Coast Guard," Canadian News Wire, 6 February 2003.

5 Jim Stanford, "The Economic and Social Consequences of Fiscal Retrenchment in Canada in the 1990s," in The Review of Economic Performance and Social Progress: *The Longest Decade: Canada in the 1990s,* Volume 1, June 2001, Edited by Keith Banting, Andrew Sharpe, France St-Hilaire, 154–5. http://www.csls.ca/repsp/repsp1.asp.

6 Ibid, 154–55.

7 Peter Nicholson, quoted in Maude Barlow and Bruce Campbell, *Straight through the Heart: How the Liberals Abandoned the Just Society* (Toronto: HarperCollins, 1995), 93.

8 Greenspon and Wilson-Smith, *Double Vision: The Inside Story of the Liberals in Power* (Toronto: Doubleday, 1996), 103.

9 Paul Martin, "Budget Speech," 27 February 1995, www.fin.gc.ca/budget95/speech/speeche.html.

10 "Agenda—Jobs and Growth: A New Framework for Economic Policy," (Ottawa: Department of Finance, 1994).

11 Ibid.

12 Linda McQuaig, *The Cult of Impotence: Selling the Myth of Powerlessness in the Global Economy* (Toronto: Viking, 1988), 95.

13 McQuaig, *Cult,* 107–9.

14 Hugh MacKenzie, "Who's really Winning? How Paul Martin got his tax cut budget," United Steelworkers News Release, 29 February 2000.

15 Dr. Chris Higgins and Dr. Linda Duxbury, "The National Work-Life Conflict Study," July 2002, www.workandfamilybalance.com/recent-research_1.htm.

16 Armine Yalnizyan, "The Growing Gap: A report on the growing inequality between the rich and poor in Canada," (Toronto: Centre for Social Justice, 1997), 45.

17 StatsCan statistics quoted in *Globe and Mail,* 9 November 1996 and *Toronto Star,* 29 July 1997.

18 "The Assets and Debts of Canadians: An Overview of the Survey of Financial Security" (Ottawa: Statistics Canada, 15 March 2001), catalogue no. 13-595-XIE.

19 Murray Dobbin, *The Myth of the Good Corporate Citizen, 2nd Ed.* (Toronto: James Lorimer & Co.), 124.

20 Mel Hurtig, *Pay the Rent or Feed the Kids: The Tragedy and Disgrace of Poverty in Canada* (Toronto: McClelland & Stewart, 1999), 10.

21 Hurtig, *Pay the Rent,* 9.

22 Ibid., 9.

23 Ibid., 10.

24 Ibid.

25 Ibid.

26 Darrin Qualman and Nettie Wiebe, "The Structural Adjustment of Canadian Agriculture," (Ottawa: Canadian Centre for Policy Alternatives, 2002).

27 Ibid.

28 Ibid.

29 Ibid.

30 Ibid.

31 Elizabeth May, interview with author.

32 Ibid.

33 Ibid.

34 Paul Martin, "The Canadian Experience in Reducing Budget Deficits and Debt," (address presented to the Federal Reserve Bank of Kansas City, Jackson Hole, Wyoming, 1 September 1995). See also Barlow, *Fight,* 215–16.

35 Ibid., 216.

36 NAFTA Commission for Environmental Cooperation, "The North American Mosaic: The State of the Environment

Report," quoted in Alanna Mitchell, "GDP value must reflect eco-health, report says," *Globe and Mail,* 7 January 2002.

37 Michelle Swenarchuk, interview with author.

38 Duncan Cameron, interview with author.

39 Erika Shaker and Denise Doherty Delorme, "Education, Limited: Monitoring Corporate Intrusion in Canadian Public Education" (Ottawa: Canadian Centre for Policy Alternatives, 1999).

40 Ibid.

41 Ibid.

42 Ibid.

43 Ibid.

44 John Demont, "Pressure Point: Federal researchers say drug companies push hard for approvals," *Maclean's,* 16 November 1998.

45 Ibid.

46 Ibid.

47 Michele Brill-Edwards, interview with author.

48 David Dodge, quote in Charlotte Gray, "There's a New Sheriff at Tunney's Pasture," *Canadian Medical Association Journal* 161.4 (24 August 1999): 426–27.

49 Demont, "Pressure Point."

50 Gray, "New Sheriff," 426–27.

51 Demont, "Pressure Point."

52 Brill-Edwards, interview.

53 Ibid.

54 Laura Eggertson, "Salmonella outbreak was Canada's worst since 1984," *Toronto Star,* 3 April 1999.

55 Ibid.

56 Laura Eggertson, "Food agency ignored risk of botulism," *Toronto Star,* 26 November 1999.

57 Paul Martin, "The Economic and Fiscal Update to the House of Commons Standing Committee on Finance," 9 October 1996, www.fin.gc.ca/update96/961009e.html.

58 Ibid.

**CHAPTER 5**
**JUDGING PAUL MARTIN**

1 Paul Martin, "Budget Speech," 6 March 1996, www.fin.gc.ca/budget96/speech/speeche.htm.

2 Ibid.

3 Ibid.

4 Ibid.

5 Jim Stanford, *Paper Boom* (Toronto: James Lorimer & Co., 1999), 196.

6 Ibid., 197.

7 Paul Martin, "Budget Speech," 18 February 1997, www.fin.gc.ca/budget97/speech/speeche.html.

8 Jim Stanford, "Winner by Default: How debt repayment has hijacked the great Canadian fiscal dividend, and at what cost," (Ottawa: Canadian Centre for Policy Alternatives, 1998.

9 Ibid.

10 Jim Stanford, "Paul Martin: 'Big Spender'— Analysis of the 1999 Budget," *Option Politiques,* Avril 1999.

11 Eric Beauchesne, "IMF pressures Ottawa to stress tax reductions. The global body says the federal government should abandon its 50-50 plan for dividing up surpluses," Southam Newspapers, 20 November 1999, www.hartford-hwp.com/archives/44/086.html.

12 Paul Martin, "Budget Speech," 24 February 1998, www.fin.gc.ca/budget98/speech/speeche.html.

13 Paul Martin, "Budget Speech," 16 February 1999, www.fin.gc.ca/budget99/speech/speeche.html.

14 Ibid.

15 Paul Martin, "Economic and Fiscal Update 1999," 2 November 1999, www.fin.gc.ca/update99/indexe.html.

16 Martin, "Budget Speech." [1999]

17 Armine Yalnizyan, "What would they do with the surplus?" (Ottawa: Canadian Centre for Policy Alternatives, 2000).

18 Ibid.

19 "Ottawa disbanded GST fraud squad in 1995," 20 November 2002, www.cbc.ca/storyview/CBC/2002/11/20/gst_scam021120.

20 Philip Authier, "Tax-cheat crackdown turns up $4.8 billion," *The Montreal Gazette,* 19 February 1997.

21 Kirk Makin, "Tax ruling costs Ottawa $1.26 billion," *Globe and Mail,* 7 March 2003.

22 *Financial Post* article, March 26, 2002, quoted in Mel Hurtig, *The Vanishing Country: Is It Too Late to Save Canada?* (Toronto: McClelland & Stewart, 2002), 346.

23 Hurtig, 346.

24 Paul Martin, "Budget Speech," 27 February 1995, www.fin.gc.ca/budget95/speech/speeche.html.

25 Bruce Campbell, "From Deep Integration to Reclaiming Sovereignty" (Ottawa: Canadian Centre for Policy Alternatives, 2003).

26 Eric Beauchesne, "Lame Buck Better Than NAFTA: Study—Trade deals get credit for only 9 percent of export growth," *Ottawa Citizen*, 20 June 2001.

27 Jim Stanford, "The Global Cheesecake," *Facts from the Fringe* 37 (23 March 2001).

28 The Canadian Exporter Registry, "Profile of Canadian Exporters, 1993–2001" (Ottawa: Statistics Canada, 2002).

29 Paul Martin, "Economic and Fiscal Update," 9 October 1996, www.fin.gc.ca/update96/961009e.html.

30 Jim Stanford, "Canada's Economic Role in North America," CAW Submission to the Standing Senate Committee on Foreign Affairs, April 2003.

31 "The Competitive Alternative" (Vancouver: KPMG, 2003).

32 Stanford, "Canada's Economic Role in North America."

33 Mel Hurtig, "How Much of Canada Do We Want to Sell?" *Globe and Mail*, 5 February 1998.

34 Hurtig, *Vanishing*, 32.

35 Ibid.

36 Paul Martin, "Notes for an address by the Minister of Finance of Canada, Paul Martin, to the Canadian-American Business Council," 10 October 1995, www.fin.gc.ca/news95/95-082e.html.

37 Stanford, "Canada's Economic Role in North America."

38 Andrew Duffy, "Canada's Roaring Economy: Tiger or Toothless Illusion?" *Ottawa Citizen*, 31 May 2003.

39 Stanford, "Canada's Economic Role in North America."

40 Murray Dobbin, *The Myth of the Good Corporate Citizen*, 2nd Ed. (Toronto: James Lorimer & Co., 2003), 140.

41 Stanford, "Canada's Economic Role in North America."

42 Murray Dobbin, "Who's minding Canada's trade negotiator?" *Financial Post*, 3 April 2002.

43 Bruce Little, "Bad Jobs Don't Make a Big Surplus," *Globe and Mail*, 27 January 2003.

44 Murray Dobbin, "The Remaking of New Zealand," *Ideas*, CBC Radio, 12 October 1994 and 19 October 1994.

45 Ed Finn, "Alternative Budget Policies and Packaging: Our ideas ignored because they don't please the markets," *CCPA Monitor*, April 1999.

**CHAPTER 6**

**WHERE WILL PAUL MARTIN TAKE US?**

1 Ursula Franklin, "Global Justice *Chez Nous*," *Monetary Reform*, Winter 1997–98.

2 Kate Malloy, "Behind the Martin Money Machine," Hill *Times*, 12 February 2003.

3 Campbell Clark, "Membership Rules Have Martin Rivals Grumbling," *Globe and Mail*, 25 January 2003.

4 Simon Tuck and Jane Taber, "Liberals Irked at Manley's 'Whining' About Rules," *Globe and Mail*, 26 January 2003.

5 Shawn McCarthy and Gloria Galloway, "Martin's Nomination Reveals Strong Support," *Globe and Mail*, 6 March 2003.

6 Hugh Winsor, "The Power Game: A brief lesson on the politics of the spin," *Globe and Mail*, September 2002.

7 Edward Greenspon and Anthony Wilson-Smith, *Double Vision: The Inside Story of the Liberals in Power* (Toronto: Doubleday, 1996), 275–76.

8 Industry Canada Web site, Lobbyists and Leadership Campaigns, www.strategis.ic.gc.ca/SSG/lr01113e.html

9 "Democracy Watch Launches Court Challenge of Ethics Counsellor's Bias, Delay and Failure to Fulfill Legal Duties in Eight Complaints," Democracy Watch Media Release, 18 December 2002.

10 Stephen Handelman, "Paul Martin: Canadian Newsmaker of the Year," *Time*, December 2002.

11 Industry Canada Web site, Public-Private Partnership (P3) Office, www.strategis.ic.gc.ca/SSG/ce01374e.html.

12 Maude Barlow and Bruce Campbell, *Straight through the Heart: How the Liberals Abandoned the Just Society* (Toronto: HarperCollins, 1995), 49–50.

13 Murray Dobbin, *The Myth of the Good Corporate Citizen*, 2nd Ed. (Toronto: James Lorimer & Co., 2003), 167.

14 For a full history of the BCNI, see Dobbin, *Myth*, 165–81.

15 Greenspon and Wilson-Smith, *Double Vision*, 21.

16 Wendy Dobson, "Shaping the Future of the North American Economic Space: A Framework for Action" (Toronto: C.D. Howe Institute, April 2002).

17 Shawn McCarthy, "Canada's Resources Help Soothe U.S. Anger," *Globe and Mail*, 18 April 2003.

18 Jack Granatstein, "A Friendly Agreement in Advance: Canada-US Defense Relations Past, Present, and Future," C.D. Howe

# NOTES

Institute, June 2002, quoted in James Laxer, "Wake-Up Call," *Dimension,* November/December 2002.

19 Ibid.

20 Wendy Dobson, "Trade can brush in a new border," *Globe and Mail,* 21 January 21 2003.

21 Tom d'Aquino, "Security and Prosperity: The Dynamics of a New Canada–United States Partnership in North America," presentation to the SGM of the CCCE, Toronto, ON, 14 January 2003.

22 Ibid.

23 David Crane, "How Would Martin Safeguard Our Independence?" *Toronto Star,* 18 January 2003.

24 CTV NewsNet, 26 April 2003.

25 Mark Kennedy, "Martin Takes Shots at Liberals," CanWest News Service, 26 April 2003.

26 Handelman, "Paul Martin."

27 "Martin: Canada Can Make History," 27 April, 2003, www.paulmartintimes.ca/the-campaign/stories_e.asp?id=523.

28 "Martin spells out vision, says Canada 'can make history,' at first Liberal leadership debate," 3 May 2003, www.paulmartin-times.ca/the-campaign/ stories_e. asp?id=534.

29 Adam Radwanski, "Why does Paul Martin want to be prime minister, anyway?" *National Post,* 1 May 2003.

30 John Andersen, interview with author.

31 Ibid.

32 "Martin promises a national home care program," 24 May 24 2003, www.paulmart-intimes.ca/where-paul-stands/stories_e.asp?id=560.

33 John Dillon, interview with author.

34 Ibid.

35 The "Tobin tax," proposed in 1978 by James Tobin, would see a worldwide tax imposed on all foreign exchange transactions. The tax would have a twofold effect: (1) it would reduce exchange-rate volatility and improve macroeconomic performance and (2) it would generate revenue to support international development efforts.

36 Greenspon and Wilson-Smith, *Double Vision,* 133.

## Chapter 7
### Keeping Our Eye on the Prize

1 Paul Martin, "Budget Speech," 27 February 27 1995, www.fin.gc.ca/budget95/speech/speeche.html.

2 Samuel Huntington, Michel Crozier, and Joji Watanuki, *The Crisis of Democracy* (New York: New York University Press, 1975), 113–14.

3 Frank L. Graves, "The Economy Through a Public Lens: Shifting Canadian Views of the Economy," (Toronto: EKOS, 2001).

4 Ibid.

5 Judith Maxwell et al., "Citizens' Dialogue on Canada's Future: A Twenty-First Century Social Contract," (Ottawa: Canadian Policy Research Networks, 2003), www.cprn.com/cprn.html.

6 Ibid.

7 "Rethinking Government (1994)," (Toronto: EKOS, 1995).

8 This article in the Canadian Labour Congress's quarterly economic review *The Economy* was based on a paper by Per Kongshoj Madsen for the International Labour Organization titled "Denmark: Flexibility, Security and Labour Market Success," reprinted in the *CCPA Monitor,* June 2000.

9 Anders Hayden, "Good Morning, I'm Your Father! Netherlands sets example: shortest hours, fewest jobless," *CCPA Monitor,* June 2000.

10 Ricardo Grinspun, interview with author.

11 Ibid.

12 Bruce Campbell, "From Deep Integration to Reclaiming Sovereignty" (Ottawa: Canadian Centre for Policy Alternatives, 2003).

13 Michael den Tandt, "Presto! Canada-US trade spat goes up in smoke," *Globe and Mail,* 8 Apr 2003.

14 Jeffrey Simpson, "Worried about US retribution? Don't be," *Globe and Mail,* 9 April 2003.

15 Ed Finn, "Where's the Money Coming From?" (Ottawa: Canadian Centre for Policy Alternatives, 2002).

16 Ibid.

17 Ibid.

18 Gavin Hales et al., "Vertical Fiscal Imbalance—July 2002," (Ottawa: Conference Board of Canada, July 2002).

# INDEX

# INDEX

(NDP), 45
New Zealand, 140
Nicholson, Peter, 45–46, 61, 93, 166
nifedipine, 110
nomination papers, 149
North America Treaty, 159–60
North American defence perimeter, 160
North American Free Trade Agreement (NAFTA). *See* NAFTA

OECD. *See* Organization for Economic Cooperation and Development (OECD)
Opposition, 41, 42–43
Organization for Economic Cooperation and Development (OECD), 166–67

Paramount Communications, 25–26
Parmalat, 113–14
pension reform, 67
Peters, Doug, 55–57
Planning and Priorities Committee, 104
political staffs, 71–72
Port Pirie (Australia), 18
postsecondary education. *See* universities
poverty, 91, 100–101, 123
Power Corporation, 5, 11
privatization, 86–87, 91; *see also* commercialization
productivity, 136–39
Program Review Committee, 74–75, 104
program spending, 10; *see also* social programs
Progressive Conservative Party. *See* Tories
PT Jawa Power, 23
public relations, 151
public-sector workers, 171–72
Public Service Commission, 72
public services, 171–72
Purple Book, 80–81, 94–96

Quebec, 39–40

recession, 65
Red Book, 5, 38, 41–48, 70, 71, 166; and deficit, 73; dis-

regard for, 75–77
Red Book III, 127
Red Cross: and Connaught, 27–28, 31; and risky blood suppliers, 29–30
refugee policy, 158
Reid, John, 34
Reid, Scott, 35
research and development, 136
rural communities, 102–3

salmonella outbreak (1998), 113–14
SAPs. *See* Structural Adjustment Plans (SAPs)
science and technology budget, 108–9
security, and deep integration, 158, 159
September 11, 2001, 159
service providers, 171–72
ships (FOC), 15–17, 18–19
social assistance. *See* Unemployment Insurance (UI)
social housing, 40–41
social policy review, 77
social programs: cuts to, 3, 53, 54, 55, 115; employment, 95, 98
sovereignty, 176–77
Standing Committee on Fisheries and Oceans (SCOFO), 91
Stanford, Jim, 92, 136
Star Chamber, 75
Strong, Maurice, 11
Structural Adjustment Plans (SAPs), 54
student loans, 128
sustainable development, 43
Sweden, 175

tainted-blood scandal, 26–35; compensation to victims, 32; document destruction, 34–35
Task Force on Housing, 40–41
tax avoidance, 174
tax cuts, 3–4, 88, 126, 127, 178–79
tax fraud, 128–30, 174
tax havens, 22–23, 129–30
Thorsell, William, 52
Thurow, Lester, 45
TINA argument, 46, 171

TLC. *See* Trilateral Commission (TLC)
tobacco industry, 25
Tobin tax, 165, 190 n35
Tories: criticism of, 42; and UI, 96, 97; *see also* Mulroney, Brian
trade, 2, 130–33, 142: with Asian countries, 131; and US, 177–78; *see also* free trade
Trilateral Commission (TLC), 170–71
Trudeau, Pierre, 68
Turner, John, 65

UI. *See* Unemployment Insurance (UI)
unemployment, 4, 56–61, 119; and NAIRU, 57
Unemployment Insurance (UI), 51, 96–99
unionized workers, 97
United Nations, and Canada, 100–101
universities, 91, 106–9
US: and Canada, 8, 156–62, 177; and NAIRU, 59; security needs, 158; shared economy, 176; *see also* deep integration
US National Missile Defense System, 8

values (Canadian), 6, 42, 172–74
voters, 180–83
Voyageur Bus Lines, 14

wage gap, 99, 122–23
Washington Consensus, 12–13, 54, 87, 168–69
welfare state, 57–58
western alienation, 164
Wilson, Howard, 26; and CSL, 19, 24; and Earnscliffe, 153–54; and tainted-blood scandal, 27, 33
workers: and 1995 budget, 77; on FOC ships, 15–16; public sector, 171–72; unionized, 97; *see also* employment; labour; unemployment
working conditions, 98

Young Liberals, 36, 37
young voters, 181